It is the author's belief that anyone who can
LISTEN to music can also understand it.

Without using a single bar of printed music as illustration,
Mr. Randolph explains his thesis that music does not tell a
story, paint a picture, or describe anything. Music is simply
about itself.

Dispensing with what he calls the "saturated-romantic"
viewpoint that reads into music what isn't there, Mr. Randolph
then analyzes the basic elements of music: harmony, melody,
rhythm, tone color, and form. He shows how music *itself*
provides an aesthetic experience; how mental transformation
into verbal or pictorial form is unnecessary and false.

After scattering the pompous ranks of music "interpreters,"
the author speaks with undisguised delight of the emotions that
music can arouse. His is an illuminating approach to new
adventures in listening.

David Randolph

This
Is
Music

A GUIDE TO THE PLEASURES
OF LISTENING

CREATIVE ARTS BOOK COMPANY
Berkeley, California • 1997

This Is Music is published by Donald S. Ellis
and distributed by Creative Arts Book Company

For information contact:
Creative Arts Book Company
833 Bancroft Way
Berkeley, California 94710

ISBN 0-88739-110-9

The original McGraw-Hill edition, 1964, had the
following Library of Congress Catalogue Number: 63-22525

Printed in the United States of America

To my wife,
Mildred,
in gratitude for decades
of help and devotion.

CONTENTS

PART ONE

How We Experience Music

CHAPTER 1

Clearing the Air

As someone who is interested in learning more about music, have you ever found yourself mystified by the technical explanations that so often precede radio broadcasts of musical works, or by the musical "analyses" printed in the booklets accompanying CDs? Do you sometimes wonder whether your music-loving friends are really able to understand the philosophical and technical discussions so often contained in the program booklets at concerts? The chances are that you have been discouraged at some time or other by the feeling that somehow you do not belong among the initiated who benefit from commentaries that supposedly describe the meaning of the music about to be heard.

As you listen to the radio or television announcer's impressive sounding script, you assume that others, possessed of the necessary insight or special training, are able to derive some practical benefit from what is being said. This is an unwise assumption. If it were possible for you to see into the minds of the other listeners, you would find that the majority of them are sharing your disappointment. They, too, as normal individuals normally interested in music, find the remarks quite as incomprehensible as you do and assume that they are intended for everyone else.

Here is one of the major sources of the unacknowledged sense of inferiority that has been imposed upon the average music lover ever since the broadcasting of good music became common. To anyone who gives the matter some thought, it is plain that the excessively technical and "philosophical" and "poetic" approaches to music appreciation have simply discouraged or misled many who might otherwise have come to enjoy the music itself.

The reasons for this development are not hard to find. In our approach to the arts in general, we are still reflecting nineteenth century ideas. Hollywood has perpetuated the picture of the composer as an eccentric, self-willed romantic individualist, lacking any sense of public responsibility. Magazine, television and newspaper feature writers, finding that the more colorful aspects of composers' lives make the best copy, have further impressed that picture upon our minds.

It is unfortunate that our basic orientation toward music has been shaped largely by literary people, rather than by qualified teachers of music. Even a painter or a sculptor would have more insight into the true nature of music than a writer, since he, like the composer, creates his work in a nonverbal medium. In any case, the literary man's prose, when he claims to speak for music, is seldom examined for its real pertinence or meaning.

Here is a typical example of the approach that *This Is Music* will seek to counteract. It might be labeled the "saturated romantic" viewpoint. The author, whose name is respected among twentieth-century writers on music, need not be identified, since this paragraph could have been written by many another musical "analyst." In these lines, his mission is to awaken your interest in Beethoven's Ninth Symphony:

The idea of a great new work ripened in Beethoven, of a recapitulatory representation of tragedy and its terrors, a proclamation of the resurrection of the spirit to eternal, inexhaustible joys. He descends to realms of darkness from the pure exaltation of his *Mass*, calls up ghosts of the past, and, lifted forever above the grasp of fate, remembers the despairing conflict in which his will once wrested for earthly joy, before he learned to know its worthlessness. Once more he experiences the change from the adoration of Nature to recognition of the true divine essence; and now, in the triumph of that knowledge, he raises a mighty hymn in praise of that Power which is stronger than all the fears and sorrows of human life. Joy greets the visitor who approaches beatification, and leads him to that Elysium where the limitations of earth are lost and the conqueror of fate finds a happiness far above the petty desires of earth.

We may sincerely question whether the author of this passage has helped us in the least to understand or appreciate the composition under discussion. Actually, there is nothing whatsoever in Beethoven's Ninth Symphony by which a single proposition contained in this quotation can be proved. If the suggestion is made that the comments are intended merely to describe an emotional reaction proper to the intelligent listener, then it must be observed that there is nothing in them that describes Beethoven's Ninth Symphony exclusively. With only minor changes, the passage could just as well claim to explain almost any extended, serious symphonic composition.

The highly fanciful literary imagery that has passed as music appreciation for several generations, if it sheds any light at all, sheds the kind that blinds through its glitter. If you have found yourself unable to perceive its relationship to the music it purportedly describes, take comfort. You are not alone.

This book is, therefore, not a conventional approach to music appreciation. In its attempt to give the untrained listener what is hoped to be a guide to the true understanding and enjoyment of music, it will sometimes take stands that are contrary to the generally accepted viewpoints, when those viewpoints are, in the opinion of the author, fallacious or misleading. In fact, much of Part One will be devoted to an attempt to free the reader's mind from many of the wrong concepts that permeate music appreciation.

The form of the book is also unconventional. Traditionally, music appreciation books begin with a discussion either of the physical nature of a musical tone, or of the music of the ancient Greeks. But no music lover, in the process of enjoying a musical work, ever listens for the acoustical and mathematical properties of a musical tone; that is a science, of interest to the acoustician and the instrument maker. Similarly, the layman who feels impelled to read a book about music appreciation is drawn to the subject not by ancient Greek music (of which very little is known, and whose few extant fragments possess little inherent musical interest, except for the historian), but by the appeal of some of the most sophisticated symphonies, concertos, and operas of the most recent two and a half centuries.

This Is Music will draw most of its examples from such works, choosing those that are likely to be familiar to the great majority of readers. Moreover, every work that will be referred to is readily available on recordings some in numerous versions.

As a concomitant of this approach, a subject may be returned to several times during the course of the book. For example, the meaning and purpose of musical form and the forms themselves are described in Part Two, while Part Three contains suggestions on how to listen for the various forms. Similarly, the concept of program music—that is, story-telling music—is discussed in Part One, while suggestions for listening to program music are made in Part Three. Since we are not dealing with a science, in which it is mandatory to present systematically a body of *facts* of increasing complexity, but with an art, which combines sophisticated emotional reactions with understanding, each succeeding discussion is intended to refine the reader's responses, as a result of the cumulative effect of one's exposure to the previous discussions and to one's own listening experiences.

It cannot be sufficiently stressed that, *in order to develop our understanding of music, we must listen to music.* There is no substitute for listening. We would not expect to learn how to swim or to drive a car merely by reading an instruction manual. In spite of the fact that no physical skill is involved, "getting the feel" of music is as important in learning to appreciate it as entering the water is in learning to swim, or getting behind the wheel is in learning to drive.

For listening to be most productive, it must be *attentive* listening. If we merely let our minds wander, the music will become nothing more than a background for our reveries. It is better to listen attentively to a short composition, or even to a single movement of a multimovement work, than it is to listen inattentively through a long composition.

Does this mean that we should never listen to music unless we can concentrate on it? No. Listen to music whenever you can, provided you are in the mood for it. While this will necessarily mean that you will not always be getting all that is accessible in the music, no harm can come from this practice. Moreover, aside from the familiarity with the music that will result from even casual listening, there will be those inevitable moments when the music will draw attention to itself because of some particularly appealing passage.

When you wish actively to increase your skill in listening and your understanding, however, devote some time, no matter how short, to *attentive* listening. The very process of developing your skill involves the pleasurable activity of listening to music, and you will naturally choose to listen attentively to the compositions that most appeal to you. You might also try a little concentrated, detailed listening to a work you are sure you do not like. The results of such an effort may surprise you.

CHAPTER 2

"Total Appreciation"— Is It Possible?

How shall we define music appreciation? *The Harvard Dictionary of Music* offers this definition: "A term that has come to be accepted as a name for a type of musical training designed to develop in the seriously interested amateur an ability to listen intelligently to the music which he is likely to encounter in concert performances and in broadcast reproductions and thus to enhance the pleasure and satisfaction he may derive from listening to music." The key points here are "an ability to listen intelligently" and "to enhance the pleasure and satisfaction he may derive."

Even as we turn to the task of learning to listen intelligently, it may be helpful to jump to the other end of the scale, so to speak, and to consider whether there can be such a thing as "total appreciation" of any extended piece of music. In other words, is it possible for any individual, however well trained, to experience a *complete* response to every facet, emotional and intellectual, of a piece of music, exactly as the composer intended it? To load the question further, let us even assume that our ideal listener is a trained professional musician. The answer will perhaps be a source of relief to those who find themselves bewildered by what seem to be the endless complexities, not only of music itself but of the *explanations* of music. For if the question is taken literally, the answer must inevitably be *no*.

One might expect a professional performer of music—say a member of a leading symphony orchestra—to be uniquely sensitized; yet it is safe to say that the hundred players of such an orchestra, while performing a work, are kept from a complete appreciation of it by the very fact that they must be concerned continually with matters of performance. The technical problems connected with the placement of the fingers, the adjustment of pitch, the degree of loudness or softness, and the achieving of precision make too many demands on the players' attention. Singers, whether singing alone or in a chorus, must also, like instrumentalists, be concerned primarily with problems of performance.

The conductor, who may be thought to have an ideal awareness of the entire content of a musical work, is similarly denied total appreciation by the fact that, at the time of a performance, his attention is devoted to the task of drawing from his players an interpretation that will—he hopes—convey the composer's intentions. So demanding is this task (assuming, of course, that his mind is not occupied with less elevated thoughts about his sartorial elegance or the effect upon the audience of his sweeping gestures) that it is unlikely that a conductor will derive from any work the full emotional response that the composer intended his hearers to have. Although he may at some time have experienced a fuller appreciation of the work at hand, at the time he is conducting it he is intent upon *producing* those responses in the audience, rather than upon experiencing them himself. One final reason why every one of the performers in a large ensemble, as well as the conductor, hears an unbalanced version of the music, is his physical locations.

Clearly, the auditor is *potentially* in a better position than the performing musician to experience the appreciation of which we are speaking. This does not mean, however, that every amateur music lover is of necessity a better appreciator of music than is the trained musician. Quite obviously, since familiarity is one of the greatest aids to appreciation, the insight that any performer gains into a piece of music as a result of his having studied it may be expected to increase his enjoyment of it when he hears it performed by someone else. Presumably, the person who is in this position is capable of achieving the greatest possible appreciation, since his knowledge of the score itself may be complete, especially if the work in question is a composition for a single instrument and requires only one performer.

What greater understanding can one have of the content of a composition than that which is based on the ability to reproduce it complete down to the last note? Realistically, however, the person who can do this is often no more able to enjoy the performance of a composition than is the person performing it. In listening to a performance by someone else, it is more than likely that such a listeners attention will be given over to an evaluation of the manner in which the work is played, rather than to the music itself. The amateur listener, on the other hand, is not concerned with either the technical problems of performance or the professional judgments that must inevitably arise in the mind of one performer as he listens to another.

For all these reasons, I maintain that the amateur listener — assuming his willingness to familiarize himself with the music—is the one who is most likely to experience the deepest enjoyment of a musical work.

Yet this does not mean that "total appreciation" is possible even for the knowledgeable amateur with no other responsibility than to listen to and absorb a musical composition. He in his turn is beset by his share of distractions. While a public concert is perhaps the best means that man has yet devised for the direct hearing of music in its full tonal glory, it cannot be maintained that sitting more or less motionless for the better part of two hours is conducive to the most complete response to music. The situation is an entirely artificial one, in which social restraints successfully stifle any physical response the music may evoke in the listener.

Setting aside the normal tendencies for the concertgoer's mind to wander, occasioned by an interest in such things as the facial expressions or the clothing of other members of the audience, or by musings as to how they manage to replace a light bulb in the high ceiling of the hall, we are faced with the fact that even those distractions that stem from our concentration on the performers also diminish the purity of our response to the music. Watching a pianist's hands, observing the fact that all the bows of the string players move in unison, or following the gyrations of a conductor are all responses connected with the music, but they have no true relation to the music itself. We can be certain that they were not in the composer's mind when he conceived his music. Yet all these factors, together with the normal personal worries that must inevitably impinge upon the mind of each one of us at some time, no matter how briefly, conspire to destroy the unbroken concentration upon which total appreciation must be based.

Let us carry our oversimplification to its ultimate point and imagine the ideal listener—a devoted amateur who has taken the trouble to familiarize himself with an entire symphony, who is comfortably seated in the best location in a concert hall with his eyes closed, and who has such power of concentration that no single extraneous thought disturbs his attention. Since we have removed all possible obstacles to this listener's response, let us see how close he can come to a total appreciation of the chosen work. As we explore the question, let us assume also that this ideal listener in a sense represents *us*. To the extent that each one of us experiences at least moments of total concentration upon the music itself, we can identify with this admittedly imaginary paragon.

In order for our listener to grasp the *entire* musical content of the symphony, it will be necessary for him to be able to recognize and remember every single melody, theme, or motive in the work. In addition, his familiarity with them must be so thorough that he recognizes them when they reappear in different guises—played by different instruments, accompanied by different harmonies, played at different speeds, broken up so that only a part of a melody appears, combined with one another, played upside down, and perhaps even played backward! He will also have to be aware of harmonic progressions and accompaniments, so that, when one or the other reappears without the melody with which it had previously been associated, he will realize that an allusion is being made.

These are but a few of the purely intellectual feats of recognition and memory our imaginary listener will have to achieve, if he is to experience total appreciation. Considering the number of melodies contained in the average nineteenth-century symphony, and the numerous transformations to which those melodies are subjected in the course of a work lasting from thirty minutes to an hour and a half, it becomes immediately apparent that such an achievement must be quite rare.

Moreover, if his appreciation is to be really complete, our listener will have to have sufficient knowledge of the music that was written before and during the same period as the symphony in question, so that he can evaluate its originality and its place in the stream of music. All of this—the recognition of all themes and their relationships, as well as the ability to pass judgment upon the value and the place of the composition— enters into the "ability to listen intelligently" of our original definition. Needless to say, the power to listen at this level is granted to few of us.

Let us now consider how our hypothetical listener might fare in his pursuit of the other main aim of the appreciation of music—namely, the enhancement of the pleasure and satisfaction to be derived from listening. Here, we are caught on the horns of a dilemma, for if our listener were so constituted that he could voluntarily disregard all his past emotional experiences as he listened to a piece of music, then he would of necessity shut himself off from many of the most important pleasures and satisfactions that music has to offer. Indeed, it might be argued that if he possessed the ability which we have credited him with—that of being able to disregard any and all distractions over a sustained period of time —there would be a likelihood that he so lacked emotional responsiveness as to be impervious to the communication that music offers!

Having finished with our mythical listener and sent him back to the fortunately nonexistent realm whence he came, we learn that there is no such thing as a total appreciation of music. Life itself does not permit the sort of hermetically sealed existence that would be required for such a response. Fortunately, however, it is not necessary. Music offers satisfactions at so many different levels that a genuine understanding and enjoyment of the art is open to everyone.

CHAPTER 3

The Five Basic Elements
of Music

There is nothing mysterious about the appreciation of music. Proof of your own potential ability to appreciate it lies in the very fact that you are reading these lines. If it were not for the existence of *something* in music that appeals to you, you would not have chosen to read a book on the subject.

As we proceed to consider the various elements in music that attract you, you may find yourself surprised by the degree of appreciation that you already have. These days, when so many of the world's great symphonies, operas, concertos, songs, and instrumental pieces are readily available on CDs and cassettes, in radio and television broadcasts, and at concerts, anyone with the slightest liking for music must of necessity have listened to some of the most sophisticated musical works ever created. Merely to "like" or to be "attracted to" one of the symphonies of Beethoven or Tchaikovsky implies a complexity of response that would amaze you, if you were to take note of all the factors involved. These symphonies are not simple works, and even what we might regard as only a slight degree of appreciation of them—merely a vague sense of pleasure upon hearing them—bespeaks an ability to respond to music at many levels.

Let us see what it is that you respond to in music.

Do you find something appealing about the famous tune from Schubert's *Unfinished Symphony?* If so, then you are responding to one of the most important elements of music —*melody*.

Do you find that you feel like tapping your foot during the march movement of Tchaikovsky's *Pathétique Symphony?* If so, then you are responding to another extremely important element—*rhythm*.

Yet observe that rhythm is present in the melody of

18

Schubert's *Unfinished* (just tap out the melody on a table with your finger, without singing, and you will isolate the rhythm), and that melody is present in even the most rhythmic portion of the Tchaikovsky march. Therefore, in the process of merely "liking" one of these works, you are actually appreciating *two* musical elements at once. While this example may not impress you by its profundity, the *principle*—being aware of what it is that you respond to—is at the root of all genuine music appreciation.

Now imagine how much less satisfying Schubert's melody would be if it were buzzed through a tissue-papered comb, instead of being played by the entire cello section of an orchestra. The melody and the rhythm would still be present as before; the difference would lie only in the quality of the sound that reached your ears. Therefore, when you enjoy the richness of the sound of the massed cellos playing the melody, you are responding to another of the basic elements—*tone color*. Your appreciation, then, really involves *three* elements.

Now, let us suppose that a pianist is playing one of your favorite songs the melody in the right hand, the accompanying chords in the left. Suppose that his finger slips as he plays one of the chords, causing him to play a sour note. Your immediate awareness of that wrong note comes from your response to another of the basic elements—*harmony*.

Let us briefly consider the more positive implications of harmony. Whether you are attracted by barbershop-quartet singing, or by an atmospheric work by Debussy, or by the powerful, forthright ending of Beethoven's Fifth Symphony, *part* of your reaction stems from your response to the harmony, which may be defined as the simultaneous sounding of two or more notes (usually more than two, as in these three examples). Thus we have found a *fourth* element in your appreciation.

Do you have a sense of completeness at the conclusion of a performance of (we will use only one of countless possible examples) Beethoven's Ninth Symphony? Are you left with a feeling of satisfaction as well as of elation? If so, part of that sense of satisfaction—of completion—comes from your feeling for *form*, which is the last of the five basic elements of music.

Perhaps you will say that you have not been consciously aware of the music's form as such. You may argue that your feelings of satisfaction and elation stem merely from the fact that the symphony ends with the full chorus and orchestra singing and playing loud and fast (by which argument, incidentally, you are acknowledging your appreciation of the work's melody, rhythm, harmony, and tone color).

In that case, imagine that you have just turned on your radio, and the first thing you hear is the final few seconds of Beethoven's Ninth. In spite of the fact that you are hearing a large chorus and orchestra singing and playing at full tilt, your reaction to the sudden outburst of sound would not be the same as it might have been had you experienced the cumulative effect of all the music that preceded it.

True, you would be hearing a climactic moment, but—as a climax to *what?* What would be the motivation—the "reason"—for that tremendous sound, from either the intellectual or the emotional viewpoint? To the extent that you found such an experience unsatisfying, it would be your sense of musical *form* that would be left unsatisfied. Whether or not you have ever thought of it consciously, you demand of music a certain sense of continuity, a "hanging together," a feeling of one passage or mood leading logically to another.

We see, in the light of all this, that you are drawn to music through an appreciation of its basic elements: its melody, rhythm, tone color, harmony, and form. At every moment in which you are listening to music, all five of them are at work to some degree, although their relative importance may change quickly, both in the music itself and in your conscious and unconscious responses to it. As you turn on your radio at random, a song or a popular ballad will emphasize melody, while a jazz orchestra will place greater emphasis upon rhythm, although, to be sure, the other elements will also be present. A work for piano will be limited, of course, to the tone color of the piano, but it will have its full measure of all the other elements. On the other hand, a work for full orchestra by a late nineteenth century romantic composer is likely to abound in contrasting instrumental colors.

Harmony of one kind or another will be present in any music that you happen upon, unless it be a rare work for, let us say, an unaccompanied flute or perhaps for unaccompanied voice, of which Gregorian chant would be the most likely example. Even in music of this sort, consisting of a single accompanied melody, you may feel a certain effect of harmony, an *implied* harmony.

Though form, too, will be present in all the music you hear, it wilt often be one of the more elusive elements. In a popular song or a folk song, the form is usually quite simple and obvious. In an extended orchestral work, such as one of the tone poems of Richard Strauss or Tchaikovsky's Overture-Fantasy *Romeo and Juliet*, the form will be quite complex and less easy to follow.

By way of this intentional oversimplification, we now come to an extremely important point. It is the fact that music can affect our *feelings*. While it would be impossible to catalogue all the varying emotional responses that we may derive from music, let us at least begin by seeing how we respond to the basic elements. Melody goes hand in hand with rhythm; change the *rhythm* of the melody of Schubert's *Unfinished* and you have changed the melody. Hum it to yourself, giving each note the same even time value, and notice that it becomes difficult to recognize, as well as dull in feeling. Play only the rhythm of the most Exciting march, without the melody, and the music loses most of its appeal. If all the notes of Beethoven's Fifth Symphony, without a single alteration of the melody, rhythm, harmony, or form, were to be played by an orchestra of harmonicas or mandolins, we would hear a radically different tonal effect from the one intended by Beethoven—and the emotional impact would be completely changed.

Just as all music, therefore, is a composite of basic elements, in which each one affects all the others, so our response to music at any given moment is the total of our reactions to all the elements.

At this point, it would be beneficial for the reader to explore these five basic elements by means of listening. Choose a piece that you have heard before—preferably a short one—and listen to it several times. With each hearing, try to concentrate on one or the other of the elements.

As you listen for melody—the "subject matter" of the music—take note of the *kinds* of melodies that are presented: their lengths, their contrasting characters, their reappearances, the way they may reappear in fragmentary form or in combination with one another.

The best way to concentrate upon the rhythm—the physical aspect of the music—is to beat the time in some fashion, whether it is by "conducting," moving your head, or tapping your foot. To the extent that the rhythm may at times be hard to follow, you will in this way be gaining an insight into the composer's rhythmic imagination and originality.

As you listen for the tone color—the sensuous aspect of the music—be alert for the contrasts in *kinds* of sounds that are offered, for the different feelings that a melody will arouse when it is played by different instruments, and for the excitement created ·by a great number of instruments playing together.

It might be unwise to attempt to discern the form at the beginning stages of listening. It is nevertheless a fact that each recognition of the reappearance of a melody will increase your awareness of form—the "ground plan" of the music.

If we wanted to be rigid about definitions, we could say that music consists of nothing but the manipulation of the five elements. The statement is correct in that there is no music in the world, regardless of the time or place of its origin, that can be based upon anything other than some combination of these five elements. Thus, to offer the most extreme contrast possible, what we may imagine as the ritual stamping on the ground by the savage appealing to his gods partakes of some of the same basic elements as does Bach's *Passion According to St. Matthew*, notably rhythm and tone color, and certainly, to a degree, form.

CHAPTER 4

Communication in Music

As one who has spent his working life with music—listening to it, conducting it, broadcasting, lecturing and writing about it— and thus perhaps ought to be a bit casual about it, I still find myself moved by the thought that when I hear a choral work by Bach, or a quartet by Beethoven, these men are actually communicating with me. How wonderful it is to realize that a man who lived as long ago as the sixteenth century—let us say Orlando di Lasso—can still reach us with a jocose little madrigal or with a somber choral work—and all in as abstract and as ephemeral a medium as sound! None the less wonderful is it to think that a contemporary composer—one who is living at this very moment, but whom we will probably never see in person—can also communicate directly with us by the very same means that di Lasso used so long ago.

The phenomenon I am describing is no different, of course, from that by which we are able to know Shakespeare's thoughts through his writings, or Michelangelo's through his sculpture and painting. I often feel that we pay too little attention to this element of personal communication in art when we place so great an emphasis upon objective analysis. The sonnet was written by a living person, the picture painted by a living person, the symphony composed by a living person.

With an apology for its personal nature, I submit the following experience because it demonstrates in brief how music can communicate its message, even when its composer is unknown and when no conscious attempt is made to analyze its effects.

Early one morning, tuning my radio to a program devoted to symphonic recordings, I found myself listening to a gentle passage featuring woodwind instruments—flute, oboe, and clarinet—with a light accompaniment in the strings. One of my first impulses was to try to figure out who the composer was. Then, caught by the mood created by that combination of melody, restful rhythm, instrumental color, harmony, and form (the passage was obviously "going toward" something), I put out of my mind all thought of identifying the composer. The effects of the music itself were more interesting. As I continued to listen, something in the music called forth a welling up of tender feelings. It was one of the most moving moments I have ever experienced in listening to music, and it was an *emotional* reaction above all; it did not come from any analysis of the themes, of the chord structure, of the form. At that moment, surely, I was appreciating the music simply as music.

Another thought came to my mind after that particular passage had ended. It was that this was beautiful music. Without knowing who the composer was—without being influenced by a name, famous or second-rate—I made my judgment. Later, as the music continued, I realized from the kinds of melody, from the particular rhythms, from the ways in which the instruments were employed, from the manner in which the harmony was used, and from the way one section of the music followed another, that I was listening to a symphony by Mahler.

Now, the point of presenting all these personal reactions.

First: when I spoke of being moved by the idea that Bach or Orlando di Lasso or Beethoven could communicate with me across the centuries, notice that I could not speak of a string quartet by di Lasso, or a madrigal by Beethoven, or a symphony by Bach. We realize, from this, that the *forms* of expression have been different at different times, depending in part upon the music's purpose, in part upon the social and economic forces at work at the given times. When we listen to any piece of music, then, we should do so with some awareness of the time in which it was composed. A string fantasy by the early English composer Henry Purcell, being a brief piece to be performed by aristocratic amateurs, although it uses many of the same notes, does not call for the same attitude in the listener as does a string quartet by the Viennese master Beethoven, who composed such works for performance by the leading professional virtuosi of his day.

Second: the means by which such an ephemeral art as that of organized sounds can be preserved for us over the centuries brings us to the question of musical notation. The whole course of music has been affected by the development of the means of writing it down. Much early music has been lost to us because no way was known to preserve it. Greek poetry, philosophical thought, sculpture, and architecture have come down to us extensively, but we know next to nothing of Greek music. Had musicians been able at an earlier stage to notate their musical ideas, and so to experiment more easily with the possibilities that would then have been open, the kinds of music we listen to today would in all likelihood be quite different.

Third: my mention of some of the emotional responses that may come from an appreciation of poetry or sculpture or painting is intended to point up the fact that there is a correspondence between our reactions to music and to the other art forms. At the same time, it is important to realize that each art form has its own characteristics and limitations. A play or a motion picture can show us an incident in a person's life that music could not possibly portray. A painter, with his visual medium, can more convincingly suggest a country scene than Beethoven is alleged to do in his *Pastoral Symphony*. We do not go to a shoemaker when we need groceries; let us not, therefore, make the mistake of demanding that music—which exists only as sounds—provide us with visual satisfactions. In its own realm, music can affect our feelings in a way that no other art can approach.

Recall how the chance passage from the Mahler symphony evoked a welling up of tender feelings in me. The most important implication of that experience is that the feelings were about *nothing specific*—except the music. Literature and the drama can cause us to have strong emotional reactions to particular people in particular situations, but it is music's unique characteristic—and its strength—that it can create feelings in us *without a specific cause.*

I mentioned the particular time of day at which I heard the Mahler passage simply to make the point that each of us has his own moments of being especially sensitive to music. Not only does responsiveness vary from one individual to another; it can also vary in the same individual from one occasion to another. The implication is, therefore, that the same piece of music can affect you differently at each hearing, depending upon the mood in which you approach it.

I also mentioned my impulse to identify the composer. Here, I was responding to social pressure. It would be unrealistic not to acknowledge the fact that the desire for social acceptance enters into our appreciation of music, no matter to how small a degree. The ability to recognize composers—despite its lesser importance in the long run—has become one of the admired intellectual accomplishments. Can it be denied that, along with the intrinsic artistic pleasures, one of the satisfactions of owning a collection of paintings, or books, or records, or even an expensive stereo system is the prestige that comes with ownership? The accumulation of knowledge is, similarly, looked upon with admiration in certain circles. The ability to recognize a composer from his style does not necessarily imply a genuine appreciation of the music; nevertheless, if the intellectual feat does not become an end in itself, the impulse is a perfectly natural one and all to the good.

There is an important implication in my judgment that the Mahler passage I was hearing was beautiful—that is, excellent—music. In judging art, it is probably impossible for any critic, or any serious listener, to be unaffected by his or her own emotional state or his prejudices.

Would my reaction to that passage have been the same if I had known beforehand that it was Mahler who had composed it? I suspect that, while my reaction would have been *similar*, by and large, it might nevertheless have been colored by preconceptions.

Then, too, to what extent were my reactions the result, not only of Mahler's writing, but also of the sensitive performance of the music? Since the performer is the means by which music is conveyed to us, it is perfectly natural that a certain portion of our appreciation should be bound up with the performance. For some listeners, in fact, the performer is far more important than the music, especially when a glamorous or highly publicized figure is involved. This is another factor that will vary with the individual listener.

Now let us look into the implications of my statement that my reaction was an emotional one, apart from any conscious thought about the themes, chord structure, or form. It is important for us to recognize the fact that, although no conscious analysis may be taking place, the very source of our emotional response lies in the composer's handling of his themes, chord structure, tone colors, rhythms, and form. Ultimately, there is nothing but the ways in which the composer uses these five elements that enables him to produce emotional effects in the listener.

Let us consider simply the matter of form. My appreciation of the passage in the Mahler symphony would have been greater had I happened to tune in at the beginning of the movement. I would then have reacted to that particular passage not only for its own immediate appeal, but from hearing it as a logical outgrowth of what had come before, and as a transition to what was to follow.

And what of Mahler's handling of the other four elements? Obviously, he could not have communicated a feeling of tenderness to me, had he had the entire orchestra playing a loud jagged, rhythmic melody, with dissonant chords. There is implied a great deal of conscious selection on his part with regard to melody, rhythm, tone color, and harmony. His melody, at that point, was of what we might call the "sweeter" kind; his rhythms tended to create an atmosphere of calmness. His choice of instruments—their tone colors, their combinations, and the number used—was determined by the sensuous and emotional quality that he wanted to create. The harmonies contributed to the overall feeling by adding a sense of poignancy. It was Mahler's particular way of handling the five basic elements—his musical style—that finally led me to identify him as the composer.

Several further points emerge from the preceding paragraphs. Observe that it is impossible to describe the effect of a piece of music in words, except in the most general sense.

Our response to music is largely conditioned by social and ethnic factors. For me, Mahler's harmonies evoked a sense of poignancy. A non-westerner, brought up to respond to a completely different musical system, would probably not only not find the harmonies poignant, he might be entirely unaffected by them. Similarly, the differences in the emotional feeling that we derive from hearing different instrumental colors and different rhythms would, we may imagine, leave the non-westerner completely unmoved. Most cultures would recognize the difference between two sharply contrasted rhythms. But even the differences in rhythm are slight, it is doubtful whether the variation in the intended emotional effect would be equally recognized by all cultures. As for melody, what we Might describe as a "sweet" melody would probably leave no such impression on a non-western listener.

"Music is the universal language" is thus a misleading adage. Had there never been an emigration of Europeans to America—had we "Americans" known nothing but the music of the Indians who were here before Columbus came—we should today probably be entirely unresponsive to the music of Mahler and Bach and Beethoven. Moreover, had it not been for the great influx of Germans to the United States in 1848, our musical scene would probably not have taken on the Germanic coloration that it has had during the last century. Our basic musical diet, partly as a result of that immigration, has been for many decades Bach, Beethoven, and Brahms.

Far from being universal, music is actually extremely specialized in its communication. Let us look at the situation in the United States. The overwhelming majority of the country's approximately 250 million inhabitants are uninterested in the creations of Beethoven, a point that is easily proved by comparing the sales of recordings by popular rock or country music singers with those of the music of Beethoven. Carrying the point further, even among the relatively small percentage of people who like symphonic music, you will find that a melody that is "poignant" to one person may be "saccharine" to another. Thus the myth of the universality of music is further cut into by personal tastes.

Think of what a complex chain of circumstances went into making my response to that passage in the Mahler symphony just what it was. My personal taste at that moment was determined not only by the immediate factors—my state of physical and mental well-being, which shaped my mood—but also by the degree to which my ethnic and social background had exposed me to music, first of all, then to serious music then to serious orchestral music, then to serious orchestral music of an AustroGermanic cast, and finally, within that specialized realm, to the individual style of Mahler! So we see that the five basic elements of the music itself are supplemented by what we might call the sixth element, the *listener*, who is usually a highly complex variable.

To summarize: Music is a means of communication of emotional states. Its forms vary with the particular needs and usages of the place and time of its origin. Our appreciation of music hinges upon the degree of our understanding of what music can and cannot do. It also varies with our backgrounds, which are determined by ethnic and social influences, and further shaped by our individual experiences. Our mood of the moment, as well as our reaction to the performer and to the performance, also affects our response to any particular hearing of a piece of music.

CHAPTER 5

The Myth of Storytelling in Music

From compositions with titles such as *The Sorcerer's Apprentice, The Moldau, The Swan of Tuonela, Death and Transfiguration,* and the like, the layman may gain the impression that music is about such nonmusical phenomena as stories, scenes in nature, and philosophies. While "program music"—that is, music that purports to tell a story or paint a picture—reached its greatest popularity with composers and audiences in the nineteenth century, and is therefore sometimes looked upon as a phenomenon peculiar to what we call "the romantic period," it was even at that time actually nothing new. There has hardly been a time, in fact, when composers have not attempted to depict in their music storms, battles, birds, murmuring streams, and countless other essentially nonmusical subjects.

Handel, a century before the romantic period, offered pictorial ideas in his oratorios, and in his *Israel in Egypt*, for example, gives the violins a running figure that, because it is played in conjunction with the chorus's "And there came all manner of flies," suggests the buzzing of flies. Well after the Romantic period had ended, a new peak was reached when Arthur Honegger pretended to take the listener for a locomotive ride in his *Pacific* 231, and Alexander Mossolov, a Russian avant-gardist of 1928, shocked sensitive listeners with his graphic descriptive piece *The Iron Foundry*.

The basic and quite familiar idea of program music, which has had thousands of applications and will doubtless have thousands more, is at least as old as 586 B.C., as demonstrated by the Greek composition of that year, now known as the "Pythic nome." Played by a single *aulos*, a reed instrument somewhat like our oboe, it purported to offer a "demonstration of Apollo's fight with the dragon," in five sections, titled: 1. Preparation; 2. Challenge; 3. The Fight; 4. Song of Praise; 5. Victory Dance.

For the listener, the question is not whether it is right or wrong for composers to portray or imitate or derive inspiration from battles, locomotives, and the insect world. Obviously there is nothing wrong with this. Rather, it is how much our knowledge of the composer's programmatic intention or Aspiration helps us to appreciate his music. Long experience with listeners' problems in understanding music has led me to the conviction that an approach to appreciation that is based on the alleged storytelling or descriptive powers of music is not only misleading, it is actually harmful, in that it encourages the listener to look and listen for the wrong satisfactions.

Rather than present all my proofs first, I shall begin with the conclusion, which is simply that music, despite all claims to the contrary, has absolutely no ability to tell a story, describe a person's character, or portray a scene. As we explore the reasons for this incapacity, we shall at the same time see what music *can* do. We shall also see why many authorities, including even musicians themselves, find it opportune to perpetuate the "storytelling" myth.

Because it consists of sounds, music does have the power to imitate some of the sounds we hear about us, and it is this ability that is the basis for most of its claimed descriptive power. Obviously, a composer can imitate the song of a bird with a flute or an oboe. But mere imitation is hardly more than a clever stunt; it is no more music than the original bird's song is music. (The nature lover who maintains that a bird's song is music should be aware that he is using the term in a loose, poetic sense. Here we are assuming that the term "music" refers to compositions consciously created by humans, rather than to sounds found in nature.)

Mention of the songs of birds may immediately bring to the reader's mind the passage near the end of the second movement of the *Pastoral Symphony*, where Beethoven imitates a cuckoo, a quail, and a nightingale. Realize, however, that this is no more than a momentary touch in a work that takes the better part of three-quarters of an hour to perform. It can hardly be put forward as the basis of an esthetic theory, especially in view of the fact that Beethoven never did anything like it again. Its very obviousness has served to draw much greater attention to those few moments of the symphony than they deserve.

On an equally obvious level is the roll on a bass drum, as an imitation of thunder. Moreover, the softness or loudness of the drum-roll can suggest distant thunder or it can place us in the middle of the storm. Let us grant immediately that music has descriptive powers of this sort, but let us also admit that such devices, and others that are similarly based merely on the trick of imitation, are too obvious to detain us Anger.

One of music's greatest powers is that of creating moods. That is what makes it so suitable as a background accompaniment to a scene in a play or opera, in the movies or on television. This is another source of the belief that music can tell a story. Appropriate music is found—or is written—for a movie. It is appropriate in that it *supports* or *reinforces* the *mood* of the scene it accompanies. If the movie becomes popular; a cassette or CD of the background music may be issued.

Some listeners will then assume that the music as such tells the story. Here, of course, the power of suggestion comes into play. The listener recalls the story of the movie; in addition, his or her memory is helped by the summary of the scenario printed in the booklet accompanying the CD, and by the title of the composition.

Because of music's ability to create moods, some of this music may be highly appropriate to the scenes it accompanies. Surely, given two pieces of music, one loud and turbulent, the other soft and gentle, and faced with the problem of deciding which piece would suggest a storm at sea and which would be more suitable as a lullaby, no listener would make the wrong decision. At first, this would appear to demonstrate that music *can* tell a story. Yet, consider all the facts. In the situation just described, the listener is armed in advance with knowledge of the content of the scene, so that there is hardly the likelihood of his making an error. But suppose the listener were to hear the music by itself, without any knowledge of what it was intended to represent; would it alone be able to portray specifically and unmistakably a storm at sea? Or, would it not simply create a feeling of excitement and turbulence? Would the quiet excerpt inevitably be a lullaby in the mind of the listener, or would it not be more likely to create just a feeling of calmness? Could it not just as well accompany *any* scene whose emotional tone is calm and gentle?

This is the crux of the problem. It accounts for the fact that the "storytelling" idea has endured throughout music's history; paradoxically, it also explains why the idea is a fallacious one. Because music is able to create a wide variety of moods and feelings, the same piece of music can be appropriate to any number of specific situations, provided they have a similar emotional tone. In a sense, music can be compared to a chameleon in its ability to take on the coloration of its surroundings. Given a storm at sea and any suitably turbulent music, the power of suggestion created by the visual concept of the storm makes the music *seem* to be a description of that scene. Yet the music, by itself, might do equally well for a fight, a mob scene, or a bad dream in which someone is being chased.

Listen to the climax of Tchaikovsky's *Romeo and Juliet* Overture-Fantasy. I submit that there is no more vivid "description" of a storm at sea in all of music—complete with tremendous waves, wind-lashed sails, and claps of thunder. Yet this passage is intended to represent the enmity between the families of the lovers! The narrative or descriptive content of the scene points our minds in specific directions; in the case of *Romeo and Juliet* our prior knowledge of the story tells us that we are dealing with the hatred between the Montagues and the Capulets. The music merely supplies the *mood* of excitement and turbulence that is appropriate to such a scene. By itself, it cannot make clear the *source* of the turbulence.

While some listeners may maintain that the music, in gradually quieting down, describes the storm's abating, it is actually doing no more than carrying us from a state of emotional excitement to a state of increasing calm. It is with our inner emotional condition—not with external events—that music deals. It is this fact—that the emotional tones of specific actions or scenes can be matched or intensified by music—that has led to the erroneous belief that music can convey a narrative or paint a scene. This, coupled with its imitative powers, is the source of the concept of "program music."

So far, we have examined extreme examples: a storm at sea and a lullaby. What about the kind of event or scene that does not involve such extreme emotional states? Suppose that we now have to decide which of two compositions would describe a quiet scene in the country and which would portray a conversation between two friends. Once again we have the advantage of knowing ahead of time the material that is to be portrayed; yet, the limitations of music as a storyteller or a scene painter are now even more apparent, in so far as there is no longer the obvious difference in emotional tone that we had in the earlier examples. As a result, the two pieces would be roughly similar in mood—so much so, in fact, that they might even be interchangeable. If no suggestion were made to the listener as to what this music was supposed to describe, it is doubtful whether he would be conscious of either scene, or indeed of any scene at all.

It is *prior suggestion*, then, that makes possible the belief that pieces with titles such as *By the Stream* are depicting scenery rather than conveying music. A flowing, uninterrupted succession of notes, which evokes no special image or comment when it occurs in a piece without a title, allegedly becomes descriptive of a "limpid stream" as soon as that visual image is planted in our minds by some title. All one can really say is that the music is *appropriate* to the scene, although it might be equally appropriate to any number of other scenes with a similar emotional tone. Without the title, the music merely creates a gentle mood and evokes certain purely musical reactions as a result of its flowing succession of notes.

What of pieces with titles like *Butterflies*, or *Children at Play*—titles that imply action? Here, by the device of having the melody "skip around," the composer presumably depicts the flight of the insect or the romping of the children. Note that the same music might serve for either of our hypothetical titles. The answer is that, with this type of music, we enter the realm made familiar through the movie cartoon. As the cartoon character ascends a flight of stairs, the music matches his steps—with an upward scale, of course. As he falls and slides, the music supplies a crash and a downward slide, all synchronized with the action. As the cat's tail is caught in the door, the music squeals appropriately.

Among Hollywood composers, this technique is known as "Mickey-mousing." Much as it adds to the effect of the cartoons, it can hardly be taken seriously as an esthetic concept or practice, since it remains at an obvious level and is merely another form of imitation, reducing music to the role of illustrator.

The inherent romanticism in man, which has manifested itself in varying degrees throughout the centuries, has caused him, both as composer and listener, to attach titles to thousands of short pieces of what is really abstract music. There seems to be an uneasiness with the abstract and a need for the concrete, as exemplified by the well-known proverb that "one picture is worth ten thousand words." Undoubtedly, the eighteenth-century aristocrat felt more at home with Rameau's abstract harpsichord pieces when they were given fanciful titles such as *La Timide* or *L'Indiscrète*, even though the titles were inherently meaningless and in most cases might have been interchanged without damage.

By the same token, the title *Moonlight Sonata* is far more appealing than *Sonata in C Sharp Minor, Opus 27, No. 2*. It matters little that the former title was given to the sonata not by Beethoven, but by a critic named Rellstab, who likened the first movement to a boat gliding on the moonlit waters of Lake Lucerne. (It might just as easily have become known as the *Lake Lucerne Sonata*.) Incidentally, Rellstab's interpretation concerned only the first movement. As a result, listeners who feel that they "understand" that movement when they see visions of moonlight are often left entirely in the dark by the other two movements of the sonata, a gently rhythmic *allegretto*, and a brusque, stormy *presto*.

Generally speaking, despite all the efforts of the twentieth century avant-gardists to establish their new kinds of electronic music, we are still under the influence of the Romantic period in our musical listening and our musical appreciation Yet, contrary to the common notion, music is *not* a language In a language, words have specific meanings. Thus, the word *house* brings to mind a specific concept that will not be confused with the concept represented by the word *ocean*. But even language is not always as specific as it might be. The word *house* still does not tell us anything about the size, color, and design of the structure. Further qualifying words, each with its own specific meaning, are required to complete the picture.

Music, however, has no melody, no chord, no tone color no rhythm, no form that can convey even as general and simple a concept as *house*. It is just as incapable of conveying, by itself, the exploits of Don Juan, the antics of Till Eulenspiegel, or the predicament of the Sorcerer's Apprentice. The only way in which we are able to learn the "story" allegedly contained in the tone poems devoted to these people (the first and second by Richard Strauss, the third by Paul Dukas) is through the medium of words.

All program music of this sort depends upon the purely arbitrary assignment of specific literary or pictorial meanings to the various melodies. We can assume, of course, that the composer exercises good judgment, so that a sweet young lady will not be represented by a series of dissonant chords. However, once a general type of melody has been chosen to represent a specific character or idea, one melody will do as well as another.

Let us consider a few well-known examples in which, it should now be clear, music is really shown to be unable to tell a story. Prokofieff's *Peter and the Wolf* is generally regarded as one of the most descriptive works of our day Its meaning is considered to be so apparent, in fact, that it is thought to be easily comprehensible by children. If this were actually the case—if the music could really tell the story—why was it considered necessary to translate the composer's original Russian narration into English? Or, to go a step further, why was any narration necessary at all?

The effectiveness of the music, which is most appropriate, depends upon a number of the standard means used by composers of program music: arbitrary assignment of meaning (the Narrator's statement that Peter is represented by the strings, the duck by the oboe, the cat by the clarinet, etc., all with their attendant melodies); imitation (the rifle shots, the bird call, etc.); "Mickey-mousing" (Peter letting down the rope); and prior suggestion (the excitement in the orchestra at the Narrator's words, " 'Look out!' cried Peter."). Thus, delightful as it is, the music tells no story, and is really no more than *appropriate* to the character, action, and mood suggested by the words.

The device of imitation is sometimes used even in ultraserious works. Strauss's *Death and Transfiguration* opens with a quietly repeated rhythmic figure. We are told that this represents the pulse beat of the dying man. In other words, "Mickey-mousing." But, clever as this is, and appropriate as the music sounds in the light of this knowledge, even so obvious and frankly imitative a device as this will still be heard as abstract music until we have been *told* what it represents.

Association is another device upon which the alleged storytelling power of program music hinges. Tchaikovsky's *1812 Overture* contains fragments of the *Marseillaise* and ends with a stirring version of the old Tsarist hymn. The listener who recognizes that the snatches of the *Marseillaise* represent the French might just gather, from the fact that the Russian anthem is played later, complete and louder, that Napoleon was defeated at Moscow—but a prior knowledge of European history will help him immeasurably here. To the listener who happens not to be familiar with the associations attached to the two melodies, Tchaikovsky's work will be simply exciting music.

Richard Wagner's use of what he called the *Leitmotiv* ("leading motive") is another example of the arbitrary assignment of meanings to purely abstract melodies and chord progressions. Not only was each character in his music dramas associated with a particular motive or melody, even such concepts as "filial love" and the "desire to travel" were assigned motives. Thus, while a character's words expressed one view, the audience could tell, by listening to the melodies woven into the orchestral parts, that his actual thoughts were quite different. Again, a very clever idea, which affords a means of gaining psychological insight into the characters. However, unless the listener is made familiar in advance with the arbitrarily assigned meanings of all these motives, he is at a loss to know what insights are being vouchsafed him.

A final example will, I hope, demonstrate how ineffectual music is as a means of telling a story or painting a picture. The French composer Vincent d'Indy wrote a work called the *Istar Variations*, based on the ancient Babylonian legend of Istar, who goes into the other world, seeking the return of her dead lover. She is stopped at each one of seven gates, and is required to remove another article of clothing in order to be allowed to pass through each gate. Finally, she stands before the seventh and last gate, and removes her last piece of clothing. Just as Istar is never entirely revealed until she passes through the final gate, d'Indy first presents the variations, never allowing the listener to hear the theme itself until the end of the work. At the end, however, he presents the theme, completely "unadorned," that is, unharmonized, to represent the state of the heroine at that moment. Certainly, an original idea, and a very graphic one. However, the music at that point would not cause a second thought in the mind of even the most susceptible listener. But let that scene be presented on television! . . .

Another concomitant of the storytelling approach is the belief in music's powers as a portrayer of character. Especially with regard to opera does the myth prevail that music can define character. It may be instructive, therefore, to consider the character of Don Juan, who has been treated not only in Strauss's tone poem of that name, but also by Mozart in his opera *Don Giovanni*. Many writers have assured us that each composer has perfectly captured, in his music, the character of the famous libertine. While we are told that the music offers us a psychological insight into the underlying nature of the Don, the only insight that the music itself really gives us (aside from the internal *musical* organization and development within the respective works) is the undeniable fact that Strauss's *Don Juan* is immediately identifiable as music by Strauss, while Mozart's *Don Giovanni* is immediately identifiable as music by Mozart!

Neither work reveals anything of the amorous philosophy or methods of the Don; instead, what each reveals is its composer's manner of handling musical material, within the framework of the style prevailing in the era in which each composer lived, and the orchestra at his disposal. Yet the fiction that a composer is a "character portrayer" lives on in almost all books, program notes, and commentaries about operas, oratorios, symphonies, overtures, and tone poems—and in newspaper and magazine reviews, too.

Let us assume for a moment that this popularly accepted view is correct—that composers *are* able to depict character in their music. In that case, our ears lead us to conclude that Nietzsche's Superman, as allegedly portrayed in Strauss's tone poem *Thus Spake Zarathustra*, bears a great resemblance to Don Juan, and yes, even to the puckish Till Eulenspiegel, for all three of these tone poems are unmistakably related in styles of melody, harmonic treatment, and orchestration. Even if we grant that Strauss employed different themes with which to "portray" the various individuals, they all bear the unmistakable mark of his pen; they have a family resemblance that reveals their single origin.

Moreover—and while this is a more subtle point, it is nevertheless an extremely important one—let us realize that a musical composition contains far more than just the melodies that are meant to represent a character or an event. Regardless of how appropriate the melodies themselves may be to the persons or things they are intended to suggest, it is what *happens* to them—the ways in which they are developed and combined or alternated—that makes the composition. *That* is what the music is *about*. And here, in the ways in which he treats his melodies, his harmonies, his orchestration—the things that go to make a "style"—Strauss is always Strauss, just as Mozart is always Mozart.

Heretical as this may sound, if the theme said to represent Don Juan's amorous passion had by some chance been substituted for the "transfiguration" theme in *Death and Transfiguration*, and then been treated in Strauss's typical manner, we would be told how well it conveyed the idea of transfiguration.

In the light of all this, the listener who tunes in his radio after a work has begun, and recognizes it as by Strauss but finds himself unable to tell *which* tone poem he is listening to, need not chide himself for any lack of musical understanding. It is only through repeated association of the music with its title—a purely arbitrary process—that a listener is able to tell which work he is hearing.

It may be instructive to consider what happens to character portrayal when a composer uses music from one of his works in another work with a different subject matter. Gluck, for example, put into his ballet *Don Juan* the music of the "Chorus of the Furies" from his opera *Orpheus*, omitting the chorus and, of course, the words. In its purely instrumental setting, the music serves equally well in the ballet and in the opera, yet no one would for a moment maintain that the character of the idealistic Orpheus has anything in common with that of Don Juan.

One more example of supposed character portrayal may be helpful. Goethe's *Faust* has been a popular subject with composers. Among the best-known treatments are Gounod's opera, Liszt's *A Faust Symphony*, Wagner's *A Faust Overture*, and the *Damnation of Faust* by Berlioz. Somewhat less familiar are Schumann's *Scene from Faust*, and Mahler's use of a scene from Goethe's drama in his Eighth Symphony Now, if the character of Faust could really be portrayed by some exceptional arrangement or combination of notes, might we not expect to hear at least a few moments of correspondence among these various works?

Yet it is impossible to find a single passage in any of the works that displays any recognizable correspondence with any portion of another. Instead, what we find is that each work follows its own *musical* course, irrespective of the character of Faust and of the incidents in the narrative, Moreover, because of each composer's individualities in matters of musical style, each work immediately calls to mind, not the portrayal of Faust by any of the other composers, but rather other compositions by the *same* composer—works having nothing to do with Faust.

Some might argue that each composer's music is his "interpretation" of Goethe's *Faust*, but we may wonder how valid an "interpretation" is if it cannot provide any conception of the person or dramatic situation allegedly being interpreted. Also, how precisely applicable to the subject at hand is any musical "interpretation," if it has more in common with the same composer's interpretations of other, widely different subjects, than it has with several other composers' versions of the same subject?

Thus we see that when Beethoven (who was somewhat strait-laced) disapproved of Mozart for having made Don Juan the hero of an opera, his reservations could have been directed only against the story, in view of the inability of Mozart's music to suggest the Don's moral outlook. And by the same token—despite what we are told—Verdi could not portray, through his music alone, the evil in Iago's character.

What a composer really expresses or "interprets" is himself. He demonstrates, not the character traits-of some real or imaginary figures, nor their actions, but rather his own creation of themes and his particular methods of handling them. He shows us how he organizes his musical materials, so that the final product appeals to our sense of musical logic and to our emotions. If Wagner's *A Faust Overture* gives us an insight into anything beyond the musical material itself, it is not into the character of Goethe's hero; it is, rather, into the rest of Wagner's music.

In view of music's inability to project scenes, characters, and stories, we are entitled to wonder how so many writers on music can be in agreement about the specific "meaning" of many works. Even those commentators who are able to leave Napoleon out of their discussion of Beethoven's Third Symphony cannot seem to ignore the fact that Beethoven subtitled the work *Sinfonia Eroica*, after he had removed the dedication to Napoleon. Thus, much has been written about how the symphony expresses "heroism" in all its aspects.

Similarly, specific thoughts continue to be associated with the same composer's Fifth Symphony except that here the music is said to be about "victory over fate." The commentators use as their starting point the remark supposedly made by Beethoven (there is considerable doubt about its authenticity) concerning the opening four notes of the symphony: "Thus Fate knocks at the door." They refer, also, to the triumphant mood that characterizes *parts* of the final movement.

Now, the fact is that, since both the Third and the Fifth Symphonies are highly organized musical structures, each contains, for the sake of musical contrast, extended sections that can hardly be attributed to the concept of either heroism or victory. Moreover, even within the movements whose prevailing moods *are* appropriate to the feelings of heroism and victory—the opening and closing movements of both symphonies—there are sections whose emotional tone does not lend itself to either of those concepts. The conventional analyses are of no assistance at all during these sections.

Let us now meet the commentators on their own ground and consider only those sections of the two symphonies which, by their predominant mood, lend themselves to being interpreted as heroic or victorious.

Each of the works is characteristic of Beethoven's mature style; they were completed within four years of each other. In the more powerful passages of both symphonies, Beethoven produced expressions of the feelings of virility, forthrightness, excitement, triumph, or what you will—including heroism and victory, if you wish—that outstripped anything that he or any other composer had produced of that nature up to that time. But—and here is the important point—despite claims to the contrary, no one can point to any section of either symphony and demonstrate that it clearly conveys the idea of heroism as distinct from that of victory. The loud, exciting portions of the *Eroica* fit the idea of victory just as well as do the similar portions of the Fifth Symphony; the climactic sections of the Fifth Symphony can be said to be just as heroic as the corresponding portions of the *Eroica*.

Here we are not dealing with distinctions as obvious as those to be found in, let us say, Moussorgsky's *Pictures at an Exhibition*, in which each section of the music supposedly describes a specific painting, nor are we concerned with relatively obvious events in a narrative, such as are alleged to take place in Rimsky-Korsakov's *Scheherazade*. While, as has been pointed out, music is not actually capable of doing any more than "backing up" the mood or emotional tone of a specific event, it is easy to distinguish between that portion of *Scheherazade* intended to suggest "The Young Prince and the Princess" and the one that accompanies the scene in which a ship is said to founder in a storm. The contrast in the emotional tones of the respective musical passages makes that distinction obvious. In the case of the two Beethoven symphonies, the distinction that commentators claim to make is between concepts whose emotional tone is identical, in compositions that are cut from the same cloth.

Both symphonies are exciting examples of Beethoven's discourses on the intellectual and emotional possibilities inherent in his melodies, or themes. The themes of both symphonies, however, are as abstract as any to be found in all of music. (Incidentally, several of the main themes in both symphonies—

in fact, in the very portions which most readily lend themselves to the heroic or the victorious concepts—are built out of nothing more than the common chord.) The opening and closing movements of both works contain some of the most exciting music ever created, but there is no one who can say what that excitement is about. While portions of those movements undeniably create the emotional tones appropriate to heroism and victory, an equally valid claim could be advanced that they express just animal spirits.

It is the merit of any piece of music that it creates its own particular kind of excitement. That excitement derives its quality from the nature of the composer's melodies and his musical idiom, from his national background and his time in history. Attempts to go further in specifying its nature or its cause cannot really be accepted as valid.

Finally, consider that most composers who have written programmatic works have also written nonprogrammatic works, usually referred to as "absolute" music. Yet the programmatic compositions and the absolute works by any one composer will be found, for the most part, to be indistinguishable from each other.

One example is the scherzo of Mendelssohn's incidental music to *A Midsummer Night's Dream*, often praised for the way it portrays the fairyland of Shakespeare's play. True, it is wonderfully appropriate music. But had Mendelssohn substituted for that movement the scherzo of his *Octet for Strings*, in the orchestral version which he himself made, the music would have been just as appropriate—and doubtless just as highly praised. The only reason Shakespeare's fairyland is not mentioned in connection with the scherzo of the *Octet* is that the latter was published as part of an abstract, nonprogrammatic composition.

If the programmatic works are really capable of delineating the stories that are attributed to them, what should we think of such abstract works, written in precisely the same musical style? What is their "meaning," when they offer no titles or stories to guide us? Only one of two possible answers is valid. If the programmatic concept has validity, then all music must be telling some kind of story. If, however, the concept possesses as little validity as we have seen in this chapter, then no music can tell a story.

CHAPTER 6

The Myth and the
Listener's Problem

Many listeners, as we have already noted, prefer the concrete to the abstract. This is likely to be particularly true in the case of the listener who is searching for the "meaning" of music. Surrounded as one is by a plethora of comment about what almost every composition supposedly represents, and often unable to tell what the music is "about" until one has read the program notes, the layman is apt to become the victim of a steadily growing sense of inferiority. One assumes that one's inability to hear the story in the music is due to one's own lack of skill. One then becomes fair game for what Virgil Thomson aptly called the "music appreciation racket."

He reads or listens to those who offer him an "understanding" of music by telling him the specific stories or pictures to look for in each composition. For the moment, at least, and for those particular compositions, he no longer has to wander in the realm of the abstract. His need for the concrete has been satisfied, and he now thinks he "understands" the music In reality, he is merely imagining the story or the picture that someone has suggested to him, relegating the music to the background as an accompaniment. Since not all the events in the story are likely to-have that extreme emotional coloration that will make their accompanying music immediately identifiable, what the layman really does is to wait for those one or two obvious moments when he can be sure that the music and the "story" coincide.

Thus, in *Till Eulenspiegel*, having been told that Till is finally caught and hanged, our listener must wait until that moment, near the end, when ominous-sounding chords unquestionably announce the hero's demise. Since the series of chords occurs only once, the listener has no problem matching the music with the event. As for the rest of the work, one has vague images of Till's antics, but since most of these are of a mischievous nature, and most of the music is lighthearted in tone, one is unable to make any specific passage correspond with the precise event it is supposed to portray. The result is a kind of general reverie about the story, with the music supplying a pleasant background.

One hears the argument, even from relatively sophisticated music lovers, that the attention given to the story or picture in a piece of music does no more than to add a harmless fillip to the listener's enjoyment. It is assumed that the layman, realizing that the story is not really to be taken seriously, gives it only momentary consideration, and then turns his thoughts to a genuine consideration of the music itself. Thus, it is argued, a brief warning to the effect that the story or pictorial idea is not to be taken too seriously should be sufficient to protect the novice listener from any false interpretation. Years of contact with the problems of the ordinary listener compel me to disagree. *The music lover of today is subjected to more influences that tend to make music seem concrete than ever before in history.* Radio and television commentators, program notes at concerts and in CD booklets, conductors and performers who comment at concerts, music appreciation lecturers, advertisements for recordings, and music appreciation books and records all tend to inundate the unsuspecting listener in a torrent of information of a storytelling or programmatic nature. Since all these media vie with one another for the commercial rewards of a mass market, they constantly seek to broaden their appeal, and it is almost inevitable that they exploit the storytelling or pictorial approach as the one that is the most immediately appealing to the greatest number of purchasers.

The Food and Drug Administration protects the consuming public to the extent of requiring the commercial processor to list the ingredients of his product on the label. Unfortunately, the consumer of information about the arts has no such protection against false, misleading, or harmful statements. The undue awe that the American public has for the printed word and for any information conveyed by the mass media adds further strength to the fallacious viewpoint. Moreover, many recognized music experts lend their names and their services to these misleading endeavors, adding to them the weight of authority.

I wish that those who regard the "storytelling" lure as harmless would attend some of the introductory sessions in my lecture series, and witness the actual results of these fallacious approaches to music appreciation. Far too much time has to be spent canceling the effects of years of exposure to the idea that every piece of music is "about" something extramusical. Sad as it is to report, many listeners confess that they still cannot hear Beethoven's *Pastoral Symphony* without visualizing dancing fauns—as the result of their having seen the motion picture *Fantasia*.

When asked what Beethoven's Third Symphony (the *Eroica*) is "about," a large proportion of my adult students immediately answer "Napoleon." And the certainty of their response is far greater than their already confessed lack of knowledge about music in general would warrant. I add with pleasure, however, that an occasional student will timidly ask *why* Beethoven's Third Symphony is about Napoleon, confessing that he has never been able to see the connection. Unfortunately, when told that *this* listener is on the right track in his inability to see Napoleon in the *Eroica*, the rest of my students are baffled, even though they soon confess that they too have not found Napoleon in the music. They assume that the symphony *must* be about Napoleon, because for years they have heard this assertion, and that it was *they* who somehow lacked the ability to discern his presence when the composition was played.

When I play the first few bars of Beethoven's *Moonlight Sonata* and ask what the music "means," someone will respond immediately with the familiar title, claiming to see a romantic scene bathed in moonlight. Again, the speed and the certainty of the answer are out of all proportion to the timidity displayed in response to practically all other questions I may pose about music. I will then play Beethoven's quietly repeated three note figure upside down, and ask whether the music still conveys the idea of moonlight. The answer is invariably a look of utter confusion, despite the fact that the mood of the music—as well as its harmony, rhythm, tone color, and form—is unchanged.

My request for reactions to a concert performance of Mahler's Second Symphony elicited a response from a woman to the effect that she and her two companions had left the concert hall in a state of ecstasy—lost in thoughts about the Resurrection. This was a listener who had already admitted that she "knew nothing" about music, and that she was not only unable to tell one Mahler symphony from another, but could not have distinguished the music of Mahler from that of any other composer. Of course, it was the symphony's nick-name that gave her something specific to think about. (The name stems from the fact that the closing movement employs a chorus and vocal soloists singing a text concerning the Resurrection.) As for the "meaning" of the other movements of the work, this same listener predictably had no answers. Her pleasure in the final movement obviously came almost entirely from her contemplation of the words. She might have experienced the same reaction by simply reading the text, with any suitable music supplying the background.

In all the cases I have cited (along with innumerable others), the layman tends to seize upon any bit of specific information with what amounts to almost a sense of relief. For that particular work, or for that single movement, at least, he feels that he is on firm ground. However, being unable to bear the story or see the pictures unless and until they are pointed out to him, the layman wrongly assumes that he has teen missing the "meaning" of the music. The ability to understand music looms up as a specialized, mystical skill, possessed only by the experts, and the lay listener turns to an "authority" for an explanation of every single work, much as a hypnotized subject waits for instructions from the hypnotist. Every time I play a recording of an unfamiliar piece of music during my lectures and then ask for reactions, the majority of my audience remain silent, not knowing what to "see" or think, and afraid to trust their own reactions. "I am only a layman. I don't know what I'm sup-posed to be listening for," the blank faces seem to say. "*You* are the authority. Please tell us how to enjoy this piece."

This is the result of the steady exposure to the influences mentioned above; a good portion of the public are drawn to music, but frightened into an esthetic strait jacket and afraid to enjoy themselves.

Older readers may recall their experiences in elementary school, when music appreciation consisted of Walter Damrosch's application of doggerel rhymes to the melodies of the famous symphonies. Everyone admits that this helped not one bit in advancing his or her appreciation of music. Many, in fact, confess that it actually hindered a true enjoyment of music, since to this day they cannot hear those works without also hearing the ludicrous words. However, to judge by the obvious amusement with which people recall these experiences, it is apparent that they do not take that sort of approach seriously. Worthless as it was as a means of learning how to appreciate music, it was less misleading than today's emphasis upon alleged concrete "meanings."

Here are only a few of the innumerable current examples of the kinds of influence to which the layman is exposed:

A recording of Aaron Copland's music for the ballet *Appalachian Spring* prides itself on the fact that it is the complete version. The principal addition to the score, distinguishing this recording from previous versions, is, according to the liner notes, a section "dramatic in nature, in which the young bride anticipates motherhood. Her reactions —joy, fear bordering on hysteria, and wonder—are vividly revealed." It should be pointed out that this claim, which asserts a manifest impossibility, was *not* made by the composer himself. Copland was certainly a sensitive enough composer; we can be certain that his music will be *appropriate* to the action of the ballet. But, as explained earlier, any other equally exciting music that Copland had written in the same style would have served the purpose assigned it here; the passage in question cannot actually "reveal" what it is claimed to reveal.

The liner notes of a recording of Richard Strauss's *Don Juan* use the technique of one commentator quoting a previous commentator. "According to Mauke, Don Juan makes three conquests in Strauss's symphonic poem. The first . . . is easy, and takes only seventy bars in *Allegro molto con brio*." (Sophisticated "Mickey-mousing"!) "The opening theme represents the philosophical concept of the multiplicity of womanly essence." (Arbitrarily assigned meaning.)

After identifying the first victim as Zerlina, Mauke says: "But this conquest leaves a feeling of disgust and lassitude, expressed in dreary chromatics. The second conquest starts on the ninth-chord in *pianissimo*. The intended victim is a blonde countess, who lives in a villa one hour's ride from Seville." (Even the firmest believer in music's ability to convey literal information might wonder about its definition of a woman's social status, the color of her hair, and the location of her residence, except that such claims are seriously made by writers who seem to know, and who appear to have the listener's interests at heart.)

"The third and tragic love is Anna. She is a G Major creature; but the chromatics of disgust are contrapuntally projected against her theme at the very outset." (Wilhelm Mauke, a German critic, seems obsessed by the idea that chromatic progressions signify disgust. If he is correct, Tristan and Isolde must have had a continuously "disgusting" affair, in view of Wagner's use of this resource in his Highly chromatic music drama.) Mauke concludes: "Then comes death by the sword of Don Pedro. Don Juan's blood flows slowly down the tremolos of the violins. ["Mickey-mousing" with a vengeance!] He expires in E Minor."

Another source of constant emphasis on the subject matter approach is our radio stations. Program directors, particularly of the smaller stations that depend upon recordings for most of their musical fare, are given to celebrating seasonal or patriotic dates with supposedly appropriate music. The following works were among those broadcast by two of New York City's leading "good music" stations on a first day of spring: the *Symphony Number One* of Schumann, nicknamed *Spring Symphony*; *On Hearing the First Cuckoo in Spring*, by Delius; *Rondes de Printemps*, by Debussy; and Stravinsky's *The Rite of Spring*. The first day of winter was the occasion for programming the concerto called "Winter," from Vivaldi's *The Seasons*, Prokofieff's *Winter Holiday*, and Tchaikovsky's *Symphony Number One*, subtitled *"Winter Dreams."*

Needless to say, these works, and others like them, are chosen solely on the basis of their titles, for there is nothing in any of them that is inherently—that is, musically—related to the title. Incidentally, the needs of *good programming*, from the *musical* standpoint, are completely disregarded on such occasions. The only criterion is that all the works have the appropriate title.

Now what of the general run of teachers of music appreciation? A lecturer at one of New York City's most famous cultural institutions, in what purported to be a discussion of Beethoven's *Eroica* Symphony, spent the major portion of the time showing his audience slides of early nineteenth-century paintings of military subjects. On another occasion this same lecturer repeated the old saw about the descending violin figure in the *"Et incarnatus est"* of Bach's *Mass in B Minor*. "It is thought by some," he said, "that this represents the angels descending from heaven." True, he did not actually say that such was the case; but how many of his listeners noticed and remembered that "It is thought by some"? Did not the descending angels gain substance in their minds because he, an authority, said so? Several hundred listeners, I am convinced, left that lecture believing that the way to understand that particular piece is to look for the angels. Bach, who wrote that musically expressive, emotionally poignant music, would surely have deplored the disservice done him in the name of education.

So prevalent have all these practices become that even performing musicians unthinkingly accept them as a valid approach to the appreciation of their art. The leader of a string quartet, faced with the prospect of a preperformance discussion of Schubert's *Quartet Number Fourteen,* nicknamed *Death and the Maiden*—a composition whose musical riches would justify hours of investigation—automatically chose the *story* suggested by the nickname as the prime focus. Again, a member of a well-known group that was about to perform Schubert's so-called *Trout Quintet* on a televised children's program began his remarks with: "Now, you all know what a trout is." He then proceeded to tell about the actions of the fish, and of their supposed representation in the music.

The two Schubert works mentioned have, of course, absolutely nothing whatsoever to do with either death and the maiden, or a trout. The first gets its subtitle from the fact that one of its four movements is a series of variations based on the piano accompaniment (not even the vocal melody) of a *portion* of a song that Schubert wrote, whose *words* concern "Death and the Maiden." The second takes its nickname from the fact that one of its movements is a set of variations on a song of Schubert's whose words have to do with a trout. A wag once suggested that the so-called *Trout* variations represent, respectively, fried trout, baked trout, broiled trout, and so on. As outrageous as this idea is, it is no sillier than some of the thoughts that have been put forth in all seriousness about this composition's descriptive powers.

Professional musicians go on spreading such interpretations partly out of habit and partly because it is an easy way out of a chore that they find uncongenial. But while many performing musicians regard the teaching of appreciation as unimportant, we might note that if they were to display the same lack of concern for accuracy in their playing, they would not find many listeners.

Much of the guilt for the continued promulgation of the storytelling approach must be laid to the writers of books on music appreciation. Typically, they make only a glancing reference to the fact that music cannot tell a story or paint a picture, before launching into extensive interpretations that do violence to this basic truth. One such book, intending "to guide the uninitiated traveler who would embark upon a journey into the complex land of music," provides a *seven page* tracing of the story of *Till Eulenspiegel*, even giving the bar numbers of the score at which each of its episodes presumably occurs.

After reading these statements proclaiming music's ability to "tell us a story," "draw clear pictures," "describe characters exactly," and "leave us in little doubt," what impression can the inexperienced listener possibly have other than that music is a means of conveying specific stories, pictures, and ideas? *That this emphasis upon the programmatic aspects of music nowhere appears in any books intended for the instruction of composers is perhaps the clearest proof of how invalid the concept actually is.*

One further source of the emphasis on concreteness—the pictures or photographs that adorned many LP record jackets. We should not underestimate their effect on the purchaser. Many record covers contain pictorial illustrations of the name of the work, furthering the impression that the music is about the subject matter contained in the title.

In view of listeners' constant exposure to all the influences we have examined, it is no wonder that they are often deeply troubled by what they consider their inadequate responses. It is hoped that the material in these chapters will show how to keep from being overwhelmed by what is, taken all in all, a nonmusical approach to music.

CHAPTER 7

Program Music
As Composers View It

What, now, of those composers who have said that they had a specific story or picture in mind when they wrote a particular work? In the light of the point of view thus far taken toward program music, how shall we regard such statements by the very creators of the music? Did their intentions really shape the music itself, to such an extent as to affect the way in which we should listen to it?

First, let us recall that the linking of music with some literary, pictorial, or philosophical concept was one of the dominant characteristics of the nineteenth-century Romantic movement. This was the period in which the composer discovered himself as a temperamental individual. The older musical structures of variations, symphonies, concertos, and sonatas, which had done so well for the conceptions of Haydn and Mozart, were retained by Beethoven and Schubert, but were filled with music of increasing freedom and emotional intensity.

As the Romantic movement progressed, composers moved away from strict observance of the classical forms, in the direction of greater freedom. As was pointed out earlier, the nature of music itself, and our tolerance as listeners—in essence, two ways of looking at the same thing—allow us to accept considerable latitude in the musical forms, provided that our sense of continuity in the *musical* sense is not disturbed. The purpose of the programmatic composers in loosening the forms was allegedly to allow them to express better the story or the extramusical idea, which was assuming increasing importance. However, despite their use of titles, plots, and similar extramusical elements, the best of these composers carefully retained their sense of musical continuity.

Berlioz, for example, conceived the idea, in his *Fantastic*

Symphony, of having a single melody, which he called the *Idée fixe* ("fixed idea"), reappear in each movement. This melody, he said, represented the woman he loved. With each appearance the melody takes on a different sound, transformed by purely *musical* means, so that it has a different emotional effect. This turns out to be an ingenious way of imparting unity to the different movements. In a sense, paradoxical as it may seem, the device gives *more* unity to the various movements than is to be found in the more classically formed symphonies of Haydn and Mozart, in which no specific device is used to unify the separate movements.

Liszt appended to his score of *Les Préludes* a quotation from Lamartine to the effect that life is merely a series of preludes to death. While this thought might suggest a chaotic sort of music, Liszt gave exceptional unity to his single-movement work by basing it upon just two melodies, each of which undergoes several transformations. The form is episodic, but there is a sense of flow from one section to another.

Much the same can be said of Strauss's *Till Eulenspiegel*, which, as we know, is said to convey the story of a medieval rogue. It is in the form of a rondo, and quite "classical" in its orderly return, after each departure, to the original theme. The music is superbly organized from the intellectual standpoint, consisting of imaginative transformations of two main melodies. Again, the needs of both the mind and the emotions are well served.

Thus we see that three of the outstanding programmatic works from the height of the Romantic period—all of which were said by their composers (directly, in the cases of Berlioz and Liszt, tacitly in the case of Strauss) to be extramusically motivated—are very well organized indeed according to *musical* precepts.

A good composer, once he decides upon his themes, naturally thinks *musically*. In other words, even though the themes or melodies may be said to represent something outside the realm of music, or even to imitate some sound in nature, any composer worth his salt will proceed to use those melodies as sources of musical growth, developing and relating them to one another according to the dictates of musical thought, which, as we have seen, are different from the ones that shape narrative thought.

Beethoven, in his *Pastoral Symphony*, develops—that is, discourses upon—the melodies that might be thought to represent a rustic scene, and it is worth noting that he himself wrote about this symphony: "More an expression of feelings than painting." Likewise Strauss, in *Till Eulenspiegel*, seeks out the possibilities for growth and variation inherent in the themes. Both of these are excellent examples of thinking in musical terms, irrespective of any extramusical associations.

However, at the moment when Beethoven pauses to imitate the songs of birds, and when Strauss, in his *Don Quixote* imitates a windmill, or the bleating of sheep, they are writing something less than good music. The cleverness of their imitations does not compensate for the poverty of *musical* thought at these points. Fortunately, moments like that are quite rare in the output of such skilled composers.

The alliance of the nineteenth-century composer with the literary interests of his day seemed to provide the perfect channel for the expression of his feelings. Some composers caught up in the prevailing thought of their time, undoubtedly *were* convinced that they were writing about the extramusical subjects that their titles suggested. For example, Bedřich Smetana, who wrote: "I have come to the conclusion that the forms of the past are finished. Absolute music is quite impossible for me." His first String Quartet, he said, aimed to present scenes from his life. Let us see how well he fulfilled his hope. The listener who is familiar with this work will recall that the closing movement starts with a gay dance. After a few minutes, the dance suddenly breaks off; there is a moment of silence, followed by an ominous tremolo. Then the first violin enters, sustaining one extraordinarily high note—so high that it is almost painful to the ear. There then follows an impassioned melody on the viola, after which the movement goes on to a somber ending.

Hearing this succession of dramatic occurrences, the listener cannot help being aware that a profound change of mood has taken place. But, graphic as Smetana may have considered this music to be, the listener, listening only to the *music*, will be left in the dark as to what it was in the composer's life that occasioned the audible drama, thus demonstrating anew how incapable music is, by itself, of conveying a narrative.

It was Smetana's misfortune to become deaf during the last decade of his life. The affliction, which eventually was followed by mental breakdown, was announced by what the composer described as a "terrible whistling sound." The piercingly high violin note that follows the sudden termination of the dance strains is meant to represent this plaguing sound. In a letter about the quartet, Smetana wrote that the sudden change of mood was "the interruption of the catastrophe, the beginning of my deafness, a glimpse into the melancholy future." But even during this intensely personal passage, like any other composer of "storytelling" music, Smetana was actually putting together an abstract structure from abstract materials. His quartet remains absolute music in the same way that a fugue by Bach or a sonata by Mozart are abstract. The impassioned melody in the viola is actually the first theme of the opening movement of the quartet.

Thus, for all the influence that this romantic approach exerted upon the course of music, it remained outside the scope of music, as we have seen, to portray specific events and pictures. In giving their compositions a literary color, composers went along with the then "advanced" viewpoint. In their more considered statements, however, when they spoke simply as musicians, they showed that they were fully aware of the true nature of music.

Berlioz, the archetype of the self-centered romantic composer, stated that "music is a substitute neither for speech nor for the art of painting." Writing in 1837, in his "On Imitation in Music," of the moment in Beethoven's opera *Fidelio* at which the basses of the orchestra play a brief figure meant to represent the rolling of a stone, Berlioz observed: "It is a sad piece of childishness, which one is equally grieved and surprised to have to complain of in a great master."

Franz Liszt himself, although he gave titles to all of his thirteen symphonic poems, and is regarded as the preeminent champion of the program concept, wrote on this very point: "The poorest of apprentice landscape painters could give with a few chalk strokes a much more faithful picture than a musician operating with all the resources of the best orchestra."

Much earlier, the composer Geminiani, a contemporary of Handel, had made the distinction between the kinds of expression to which music was suited. While approving music that could "express Sentiments, strike the Imagination, affect the Mind, and command the Passions," he condemned the music which imitated "the Cock, Cuckoo, Owl, and other Birds." The latter, along with other imitations, he maintained, were merely tricks that belonged more properly to the domain of "Professors of Legerdemain and Posture-masters than to the Art of Musick."

Gustav Mahler, although he published his symphonies with no indication of any program, allowed descriptive subtitles to be associated with the individual movements at their first performances. Yet he was vehement in his opposition to programs, and maintained that verbal descriptions were both unnecessary and annoying. "The audience," he said, "should be left to its own thoughts about the work that is being played." He properly intended his music to convey emotional states without calling for any specific causes.

Rimsky-Korsakov's colorful symphonic suite *Scheherazade* is one of the prototypes of program music, and writers outdo one another in detailing the events it supposedly describes. It is true that, following the custom of his era, the composer paved the way for such an interpretation, by speaking of the solo violin as "delineating Scheherazade herself telling her wondrous tales to the stern Sultan." But so far did the literary detectives go in their tracing of the story that Rimsky-Korsakov later withdrew the labels that he had given to the various melodies.

He wrote in his memoirs: "In vain do people seek in my suite leading motifs linked unbrokenly with ever the same poetic ideas and conceptions. On the contrary, in the majority of cases, all these seeming *leitmotivs* are nothing but purely musical material or the given motifs for symphonic development." He wrote further that he had originally intended to title the four movements "Prelude, Ballade, Adagio, Finale." But so deeply entrenched is the appreciation-through-storytelling concept that commentators still explain that the second movement shows the Sultana "launching into a story told by a wandering Oriental beggar."

The English composer Frederick Delius is on record to this effect: "Music does not exist for the purpose of emphasizing or exaggerating something which happens outside its own sphere.... Music should be concerned with the emotions, not with external events. To make music imitate some other thing is as futile as to try to make it say 'Good Morning' or 'It's a fine day.' It is only that which cannot be expressed otherwise that is worth expressing in music." (In spite of this statement, consider the literary achievements that are all too often credited to Delius's tone poem *On Hearing the First Cuckoo in Spring*.)

What of Richard Strauss himself, by reputation the most successful storyteller in music? You will find attributed to him the statement that the time will come when music will be so specific in its descriptive powers as to make clear the distinction between a knife and a fork. He is also said to have maintained that a certain plucked chord occurring near the end of Berlioz's *King Lear* Overture represents the final snap in the mad Lear's brain. Certainly, Strauss was one of the outstanding *musical thinkers* of all time, but either of those statements opens to question his reputation as a *thinker about music*. In a sense, though, Strauss was merely carrying to its logical conclusion the entire programmatic approach to music. This is the kind of thinking that leads the ordinary listener to feel that he cannot enjoy the *Fantastic Symphony* unless he is able to hear the fall of the fatal ax, or Bach's *Mass in B Minor* unless he can visualize the angels descending from heaven.

Strauss followed a rather curious course in relation to the narratives of his own tone poems. As each one appeared, it was his custom to announce that it was to be listened to as absolute music. Then there would appear lengthy analyses by various commentators, telling the story that the music supposedly conveyed. Although he is reported to have joked at the expense of these commentators, Strauss did not repudiate them publicly. As a result, these analyses, purporting to give the "meaning" of every work down to the last detail, have become the standard explanations of the works.

One of Strauss's admirers, Ernest Newman, annoyed by his repetition of this practice, wrote: "With each new work, there is the same tomfoolery—one can use no milder word to describe proceedings that no doubt have a rude kind of German humor but which strike other people as more than silly."

Let us listen to Strauss himself on the limitations of the programmatic concept. In 1929, long after he had produced the last of his tone poems, he wrote: "Program music is only possible and is only raised to the level of the artistic when its creator is above all a musician possessing imagination and vision. Otherwise he is a charlatan, for even in Program music, the first and most important question is ever that of the worth and strength of the musical idea." What a pity that this statement is all but unknown, while all the alleged stories contained in the tone poems are endlessly repeated!

Thus we see that good composers realize the true function of music. They may be led by the conventions of their day to join in the practice of ascribing extramusical meanings to their works. It is conceivable also that some of them were motivated by practical considerations as well, since the public's fancy can more easily be caught by an imaginative title than by an opus number, by the promise of pictorial revelations than by the sober listing of a symphony's four movements. Might this be one of the reasons why Strauss, as a practical businessman, did not repudiate publicly the detailed programs written by others about his works?

At this point, I should perhaps remind the reader that most of the nicknames suggestive of stories by which certain compositions are known were not in fact given them by their composers. The names associated with Haydn's symphonies such as *The Hen, The Bear, The Miracle,* and *The Queen,* were added by commentators, as was the *Jupiter* to Mozart's Forty-first Symphony.

Beethoven himself appended the words *Pathétique* to his piano sonata, Opus 13, and *Farewell, Absence, and Return* to the sonata, Opus 81a. (The title *Appassionata* was given to his Opus 57 by the publisher.) But notice that these words do not describe people or things; they have to do with states of feeling. Even so, the word *Pathétique* is suited to only the first movement of that sonata; the moods of the remaining two movements in no way fit that description. And, other than the fact that the movement of Opus 81a marked "Return" is in a gayer mood than either of the first two movements of that work, no one can tell, without the title, that its gaiety is occasioned by the return of an individual after an absence.

Another use of the nickname *Pathétique*—that connected with Tchaikovsky's Sixth Symphony—was the suggestion of the composer's brother—made, incidentally, after the work had been completed. It, too, is applicable only to portions of the symphony.

Anton Bruckner subtitled his Fourth Symphony the *Romantic,* but not until two years after he had completed it. He is said to have referred to the opening movement as a scene out of the days of chivalry, the second movement as a rustic love scene, the third as a hunt interrupted by a festive dance; and as for the fourth movement, he himself said, "I'm sorry, but I have forgotten just what it was about." This, from the composer himself! If the music could not suggest the alleged story to the very man who had created it, we are certainly justified in feeling that the supposed connection between story and music must have been tenuous indeed.

To summarize: Despite the fact that composers have sometimes said that their music tells a story, either in direct statements, or by implication through their titles, or by tacit approval of the descriptions written by others, all of them—once they have entered the actual realm of *music*—have thought in accordance with the needs of musical growth and development.

There may be occasional moments of apparent correspondence between the "story" and the music, but these, we have seen, are the result of prior verbal suggestion. The story cannot be divined from the music itself, without the verbal suggestion. Aside from the moments of sheer imitation, which are not worthy of serious consideration as illustrations of an esthetic concept, most of the instances in which the story and the music seem to correspond are the result of a similarity in emotional tone between the event supposedly depicted and the music at that moment.

The remarks of two English critics bear directly on these points. Donald Francis Tovey warned us against taking the suggestions of titles literally. "We shall only misunderstand Berlioz' intentions," he wrote of the composer's *King Lear Overture*, subtitled "Tragédie de Shakespeare," "so long as we try to connect it with Shakespeare's King Lear at all. What Berlioz' has achieved is exactly what he has attempted; a magnificent piece of orchestral rhetoric in tragic style, inspired neither by particular passages in literature nor by particular events in Berlioz' life.... Let us frankly call this overture the Tragedy of the Speaking Basses, of the Plea of the Oboe, and of the Fury of the Orchestra."

W. J. Turner went still further in his condemnation of the whole programmatic idea by including vocal music: "The text of an opera, the words of a song, the program of a symphony or tone poem, or whatever name in the future may be given to any musical composition, is of *no importance or significance whatever*. I know this will be going too far for the majority of musicians; nevertheless l am convinced that it is true, literally and strictly true."

CHAPTER 8
Music and Words—
The Varying Relationship

The words that are sung to music may be, in some compositions, of supreme importance; in others, the text will be completely subservient to the communication of the music itself. These are the extremes. In the great majority of instances, as we shall see, the music is the dominant element. There are many examples in which the text and music appear to be so well matched that they seem meant for each other, but we should be aware at the outset that the fundamental relationship between music and words is nothing more than *compatibility*.

Many exponents of music appreciation, as we have discovered, are excessively concerned with literary aspects even in their approach to purely instrumental music. It is perhaps only natural, then, that they go to extremes when the composition they are dealing with contains a text—be it opera, choral work, or song for a solo singer. Because the concrete thoughts contained in the words lend themselves so easily to discussion, many commentators deal less, or not at all, with the music, giving the listener the unwarranted impression that the work is "about" the text, and that the music merely supports the words. Many singing teachers and choral directors also sin in this direction, often leaving singers and others with the conviction that the music is a "translation into sound" of the text.

The nonspecific nature of music has been demonstrated in the preceding chapters. As a reminder, let us repeat that there is no music in existence that can by itself convey a verbal thought. To this axiom we may add that there is no music in existence that can do anything but *hinder*, to some degree, the listener's comprehension of any words that may be set to it. Further, the greater the *music* is, the more the comprehension of the words is likely to be hindered by listening to them simultaneously.

These statements may seem to be paradoxical, coming from one who, as a conductor of choruses, demands from his singers the utmost clarity of diction and a complete understanding of the text, regardless of the language in which it is sung. The resolution of this seeming paradox will, I hope, provide us with an insight into the true nature of the relationship between music and words.

If evidence is needed of music's inability to convey the sense of words, it may be found in the historic fact that much vocal music was originally written to accommodate entirely different words from those with which it ultimately became associated. An outstanding example is the chorus "For unto us a Child is born," in Handel's *Messiah*. This music, despite the sacred atmosphere now associated with it, was originally a love duet composed to the Italian words: *"No, di voi non vo fidarmi, cieco Amor, crudel belta"* ("No, I no longer wish to trust you, blind love, cruel beauty.")* The music occurring later in the chorus, for the words "And the government shall be upon His shoulder," was originally a setting of words accusing a lover of faithlessness!

The choral literature and songs offer many similar examples. No fewer than 638 bars of the approximately 2300 bars of Bach's *Mass* in *B Minor* consist of music that Bach had already composed for different words. Although the original words were for the most part on religious subjects, they were unrelated to the meaning of the Latin words of the Mass. In one instance—the chorus *"Osanna in excelsis"*—the music was originally composed to secular words.

As we explore the true relationship between words and music, let us consider several facts about the nature of each medium. First, they have in common the fact that they make their effect in time. This makes for a certain correspondence in their emotional effects. Increased speed causes greater excitement in music. With spoken words, one gets the same effect. Thus, *compatibility*.

Now, reread the preceding paragraph, ignoring for the moment the sense of the words. Notice the way in which time was used. The paragraph begins with the longest sentence, and

* Incidentally, here is the explanation of the awkward accent on the word *"For."* It was well suited to the original Italian word *"No,"* but became inappropriate when Handel substituted the English text.

each sentence thereafter is shorter. If this had been a speech in a play, in which some exciting news were being imparted, the playwright might have given his messenger shorter and shorter sentences to heighten the emotional excitement of the ultimate disclosure. This treatment is equally useful in music; composers—particularly of the Romantic school—often use the technique to heighten excitement.

There are other obvious similarities between music and words. A rise in the pitch of speech usually denotes increased tension; a melody also reveals this phenomenon, although in a more subtle way. And dynamics— that is, loudness and softness—affect us similarly in both words and music.

Now, taking the exciting paragraph in our imagined play, a composer might set it for a solo voice and orchestra, prescribing that the music be played faster and faster, while preserving the shortening of the sentences or units of time and also making full use of the other resources of pitch and dynamics. Thus, the emotionalism would be heightened, and the appropriateness of the music to the words would increase our sense of the compatibility of the two. For the sake of completeness, we must add the fact that the composer could also set to the same sort *of* music the nondramatic paragraph I wrote for my example, and a listener who did not understand English, hearing it sung in a dramatic manner, would derive from the *music* an excitement that is not contained in the text.

The extent of the compatibility depends in part upon the degree to which the words are comprehensible. There are, indeed, many instances in music when the words are understandable, and the results can be dramatic or moving in the extreme. But in most of- those cases, the drama is contained in the words, with the music merely reinforcing the mood.

Let us for the moment maintain that *anything* that in any way hinders the natural flow of the text is to be regarded as reducing the supremacy of the words. Any repetition of words or phrases, or any holding of a syllable beyond its normal speech length for the beauty of its sound is, after all, something of a hindrance to intelligibility. Even if they do not actually make the words incomprehensible, such devices open the way, in principle, for a shifting of the emphasis toward purely musical values.

The only music that would preserve the absolute supremacy

of the words, under the conditions outlined, would be a kind of musical declamation. In order to be completely faithful, the rhythm of the vocal line would have to preserve the natural rhythm of the words at every point. Rhythm, which is a breaking up of the element of time, is a phenomenon shared by both words and music. Here, because of the qualities peculiar to each medium, we meet with the first divergence between their respective needs, the first rift in their compatibility.

A simple demonstration will make the point clear. Go back to the paragraph before this one, and read aloud the sentence beginning: "The only music . . ." Next, substitute the syllable "da" for each syllable in that sentence, and say the entire sentence out loud, preserving the natural speech rhythm and the natural accents *exactly* as they occur in the original sentence. Do not succumb to the temptation to "even out" the syllable lengths.

After this experiment, perhaps you will appreciate how complex the rhythm of natural speech is. Can you think of any piece of music, instrumental or vocal, whose rhythm is so free and so complex? Notice, also, the excessive lengths of the phrases; before you have reached the second comma, you have been exposed to so many different rhythms that you can find nothing to unify them. If you were to say that sentence out loud in the *da* version to someone who had not read it, he would be lost, unable to find any regular beat that would give him a sense of continuity.

To see how the rhythms of music differ from the rhythms of words, speak (do not sing), by means of the syllable *da,* the first few lines of "The Star Spangled Banner," as they occur in the anthem. As you *da* the rhythm of the familiar "Oh-ho sa-ay ca-an you seeeee . . ," notice how the rhythm is made to fit a regularly recurring beat; then notice how the same rhythmic pattern reappears, even though it is not found in the natural rhythm of the words. Finally, observe how certain syllables are held beyond their normal speech length, and how the general speed of the words, in the musical version, is much slower than it would be if those same words were to be spoken. All these qualities are common, in some degree, to all vocal music. Thus, music destroys even the rhythms of poetry, by superimposing its own rhythmic needs.

Music exploits its effects in the realm of the senses; therefore, the singing voice wants to hold on to vowel sounds for the sake of the beauty of the tone. It is impossible to sing the consonants "d," "t," and "p." Hardly more satisfactory are the buzzed sounds such as "z," or the hummed sounds such as "n" and "m." Therefore, the singing voice, for purely musical reasons, seeks out and holds on to the vowels. The resulting distortion of the natural verbal rhythms for the sake of musical needs places the words at a disadvantage by tending to diminish their intelligibility.

There are several more sources of incompatibility between words and music, alongside which the ones so far mentioned sink into relative insignificance. These stem from the fact that music and words, despite their moments of superficial correspondence, actually inhabit two different realms.

Inherent in the nature of words is forward motion, in order that they may fulfill their narrative function. Verbal continuity depends upon a succession of different ideas, if intelligibility is to be maintained. Even in those instances in which a single subject is being discoursed upon at length (for example, our present discussion), each idea must be followed by a different idea. This is not the case with music. Words produce concrete literary and pictorial ideas; music does not. A piece of music constructed on the verbal principle—that is, on a succession of different ideas— would lose its sense of unity.

Music, by its very nature, requires various kinds of *repetition*. Phrases are repeated; ideas or motives— fragments of melodies—are repeated, usually with some kind of change; entire sections are repeated, either immediately or after a digression into contrasting music— which also contains its own repetitions. These repetitions are not caprices; they give unity to music and are necessary to music's very existence. Note how far removed this repetition is from verbal thought, and how ill-suited it is as the companion of concrete, verbal ideas. The needs of music and words are not only lacking in compatibility on this point, they are actually *opposed* to each other.

The opera character sings "I must hurry" over and over again, but doesn't leave. The composer, having chosen his musical theme to accompany the singer's "I must hurry," needs to linger over that melody—to work out its possibilities for musical development. The singer, standing there and repeating the words to music that develops and culminates, is supplying evidence of one basic source of incompatibility between verbal and musical communication.

Again, in many arias in operas or oratorios, after considerable music has been sung, the singer goes back to the beginning and starts over. This is a recognized *musical* form—the *da capo* (Italian for "from the beginning") aria, which prescribes that a song shall have a beginning section, a contrasting middle section, and then a complete repetition of the first section. But this symmetry is a musical conception, not a literary one. The words have to go along willy-nilly.

Contrary to the impression conveyed by many writers, the way to an understanding of vocal music is only occasionally through the words. Granted, that in some compositions the words are so important that they seem to be the music's sole reason for existence; in such cases, a failure to understand them will deprive the listener of a good portion of the emotional effect contained in the combination. But at the opposite pole of this relationship, there are those vocal works in which the music is so much more important that the words are almost dispensable; in such cases, the music would make the greater part of its point even if the vocal parts were played by instruments.

Between these two poles there is every shade of emotional experience open to you as a listener to vocal music, and what we have discovered so far suggests the error of any definition that implies that there is a rigid, never-changing relationship between words and music, in which the music is the "expression" of the words.

The relative importance of one with regard to the other changes constantly, even within a single work. In the music of Bach, for example, we find both extremes represented. Moments of the *Passion According to St. Matthew* are completely dependent upon the words for their full significance. Yet large portions of that same work, and of his *Mass in B Minor,* are abstract music, in which the meaning of the words is completely subordinated to the music. Both are works with religious texts; both involve the same performing bodies—chorus, soloists, and orchestra—and both are in the same style, yet they demonstrate the poles of the relationship between words and music.

One of the most telling examples of the supremacy of the words is the section in the *Passion According to St. Matthew* in which Pontius Pilate asks the crowd to choose which man shall be released. The chorus responds loudly with the single word "Barrabam!" intoned in almost the natural rhythm of the name. Here, the drama is in the narrative, with the music relegated to the subordinate role of merely supporting the story. The action is narrated by the Evangelist, and the question is asked by Pilate, in the musical idiom known as "recitative," which is speech set to specific pitches, or notes, accompanied by occasional chords that keep the musical progression clear. While there are extremely beautiful and moving recitatives, most examples of this sort are of limited interest from the purely *musical* standpoint, and so is this one of Bach's.

The fact that the chorus responds with its "Barrabam!" in an eight-part musical chord is also of very limited interest, from the purely musical viewpoint. Musically, there is little justification for that isolated chord. It is neither led up to nor followed by, any *musical* ideas related to it. The listener who hears this portion of the work without understanding the text knows only that a single, brief, dramatic outcry has taken place. Yet, with a knowledge of the narrative content of the words, this becomes one of the most exciting moments in the realm of music-drama.

Another instance of complete supremacy of the words occurs at the end of Puccini's opera *La Bohéme.* As the hero, Rodolfo, realizes that the woman he loves is dead, his anguished singing of her name "Mimi!" over an impassioned accompaniment in the orchestra, demands an understanding of the situation, if the full emotional effect of the drama is to be realized.

Although it is at the other end of the emotional scale, one of the climactic moments in Debussy's opera *Pelléas et Melisande* also demonstrates this extreme. At the point where the hero and heroine declare their love for each other, the orchestra falls entirely silent; Pelléas quietly intones the words *"Je t'aime"* ("I love you"). Mélisande's answer is also almost more spoken than sung: *"Je t'aime aussi"* ("I love you also"). Again, although the music up to that point has contributed to the establishment of the mood, it is the words, with their specific meaning, that make the passage significant. The listener who did not understand the language would not even suspect that he was witnessing a love scene.

At the very end of Schubert's dramatic song *Erlkönig (Erlking),* the hushed and musically simple phrase *"in seinen*

Armen das Kind war tot" ("in his arms the child was dead"), depends upon a comprehension of its verbal significance if it is to be appreciated fully. Here, too, the music becomes completely subservient to the needs of the words.

Notice that in all the cases described, the key words or phrases are sung only once, in accordance with their narrative demands. The setting of such words always takes the form of some kind of musical declamation. In every case, the musical needs are sacrificed to the dramatic needs; in every case, the words might have been set to any other music with a similar mood and in a consistent style. The main function of the music, here, is to *underscore* the emotional tone of the words; it has hardly any life of its own.

Let us now move on to the kinds of vocal music in which the balance is not quite so weighted in favor of the words. Here is the middle area that encompasses most vocal music. Not all texts are as dramatic as the ones just discussed. Therefore, composers are, for the greater part of any vocal work, free to concentrate on the musical aspects of their compositions.

The texts of most songs and arias are essentially statements of *attitudes*. What the music does is to underscore the emotion *of* the words. There are, of course, limits to the extent to which music can convey specific emotions, stemming from its inability to be concrete. However, within these limits, we can say that what vocal music "expresses" is not the specific ideas of the words, but their over-all emotional tone. Thus, we may say loosely that the music "expresses" the emotions inherent in the words.

It is the capturing of a basic emotional tone that enables a composer to set several verses of a poem to the same music. The varying ideas, images, or facts contained in the different verses are things that the music itself cannot depict; as long as all the verses have approximately the same emotional tone, the music that is appropriate to the tone of one verse will be appropriate for all.

The famous aria *"La donna è mobile"* ("Woman Is Fickle") in Verdi's opera *Rigoletto* is an example of this kind of relationship between music and words. Despite all that has been written about how perfectly it expresses the fickleness of women, it does no such thing. It is merely a song for tenor and orchestra—a consistent and logical piece, from the purely musical standpoint—whose mood is fairly lighthearted.

Without a knowledge of Italian, no listener could tell that the subject of the aria is the fickleness of women. In point of fact, it is not. The fickleness of women is the subject of the *text;* the subject of the *music* is the melody that Verdi wrote. The text goes on to explore the various facets of the fickleness of women. The music goes on to explore the melody—which means not only the notes, but also the rhythms, the harmonies, and the relationships of keys, in addition to the sensuous qualities of the orchestration and of the sounds of the human voice.

Recall the point made earlier: the text is developed by the addition of different intellectual ideas- the music is developed by the repetition of the same few ideas, varied, extended, and transformed. The fact that the text and music of our example seem to go so well together—once you know the words—attests to Verdi's skill in providing the words with music of an *appropriate* emotional tone.

Verdi refused to let this aria be rehearsed until just before the opera was given its first performance, for fear that it would be sung all over Venice even before the premiere took place. He was not afraid that the words would attract that much attention; he correctly knew that it was the tunefulness of his music—the construction of the entire song as a musical entity—that would make the aria so appealing.

It is the matching of the emotional tone, then, that is the basis of the correspondence between words and music. Another instance is the contralto aria *"Erbarme dich, mein Gott,"* ("Have mercy, Lord, on me") from Bach's *Passion According to St. Matthew.* Considered from the musical standpoint alone, it can be regarded abstractly as a balanced structure, since it is in the *da capo* form already described. Moreover, it features a violin solo along with the vocal solo and since the identical melodic material is used by both violin and voice, the movement can be looked upon as a miniature concerto for two instruments. In short, the music is developed according to purely musical needs.

The text—a plea for mercy—consists of four brief verbal phrases that are repeated a number of times. The emotional tone of the music is so perfectly matched with that of the text that this is an instance in which the two seem to be made for each other. However, provided that the music is sung and played with suitable tenderness, one can listen to it without a knowledge of the words, and still be deeply touched.

The over-all attitude of the text is one of supplication; there is no "story" during this aria—no exciting incident that would bring forth an extreme dramatic interpretation at any one point in the music, such as the phrase *"das Kind war tot"* in Schubert's *Erlkönig.* Therefore, the only emotional tone that can be derived from the text is one of tenderness or gentleness.

Unless the listener knows German, the words, even when sung with all the expression that the singer can muster, cannot convey the fact that this is a plea and a supplication. The listener will know only that something gentle and tender— perhaps even "urgent"—is being expressed, with its attendant emotional overtones.

This is the situation that prevails in any number of socalled "art songs" (or, in German, *Lieder),* for voice and piano, by Schubert, Schumann, Brahms, or Hugo Wolf. It is customary to point to the importance of the words in this type of music. There is no question that, ideally, for the fullest appreciation of both the words and the music, an understanding of the text is necessary. Yet, so expressive are some of these *Lieder* that it is possible to respond to them without understanding their *words.* This phenomenon gives us an insight into another aspect of the relationship between words and music. In such an experience, we are calling mainly on the expressive powers of the music, rather than on the specific concepts contained in the texts.

Many of the texts that those composers set to music were fine poetry, but not all of them were. Moreover, there is a limit to the number of times that we can be stirred by a poet's comparison of a beloved with a flower, or upon hearing her eyes described as limpid pools. These are some of the commonplaces of Romantic poetry— just as there are, frankly, commonplaces in some of the musical settings. In many instances, it is probably better not to be aware of the specific verbal concepts, in order to leave oneself free for the emotional effects of the music.

However, if the specific words of these songs are not always important to the listener, they are all-important to the singer, who must be completely aware of the text in order to make his or her interpretation as emotionally convincing as possible. While neither the music nor the singer can convey specific verbal meanings to the listener who does not understand the language in which the words are sung, what the singer can do is express, by the quality of vocal tone and by an emphasis upon certain key words, the essential emotional tone of the text.

In the light of this, it now becomes necessary to alter slightly the implication that the enjoyment of these songs is a purely musical phenomenon. It is not. If the vocal line were given, say, to a violin or an oboe, the ultimate effect of the song would be different. The singer, performing, let us say, the word "bitterly," might emphasize the first letter, using the hardness of the consonant for its increased emotional effect. The violinist might even go so far as to accent that note, but the effect would not be the same. We would be denied those particular emotional qualities that reside only in the human voice.

In the same civilization, human feelings are expressed through similar vocal coloration, regardless of the language. That is why it is possible for a singer to convey the appropriate emotional tone to a listener who does not understand the language in which the music is sung. However, music can go no further than this. Music's limitations in this area might be compared with what can happen when one talks to a baby. It is possible to say horrible things to an infant, and provided that the tone quality is suitably gentle, the child will respond with a gurgle of pleasure.

The most sophisticated vocal music in the world suffers from a similar limitation when it is sung in a language that is not understood by the listener. Yet, by the same token, it is the very fact that *emotional tones* can be conveyed that enables us to enjoy vocal music—to feel that we have had an emotional experience— even (as is so often the case) when we have not understood a single word.

It is the indeterminate quality of music's emotional expressivity that would make it possible for music such as Mahler's *Kindertotenlieder* ("Songs on the Death of Children") for solo voice and orchestra—whose intent is obviously the expression of sadness—to serve just as easily to express the quiet joy of love. Such a statement will probably cause objections from singers and singing teachers, who will claim that Mahler's music beautifully matches the heart-rending text (which it does), but the point is that the dynamic aspects of quiet joy are similar to those of sadness. Had the *texts* of the first four of Mahler's songs dealt with the joys of love, the music would have been equally apt. The fifth song is, for the most part, a turbulent one, the text of which is the parent's statement that he should never have allowed the children to go out in bad weather. The music, which suggests the tempestuousness of the weather, could just as easily indicate the tempestuousness of the lover's feelings, since music, as we have seen, is very well able to suggest the *condition* of turbulence, but cannot attach it to any *cause*.

Because the tone quality of the singing is an important variable, a good singer will learn to convey the emotional content of the music by means of diction, the coloration of the vowels, the general tone quality, and even by facial expressions. There is, unfortunately, a tendency on the part of many singers, soloists and chorus members alike, to sing everything with the same tone quality. Even when that tone quality does have a certain finesse, the concentration upon sheer beauty of sound sometimes robs the music of its drama. Therefore, a good conductor will seek out the dramatic or emotional implications of the words, and see that the singers express those implications in their vocal tone.

Moussorgsky's opera *Boris Godounov* contains a scene in which a village idiot, off by himself in a deserted wood, laments the fate of Russia. When the music is properly sung, the cumulative effect of the story, along with the appropriateness of Moussorgsky's music at that point, makes the scene extremely moving. But if the emotional impact of this scene is to be fully realized, the singer must project the attributes of the idiot. He must invest his singing with a weak, pathetic quality. When the singer is primarily concerned with producing beautiful sound, the scene lacks impact. Moussorgsky's music, for all its appropriateness, cannot convey the necessary emotional feeling without the proper treatment of the words.

But even when the emotional tone of the music seems perfectly matched to the emotional quality of the words, we must remember that we are not matching equal things. The *emotional content* of the words, which is one element of the match, is not inherent in the *sounds* of the words. Words are really signs that stand for arbitrarily assigned meanings. They have no meaning in and of themselves. To "understand" a series of words, or to draw from them their emotional significance, our minds have to consider their assigned meanings, and by an intellectual process, draw conclusions. Granted that this process takes place in the normal mind at a very rapid rate, the fact nevertheless remains that an intermediate process is required.

That is not the case with music. Because music has no "meaning" outside itself (disregarding the arbitrarily assigned meanings that we find in program music), its emotional effects act upon us directly, and we respond without need of the intermediate process The intellectual consideration of meaning—that is necessary to a comprehension of the emotionalism of words. (We are, remember, discussing here only the *emotional* effects of music and words. A process of intellectualization is indeed required if one is to understand fully the relationships among the various sections of a musical composition, or the transformations of themes. But that is not the point under discussion at the moment.)

So far, we have explored two of the three stages of the relationships between words and music: first, that in which the words are supreme; second, that in which the two are on a somewhat more equal footing. Now, notice that a curious state of affairs exists in the relationship. When the words are extremely dramatic, as the case of the outcry "Barrabam!" or the declaration of love in *Pelléas et Mélisande,* or the final revelation of the death of the child in Schubert's *Erlkönig*—they take precedence over the music. When they are not of the most dramatic kind, the words are in danger of being subordinated to the needs of the music, as in the case of *"La donna é mobile"* from *Rigoletto,* and the *"Erbarme dich"* from the *Passion According to St. Matthew.* In each of the latter instances, the words contribute their emotional essence, but the music continues on its own course. More often it is the music that dominates. It is this fact that is too often overlooked by commentators who find the more obvious specific meanings of words easier to discuss.

Another serious source of the incompatibility of words and music is the fact that music, unlike words, exists in a vertical as well as a horizontal sense. An analogy will make the point clear. The script or "score" of a poem or a play is one continuous line of words. The fact that the lines appear under one another, as they do on this page, is merely a matter of convenience. Your mind grasps the content of what you are reading now, and moves along, we may say, on a horizontal line representing time. When you hear poetry read aloud, or hear the words in a play, the horizontal effect is inescapable.

Unlike the printed page of literature, the visual make-up of a musical score has a direct bearing on the nature of music as an art. It is part of the very nature of music to have many different things going on simultaneously. These are represented to the eye by the physical appearance of the score. Each line in a musical score represents the notes played by a different instrument or sung by a different voice. These lines are placed one under another on the page, with the understanding that they will be performed *simultaneously*.

In a play, it is difficult to follow the ideas of two or more people who are speaking simultaneously. But simultaneity is the normal situation in vocal duets, trios, quartets, quintets, and choruses.

Let us take one of the simplest forms of concerted vocal music, a hymn written for soprano, contralto, tenor, and bass, all singing simultaneously. In order to make the situation as nearly ideal as possible for the comprehension of the words, let us assume, as actually happens in most hymns, that all four parts are singing the same words at the same moment, in the same rhythm. Let us assume, also, that the composer has taken care to match the mood of the music to the prevailing mood of the words. If the diction of all the singers is reasonably good, and the singing is properly expressive, there should be no barrier to our understanding of the words. Remember, though, that just as in the case of "The Star Spangled Banner," the words will not have their natural rhythm, but will be in some form of artificial pattern in order to suit the needs of music. This often results in giving the strong accents to unimportant words, such as "of" or "and." Already, the music has superimposed its requirements upon the words.

Now, realize that all four parts are actually singing different music. Four different musical concepts are being presented simultaneously. While it is true that, in this very simple composition, the bass line will for the most part supply a foundation for the more important melody in the soprano, it will nevertheless have its own interest, in a purely musical sense, apart from the words. Similarly with the contralto and tenor parts.

Then there is the fact that a certain amount of interest will be contained in the harmonies—the progressions from one chord to another. These, too, will live a life of their own, within the realm of music. It exists quite apart from the words, and would exist if there were no words at all.

Thus we see that, even in one of the simplest imaginable examples of the mating of words and music, despite the moments of seeming correspondence between the two— which stem, of course, mainly from the correspondence in mood— the musical lines follow their own destinies.

Let us move on to a more complex but equally familiar type of vocal music—a round, such as *Three Blind Mice.* Here the music consists of overlapping strands of melody. When the first voice moves on to the words "See how they run," the second voice enters with "Three blind mice." At the entrance of the third voice, the listener takes in no fewer than *three* different sets of words at the same time. This is a wonderful device for making the music itself more interesting, but notice what an antiverbal practice it is. How can the listener be expected to hear and grasp the meanings of three or more sets of words heard at the same time?

Now let us see what can happen in more sophisticated music. To demonstrate how incomprehensible the words of choral music may become when they follow the destinies of the musical motives to which they are set, here are two words as they occur in three bars of the *"Kyrie eleison"* ("Lord have mercy upon us") of Bach's *Mass in B Minor.* The five parts, or voices, are heard simultaneously, and a vertical line at any point will indicate all the different words or syllables that are being sung at the same moment.

1st Soprano	e—— le——— i-son, e-le ——— i-son,
2nd Soprano	-son, e- le—i-son, Ky—ri-e e-le-i-son,
Contralto	— i-son, e- le –i—son, Ky—ri - e e – lei —— son,
Tenor	— i-son, e——le i— son, Ky-ri-e e—le -
Bass	-son, e- le–i—son—, e—le———————

These two words are the entire text for fourteen minutes of music. Just *one* hearing of the words is enough to convey their verbal meaning (provided, of course, that we understand the language). Certainly their repetition during the music that follows cannot be regarded as in any way elucidating the verbal sense, since everything about the music conspires to minimize the comprehensibility of the words as such. If we assume that Bach thought the numerous repetitions of the words necessary in order to impress their message upon the hearer, his opinion of his listeners' mental acumen could not have been high. On the other hand, he has set the two words to some of the most complex music he ever wrote—music that requires considerable knowledge and experience on the part of the listener for the full appreciation of its subtleties.

The point here, and in hundreds of other cases where the music is built along similar principles, whether with sacred or secular texts, is that the composer is writing abstract music. The *musical* thought reigns supreme. In this type of music, once the composer has chosen a melody, theme, or motive whose general mood matches the mood of the words, he proceeds to develop it in accordance with musical dictates; the words are merely made to fit.

This explains why Bach, elsewhere in the *Mass* in B *Minor,* could use the same four-voiced fugue for two separate portions of the text, the *"Gratias agimus tibi"* ("We give thanks to thee") and the *"Dona nobis pacem"* ("Grant us peace"). No music can convey the actual meaning of either text; yet their emotional tones are sufficiently similar so that there is nothing to prevent Bach from using the same music for both texts. With music of this sort we have reached the polar opposite of music in which the words are dominant.

During the course of still another section of the same *Mass in B Minor*—the chorus to the words *"Confiteor unum baptisma"* ("I acknowledge one baptism")—Bach has two melodies, each with its own separate set of words, going simultaneously, and each subjected to the overlapping treatment described above. Then, as if this were not enough for the ear to cope with, he complicates the texture by adding a third melody.

Surely, it is the *musical* mind that is in the ascendancy here. The words—aside from the fact that each set remains associated with its respective melody—have nothing to do with determining the shape of the music. The vocal parts are essentially abstract instrumental parts, distinguishable from the actual instrumental parts only by the fact that they have the coloration of the human voice.

Samuel Pepys, although he wrote his diary long before Bach composed the *Mass in B Minor,* gave a valid insight into the nature of such vocal music when he wrote about his own contemporary music: "I am more and more confirmed that singing with many voices is not singing, but a sort of instrumental musique, the sense of the words being lost by not being heard, and especially as they set them with Fugues of words, one after another; whereas singing properly, I think, should be but with one or two voices at most."

Here, it might be advisable to investigate the ability of "sacred" music (oratorios, masses, Passions, cantatas, and hymns) to express religious thoughts and feeling.

No series of notes can be demonstrated to contain, in itself, a religious thought or sentiment, just as none can be proven to be, per se, irreligious. All music is organized sound. All music is made up of the same ingredients. The differences lie in the ways in which they are organized.

True enough, certain styles of musical organization have come to be accepted as the "church" style. For example, the combination of slow tempo and certain types of harmonic progressions are regarded as the "devotional" manner. Even though we may be able to recognize this style immediately, we must nevertheless acknowledge that there is nothing absolute about it. It is solely the result of convention.

There was a time, during the sixteenth and seventeenth centuries, when sacred and secular works were composed in the same style. Even in the eighteenth century, church authorities complained that the masses of Mozart and Haydn were too operatic in character.

The use of the organ in secular music may suggest religious music, simply because we so readily associate the organ with the church. But there is nothing inherently sacred about either the instrument or its sound.

Many listeners, of course, do have a genuine religious experience as they listen to the religious works. But it should be borne in mind that this is, in part, the result of the religious feelings that the listeners bring to the experience, as well as of the emotional appeals of the music. Even ancient traditional melodies, such as are found in Jewish liturgical music—or the Gregorian chants in church music—cannot in themselves convey religious thoughts. It is the strong emotional associations with the melodies, together with the words, that enhance the religious experience.

We find that music, by itself, without benefit of a text, cannot reveal whether its intentions are sacred or secular, and the emotions evoked by the music—exultation, excitement, joy, sadness, and so forth—cannot be identified as either sacred or secular in origin. The overtures to many of Handel's operas are identical in style, form, and orchestration with the overture to his oratorio *Messiah,* and audiences are not impelled to think religious thoughts when listening to one of these works. The devotional frame of mind with which many listeners hear the overture to *Messiah* stems from their knowledge of the fact that it is part of a work whose *text is* on a sacred subject.

As pointed out earlier, both Bach and Handel, in some of their greatest religious works, used music that they had previously composed to secular texts, simply substituting religious words. If the *music* could actually express the religious ideas that some listeners now attribute to it, then logically the original versions of the same pieces should imbue the listener with religious feelings, despite the secular texts. This would then be contrary to the original purpose of the music. Thus, when music is said to express religious feelings, it is as a result of prior suggestion by the title or the text, or because of the conventions of musical style.

Yet even the matter of style, as has been pointed out, is not absolute. Neither a frenzied revival meeting, with its shouting, stamping, and "jazzy" singing, nor a mass composed in an extremely dissonant, modern style, can be said to be in the conventional "church" or "sacred" style. But each must be considered to be as sincere and as valid a form of religious supplication as is a serene mass for unaccompanied chorus by Palestrina, or an elaborate setting of the Passion story by Bach.

To maintain that music can express religious convictions commits one to accept the corollary that it can express irreligious thought. Actually, there is nothing, except possibly esthetic sensitivity, that could prevent a chorus of atheists from singing the *"Credo"* of Bach's *Mass in B Minor* and putting a *"non"* before each *"credo"*—meaning "I do not believe." There would be those who would object to this adaptation, but their objection would not alter the fact that Bach's *music,* though unchanged, would now lend itself with equal strength to conveying the steadfastness of the concept of disbelief.

It is the inability of music to express a religious thought, we may conclude, that allows nonbelievers to enjoy listening to the so-called religious works. They listen for the musical and emotional content. And just as nonbelieving composers write such works, so performers often sing or play them even when the texts contain avowals with which they do not agree. Ultimately, *any* music with a religious text may be regarded as religious music, although it is *only* the text that makes it so.

CHAPTER 9

The Place of Words
in Vocal Music

Composers have often taken advantage of the fact that words carry with them their own specific suggestions and imagery.

In the madrigal, a form of music for several unaccompanied voices popular in the late sixteenth and early seventeenth centuries, composers would seize every opportunity to convey as vividly as possible each pictorial allusion. This characteristic is demonstrated by a madrigal for six voices by the English composer Thomas Weelkes, called *As Vesta Was from Latmos Hill Descending*. The word "descending" is set to a downward-moving scale; at the appearance of the word "ascending" the voices move upwards The phrase "came running down amain" calls for a series of downward-rushing notes in each of the voices.

This kind of writing would seem to fall into the realm of program music. It must be once more recalled, however, that once the madrigal composers had chosen a musical idea that seemed appropriate to the literary one (as in the examples given above), they were careful to treat that idea in purely musical terms. Thus, the downward-rushing scales were the occasion for the writing of some complex, contrapuntal music—music that would make sense even if it were played on instruments.

Later in that same madrigal these words occur:

First two by two, then three by three together,
Leaving their Goddess all alone.

The words "First two by two" are sung alternately by groups of two voices at a time; the words "then three by three" are sung by groups of three voices. At the appearance of the word "together," all six voices are heard at the same time. They all continue through the words "Leaving their Goddess." Then suddenly, after the richness of the six-voiced writing, the words "all alone" are sung by a single soprano.

This kind of composition has an undeniable charm, even though, three and a half centuries later, we may sometimes find it naive. But recall that this music was composed in an era when a single extended movement, based on one or two themes, was a rarity. In the madrigal, each line of the poem was given its own musical setting. That is, each verbal line was associated with a particular musical motive that was explored in the purely musical sense. Then that motive, or "theme," would be dropped and a new one brought into play, in connection with each of the subsequent lines of the text. The over-all form of a madrigal, therefore, was somewhat episodic. However, within the section in which any one musical motive was treated, the music was of a very high degree of sophistication, and sometimes of extreme complexity. The English authority Donald Tovey had this to say about the madrigal's symbolism: "For the critic [the] illustrative aspect has the danger that it may distract his attention from purely musical values. But in the first and last resort the composer is more interested in music than in words."

There is a tendency to point to symbolism as the key to the understanding of the vocal work in which it occurs. Reference is often made to the symbolic meaning allegedly contained in the *"Et in unum Dominum"* section of Bach's *Mass in B Minor.* The soprano solo is followed, one beat later, by the contralto solo, singing the same words to the same notes. This, the well-known musical device of "canon" (see Chapter Seventeen for a discussion of this compositional technique), is interpreted as symbolizing the conceptual unity contained in the words "(I believe) in one Lord."

But the writers who point to this as a way of interpreting the "meaning" of the music are silent about the fact that, later on in the same duet, Bach continues the canon, although with words that do not imply the idea of unity. The proponents of this interpretation also find themselves confronted with the disturbing fact that, in one version of this same duet, Bach has the voices sing the word *descendit* to an *ascending* melodic line!

This same viewpoint leads to a cul-de-sac when, elsewhere in the *Mass,* Bach sets the words *"visibilium omnium et invisibilium"* ("all things visible and invisible") for full chorus and orchestra, including trumpets and drums. How can the concept of invisibility be conveyed by such a large amount of sound?

Some commentators have admitted to being perturbed by these examples. But would they not be more easy in mind if they realized that what they are propounding is actually a matter of *religious* symbolism only, and usually applies only momentarily? It is not a key to the understanding of the *music,* since it is superimposed upon the music from without, and is nowhere implicit in it. If it were implicit, it could properly be expected to apply more consistently than it does.

The idea of "word painting" is usually pointed to as a means of appreciating not only choruses and arias in oratorios and operas, but the songs or *Lieder* referred to earlier. We can grant immediately that, when a composer sets to music a text having to do with, let us say, a soldier's feelings in battle, the music will be suitably martial, and that, as the soldier's feelings turn to thoughts of his beloved, the music can be expected to take a gentler turn. Spinning songs can be expected to have a constantly moving accompaniment, as can songs whose texts are about flowing streams.

But while these things are hardly more than momentary felicities, we are too often given the impression that they are the key to the understanding and appreciation of the song at hand. Extremes are reached as in the comments about Schubert's song *"Die Stadt"* ("The Town"), in which the poet imagines himself being rowed away in a boat. We are told that a series of broken chords in the right hand of the piano accompaniment represents the steady splash of the oars! In the same composer's song *"Die Forelle"* ("The Trout"), it is said that the repeated figure in the right hand of the piano accompaniment represents the motions of the fish! Such examples could be multiplied endlessly.

By concentrating on these minor details, we divert our attention from the truly important aspects of the songs, which are the ways in which the musical ideas are developed and contrasted. As we pointed out in the discussion of program music, the important thing is not the fact that a figure in the piano accompaniment can be likened to the actions of a fish! It is, rather, what happens to that figure—the ways in which it changes, as the song moves into different harmonies. This, along with the course of the melody itself, is what the music is "about."

Schubert's *"Am Meer"* ("By the Sea") has been called "the greatest of all songs of the sea," but we may question whether the music has anything to do with the sea. The song, instead, is a wonderful example of the expression of a mood of sadness, with very limited musical means. Moreover, the main melody is an exquisite thing in itself, as are the harmonies that accompany it. The listener who loses himself in reveries about the sea will miss the message of the music.

Another of Schubert's songs, *"Der Doppelgänger"* ("The Double"), is even more economical in its use of musical material, since the four somber chords with which it opens are repeated almost identically for fully two-thirds of the work. The vocal line soars above it imaginatively, supplying variety, while the repetition of the four chords supplies unity to the musical thought. As the piano plays the series of four chords for the last time, Schubert changes the harmony of the final chord. The effect is indescribable. It is nowhere called for or justified by the text, and that one subtle change has no verbal equivalent because it exists in a realm entirely separate from words. The reason for it lies within the realm of Schubert's *musical* imagination. To be unaware of it, because one is lost in the story of the text, is to deprive oneself of one of the beautiful moments in music.

Obviously, the texts of both *"Am Meer"* and *"Der Doppelgänger"* contain their own drama. Moreover, as we have seen, an understanding of the texts helps the performers to shape their interpretations. But if one were to hear both songs without a prior knowledge of the words, it is questionable whether one could tell which song was about the sea and which was about the "double" ! It is the *musical* subject matter of each song, and its *musical* development that is of prime importance. The music should not be relegated in the listener's mind to the role of merely illustrating the words.

A similar concentration upon musical values is justified, I feel, in music involving two or more voices, as, say, in an operatic quintet. In a number of these instances, the various characters in the opera may be singing different words at the same time, suggesting another example of the incompatibility of words and music. Music such as this, despite the individual thoughts or emotions expressed by each individual singer, tends to become abstract music.

Much choral music, too, should be enjoyed as abstract music. An outstanding example is the choral finale of Beethoven's Ninth Symphony, which is customarily said to be about joy and the brotherhood of man, as if this were the key to the understanding of the music. This is a misconception. It is no more about joy or brotherhood than any piece of music is "about" its text. Granted that laudable sentiments are contained in the text. The *music,* however, is not concerned with these concepts; it is, instead, a gigantic "Theme and Variations"—as abstract a musical form as one can find anywhere. But this time the "instruments" for those variations are a chorus, four soloists, and an orchestra.

The music is about one main "idea"—the broad first melody of the movement. Later on, for contrast, Beethoven introduces a new idea; but it is a purely musical idea—another melody. Then, as the music unfolds, he combines both ideas. If you would know what the choral finale of Beethoven's Ninth Symphony is "about," you have merely to familiarize yourself with the two melodies, and follow what happens to them in the course of the music. Paul Henry Lang, the critic and historian, points out that Beethoven's music "did not arise from the poem. Rather, the poem joined the music. The theme. . . of the 'Ode to Joy' is a typically instrumental thought of purely symphonic qualities.... The text itself mattered little to Beethoven once he was actually proceeding with its musical elaboration."

Incidentally, it is an accepted opinion among those familiar with German literature that Schiller's "Ode to Joy" is not first-rate poetry, despite its lofty intentions. The music, on the other hand, remains for the most part at a high level. Therefore, it is not only beside the point to regard the text as the clue to the understanding of the Ninth Symphony; it is also unfair to the music.

We now see another point at which words and music "part company," so to speak. While a good text cannot improve a bad piece of music, good music can be written to a bad text. The most devout expression of religious thoughts cannot make an oratorio good, if the music is bad. Whatever qualities of "goodness" there may be remain confined to the text, and cannot be ascribed to the music, if it is dull. By the same token, however, there may be some comfort for the person concerned with the words in the realization that bad music cannot spoil the sentiments contained in the text. This is a further indication of the fact that words and music function in different realms.

It is a pity that, because of undue word-orientation, the public has never really been receptive to vocal music sung in abstract sounds. It is possible to conceive of works in which the composer drew upon any syllables that met the needs of his music. He could use those vowels, or combinations of sounds, that help convey the emotional coloration of the music. Consonants might be used to heighten the emotionalism at the proper places. In choral music, particularly, the composer's freedom to choose abstract syllables would afford a means of eliminating the hissed "s"'s that so often disfigure the musical effect when large groups are singing.

Given a free hand to use any kind of vocal sounds in accordance with the needs of the *music,* the composer would also be free from any need to set words in a particular rhythmic pattern. Furthermore, translations of the vocal parts would not be necessary. Composers with a humorous turn of mind have set to music such nonliterary texts as copyright notices and florists' catalogues, and have been condemned for their trouble. Musically, however, they were on the right track.

Because of the unwarranted emphasis that is placed on verbal texts, much beautiful and once admired music is no longer performed. This is particularly true in the case of operas with weak stories. If our orientation permitted us to assign the proper degree of unimportance to the role of the words, we might enrich our musical life by reviving at least sections of these works in concert form.

Those who object to concert performances of oratorios in which certain sections are omitted, or performed in other than their original order, are more concerned with words than with music. Granted that some choral works, or at least portions of them, admit of no excisions or alterations. The beginning of the second part of Bach's *Passion According to St. John* is a case in point. The recitatives, which carry the story forward, and the responses of the crowd (the chorus), are not separate and complete musical movements. Rather, they are brief, dramatic interjections which, because of their incompleteness, demand that they follow immediately one on the heels of the other. The narrative is so dramatic, and is so well seconded by the music, that to eliminate any section would be to disturb the continuity of the story.

Except for a few sequences, however, this is not the case with Handel's *Messiah,* or with his *Solomon.* The only dramatic portion of the *text* of *Solomon*—a seventeen-minute scene culminating in the two women contending for possession of the child—is set, unfortunately, for the most part to recitative that seldom rises above the routine in musical interest. If one is to perform the one section of this scene that is musically interesting—the trio with Solomon and the two women— the text demands that one also perform all the dull recitatives leading up to it.

Much of the rest of *Solomon,* however, contains beautiful music, with admittedly unimportant texts. The work, which is far too long for modern tastes, can be performed with the dull portions eliminated, and with some rearrangement of the order of the remaining sections, in order to supply musical contrast. Thus we are left with a series of exquisite musical numbers for solos, duets, and choruses, with platitudinous texts. But since the musical numbers thus preserved are so beautiful *as music,* what does it matter that their texts are routine expressions of love and conventional, flowery praises of Solomon?

I am not suggesting the thoughtless chopping up of oratorios. Certainly, wherever possible, the continuity of the text should be preserved. (Of course, when a choral work is performed as part of a religious ritual, the text will be expected to be given precedence.) But I feel that listeners would derive more enjoyment in the concert hall from oratorios and operas that are too long for present-day tastes, if they were regarded less as means of conveying a narrative or delineating character, and more as collections of beautiful, contrasting musical numbers, each with its own inherent musical interest.

The undue "word-orientation" sometimes blinds us even to these musical beauties. One of Handel's biographers, in his discussion of the oratorio *Saul,* states flatly that the work "should end" at a certain point in the text, and laments the fact that, because of "the necessity for a cheerful finale," Handel added "sundry exhortations." But, after having discussed the other music at some length, he makes no mention whatsoever of the music to which these words are set, giving the impression that, because the words are anti-climactic, this concluding section of the oratorio is not worthy of our consideration. Actually, it is a magnificent fugue, on an arresting *musical* theme, and includes some of the finest writing in the entire oratorio.

It is also customary to perform certain choral works only in those seasons to which their texts are appropriate. The music itself makes no such distinctions, however, and could be enjoyed equally well throughout the year. This concentration upon words also draws audiences to those oratorios whose texts are appropriate to certain holidays, and tends to keep them away from works whose texts are not seasonal, but whose music is equally as beautiful as that of the more popular works.

Here is final evidence of our excessive word-orientation. Anyone who has ever attended a choral concert is familiar with the periodic moments when the music is covered by what sounds like a sudden rush of water, a sound that results from the fact that the entire audience is simultaneously turning the pages of the booklets containing the text. This would seem to be an encouraging sign of the audience's interest in the music. In reality, it is an indication of the fact that audiences are, for the most part, lost in the words.

CHAPTER 10

Are Composing and Performing Emotional Outlets?

There is a great likelihood that most listeners, at some time or other, have found themselves unable to derive from music the emotional experience that they think it should give them. True, a piece of music can be exciting, especially if it is loud and rhythmic; a sentimental song can bring tender memories; the violin section of an orchestra, playing a broad, sweeping melody, can create a pleasant "romantic" feeling in us. Yet somehow we do not often have the overpowering, gripping, emotional experience that we think we ought to get from what is often described as "the most emotional of the arts."

Most of us would probably admit that we seldom get from music the kind of excitement that a good mystery movie will give us—the kind in which we can actually feel our hearts pounding. Nor does a piece of music often create in us the "lump in the throat" that we feel at the end of a television drama, when the boy finally gets the girl. We may feel that something is wrong with *us*, since we are not responding to music to the degree we have been led to believe we might.

It is easy to understand why the average music lover is under the impression that music is the language of the emotions. After all, it has been so described for centuries. Then, too, motion pictures, in their fanciful dramas about composers, have led us to believe that there is a direct relationship between the composer's emotions and his creation of music. This relationship can be summarized as follows: composer feels deep emotion (usually because he has been rejected by the woman he loves); composer goes, stricken, to the piano; composer, in the white heat of inspiration, turns out a masterpiece embodying his suffering. Presumably, each time we listen to the piece in question we, in turn, are expected to feel that suffering exactly as it was experienced by the composer. Unfortunately, this view has been fostered at times even by composers. No wonder, then, that it has gained acceptance with many music lovers.

Let us first dispose of the stereotype of the composer supposedly pouring his heart out on paper—giving vent to his emotions as an act of release. A single example should suffice to show that it is a misconception. Consider one of the best-known and most "emotional" works in music, Beethoven's Ninth Symphony. The work takes approximately seventy minutes to perform. Anyone, whether able to read music or not, cannot fail to be impressed by the size and complexity of the printed score— a 296-page tome. Merely to write the notes of that score, without taking the time for any of the thought that went into its creation, would take weeks of work.

Leaving aside the large body of purely technical matters that have to be considered by the composer, but which are never mentioned in the usual dithyramb about the process of musical creation—the limited range of each instrument, their individual characteristics, the complexities of musical notation—there is the problem of the conceiving and shaping of the music. The creation of the Ninth Symphony occupied Beethoven for *ten years,* during which period he wrote many other works as well.

Now, is it reasonable to assume that Beethoven remained in a state of continuous inspiration over the Ninth Symphony during that entire period? Is it not more likely that the music was the result of conscious thought and planning, purposefully returned to from time to time? The melodies themselves, which may give us a feeling of being inevitable, were, as a matter of fact, rewritten numberless times, until Beethoven's mind told him that they had finally been given their ideal shape. The point is that Beethoven not only *understood* the nature of the listener's responses to music, but consciously *planned* his music in order to elicit these responses.

Curiously, when we imagine a painter at work, we usually think of him as very carefully applying a brush stroke and then stepping back in order to consider its effect. In this instance, the popular notion about creativity coincides with what may be seen by those who have ever actually watched an artist at work. At no point is he ever to be seen in a paroxysm of emotion, and then in a state of relief, as the result of having expressed his emotions. If only the popular conception of the composer at work were revised so that it showed the composer going through a process similar to that of the painter, consciously and deliberately planning his emotional effects, we should have a much more accurate picture of the true state of affairs.

In one of his letters, Mozart explained that, when he depicted feelings and emotions in his works, he did not actually experience them. Instead, he consciously brought his intelligence and skill to bear in order to delineate them. What Mozart or any other composer does is to employ those patterns or devices that he knows from previous experience to be likely to produce the effects he desires in the listeners. (The fact that the responses will not be identical for all listeners need not detain us, since it does not alter the applicability of the basic principle.) This is a conscious act on the part of the composer, requiring the application of reason and skill in the manipulation of his materials.

The extent to which he is able to create the desired effects in the listener is the measure of his skill and his talent. Any sense of emotional release that the composer may experience stems from his feeling of satisfaction at having accomplished what he set out to do. Thus, when a composer writes what he considers a good funeral march—"good" in the sense that it conveys the requisite feeling of solemnity—his reaction may be one of elation. That this is the case is suggested in a statement made by Verdi: "I am working on my *Mass** and really with great pleasure."

An analogy from literature may help us to get the proper perspective on the composer's "inspiration." No one would maintain that Shakespeare had to feel in an evil mood or be evil every time he sat down to write the part of Iago. It was sufficient for him to understand the nature of evil in order to be able to plan Iago's strategy and to determine the words to put into his mouth. Similarly, a composer understands the nature of our feelings and moods, and knows how to evoke them. To believe that Beethoven had to be sad every time he addressed himself to the task of composing the funeral march of the *Eroica Symphony* would be as wrong as believing that Shakespeare had to get himself into a vengeful mood as a prerequisite to his writing lines for Iago.

It is customary to assert that a creative artist must at some time have experienced the emotions that he conveys in his work. The assumption is that the composer, for example, in order to portray a convincing feeling of anguish in his music, calls on his recollections of his own previous anguish. We may doubt this, if only for the reason that composers express feelings by means of conventionalized formulas. There is every reason to suppose that a composer, having listened to and observed the effects of other composers' music, adopts—and sometimes extends—the basic modes of expression for his own music.

On the larger scale, this common heritage of expressive devices accounts for the fact that so many Baroque concertos, regardless of who composed them, seem indistinguishable from one another, and that so much of Mozart's music can be mistaken for Haydn's. The composers were not copying one another's actual "emotions"; instead, they were all drawing upon similar *musical* conventions for conveying feelings of sadness, joy, or exhilaration. Although the fourteen-year-old Mozart, in one of his early divertimentos, wrote a slow movement that seems to embody the suffering of a mature adult, we are not justified in assuming that he actually experienced a

* Actually, his *Requiem.*

depth of emotion beyond his years. Instead, he was using the modes of expression that were current in his time. His precocity lay in the development of his musical abilities, not of his personal traits.

Let us now examine the oft-repeated claim that composers demonstrate the strength of their religious feelings in their music. The truth is that a composer's religious faith is no more capable of being expressed in music than is his social outlook, his patriotism, or his morals. The strength of a composer's religious convictions can be judged only as a noncomposer's are. That he writes a good deal of music with religious texts, and thus puts his skill at the service of his church, *may* be an indication of the fact that he is devout. But we must also realize that much religious music has been composed on commission, by both believers and nonbelievers. (When Bach, a Lutheran, was asked to compose for the Catholic Church, he used some of the music he had previously written for the Protestant service, substituting Latin words.)

In his *Mass in B Minor,* Bach sets the words *"Credo in unum Deum"* ("I believe in one God") so that the tenors of the chorus intone the words to the melody of an ancient chant, while the cellos and basses of the orchestra play a series of evenly spaced, loud notes. The unchanging rhythm and the strong dynamics of those notes are often pointed to as musical evidence of the strength of the composer's personal beliefs. Bach was a devout man, but those powerful notes in the cellos and basses do not necessarily convey the steadfastness of their composer's faith. The writing of loud, equally spaced notes is a technique available to all composers, regardless of their religious beliefs, for use in secular as well as sacred music. The literature abounds in such examples.

Any assertion that certain music demonstrates the depth of a composer's religious feelings is based on a purely arbitrary ascription of meanings not inherent in the music itself. *Any* powerful passage may be said to express a strong conviction about the text that accompanies it, just as any quiet, contemplative passage, which would create only a feeling of calmness without a text, may be said to convey a devotional attitude, once a religious title or text is added.

Another prevalent assumption— that the greatness of a composer's religious music stems from the extent to which he is inspired by religious feelings— would lead us to the conclusion that, given two composers with equal creative ability in music, the one who is more inspired by religion will be able to write the greater music. In this case, we are faced with dilemmas. First, there is the fact that a number of the admittedly greatest "religious" compositions—the Requiems by Verdi and Brahms and Berlioz— were composed by agnostics or nonbelievers.* Second, even great composers who were known to have been devout believers have produced dull sacred music.

There are routine sections in the Bach cantatas, in his Passion settings, and even in his Mass in B Minor, and there are routine movements in the oratorios of Handel and in the masses of Mozart, Haydn, and Schubert. Is it not the lack of musical craftsmanship that accounts for the many inferior works with religious subjects, now justly forgotten, that were written by devout composers, all of whom had all the requisite religious inspiration?

Then, too, there is the fact that Handel, who is today regarded as among the greatest composers of religious music, and whose lifelong, strong religious convictions are known, did not begin composing oratorios until late in his career, after he had composed more than forty operas. It might be assumed that this change was the result of a growing spirituality, but his biographers inform us that Handel continued to compose operas until the competition became so keen that he could no longer fill a theater. He then concentrated on the writing of oratorios.

What, now, of the performer, who is commonly thought to indulge in an act of self-expression when he plays a piece of music? This self-expression theory, which assumes that the making of music is the direct outcome of an intensely felt emotion, makes no distinction between good and bad art. Imagine a child who has just been severely punished. Under the direct influence of his anger, he goes to the piano and bangs on the keys to his heart's content. This is self-expression, without any question; for that child, it is a completely valid means of working off an emotion. Moreover, he is using a sophisticated medium—the sounds of the piano. But the result is obviously not what we would call art.

---

*Dvořák who was close to Brahms, said: "What a great man. What a great soul. And he believes in nothing!"

In order to point up the difference between the expression of emotions and art, let us go one step further with this situation. Suppose the person were a young music student, and had in his repertoire a vigorous, loud piece. It is hardly likely that under the influence of his strong emotion—anger—he would want to play that piece, for in order to perform it he would have to curb his emotional feeling sufficiently to enable him to perform a task that calls for a high degree of coordination. In other words, we would no longer have the unbridled expression of an emotion; instead, we would have a controlled, deliberate, artistic performance.

Carry this situation still further, and we get an insight into the real relationship between music and the emotions. Suppose, now, that our overwrought person is not a child but an adult. He has in his repertoire Beethoven's *Appassionata Sonata.* Since the title means "impassioned," what selection could be more appropriate to the expression of his turbulent emotions? And, to be sure, there is some violent music in that work. But what does our pianist find as he sits down at the piano, intending to express his stormy emotions? Beethoven begins the work with a *very soft* statement of the main melody. He repeats this theme—still prescribing that it be played softly— and then he extends the passage with material from only the last two bars of the melody. If the pianist plays according to Beethoven's directions, he will have been producing no sounds louder than a whisper for a considerable length of time.

Finally, when Beethoven again returns to the main melody, our pianist can give vent to his feelings, since now there is a series of chords to be played *fortissimo.* But note that the pianist cannot bang out just *any* chords, to relieve his emotions. He has to play the chords that Beethoven has specified, and at the speed specified. Yet even this carefully calculated outburst lasts only a moment; Beethoven immediately calls for a return to the softer dynamics. After allowing the pianist only two more such brief outbursts, Beethoven introduces another melody, this one broad and flowing. Our pianist must wait until considerably later in the movement before he can again find release for his more turbulent feelings.

The truth of the matter is that, even in such emotionally motivated music as the *Appassionata,* what we find is far removed from the unbridled expression of emotions. The act of performing is twice removed from self-expression: first, as we have seen, by the fact that the performer cannot give vent to his own emotional state; second, by the fact that his ability to follow the composer's directions successfully requires the careful application of skills that are the result of years of intensive practice. Thus the act of performing is hardly mere emotional expression.

Now consider the state of affairs in which the professional musician finds himself. Since concerts are planned long in advance, the solo recitalist must decide what music he will perform many months hence, without the slightest idea of what his emotional state will be at the time of the actual concert. Not only must he reconcile himself to going through a series of works in widely different styles in the course of a single evening—he is also required to progress through the varying movements of a single work, with their preordained, contrasting emotional coloration, and with hardly more than a few moments' pause between them.

In the course of a tour, an artist or ensemble may perform the identical program at concert after concert, perhaps as many as twenty or thirty times. Most artists will readily agree that their later performances are likely to be better than the earlier ones—so much so, in fact, that they try to schedule these later performances in the cities with the more influential newspaper critics.

Concerts, therefore, are hardly occasions for the self-expression of emotions; they are, instead, proving grounds in which efforts are made to polish the performances. Effects are planned and tried. To be sure, many of them are in the direction of making the performances more emotionally appealing to the audiences. In the case of ensembles, discussions usually follow each performance, in which the effectiveness of the various approaches is soberly evaluated, and changes in the interpretation are made accordingly. All this is a conscious and deliberate process.

The player or singer in a small ensemble is even further restricted in matters of self-expression than is the solo performer. The latter, under the impetus of a spontaneous feeling, is free to change his interpretation somewhat during performance. The members of a group cannot afford such last-minute manifestations of self-expression, because of the need for maintaining a unified approach with the other members of the group.

Orchestral players are possibly the most restricted of all. While many are exceptionally skilled artists in their own right, it is a fact that the very last thing that would be tolerated of them in an orchestral performance is any expression of their own individualities. The measure of a good orchestral player depends in part upon the extent to which he or she can submerge his individuality and blend with the others, in accordance with the conductor's dictates. Perhaps this accounts, to some degree, for the utterly blank expressions that one so often finds on the faces of the players of even our finest orchestras.

If the full truth were known, the average concertgoer would find an even more curious situation. The fact is that when a member of an orchestra is not required for a particular work on a concert program, he or she almost invariably remains backstage, chatting with the other players who are not needed for that work. It is the extremely rare player who takes a seat in the auditorium, or stays in the wings, in order to hear the music in which he is not involved.

During a performance, it is possible for a conductor to elicit from skilled players all the emotionalism that he or she wants, merely by asking them to play *espressivo*. There is not a professional player in existence who does not understand what that word means, and who cannot imbue his or her playing at will with all the warmth and emotionalism that any conductor would want. This is done consciously, on demand, and without the necessity for any emotional involvement on the player's part. Since this emotionalism can be achieved without any perceptible change in the traditional blank expressions of the players, we may safely assume that the effect comes from the application of their technical skill and because of the technical possibilities of their instruments.

Before leaving the performer, we might consider amateur choral singers. In relation to our topic, they are the ideal performers. As opposed to the approach of the jaded professional musician, amateurs sing only because they want to, and they may even pay a fee for the privilege. There can certainly be no doubt of the sincerity of their music-making. Yet choral singers are subject to the same technical considerations as those that concern the professional musician. They must devote their entire attention to the best possible realization of their own vocal lines, so that they take their proper place as a part of the complete musical fabric. Not having trained voices, they must concentrate all the harder on producing a satisfactory tone quality. With all these things on their minds, it is perhaps remarkable that they are able actually to *enjoy* the experience.

What is the true nature of the emotional experience of amateur choral singers? A good portion of it comes solely from the phenomenon of participating in a concert. The excitement of the public appearance, sometimes with professional instrumentalists, is an exhilarating experience in itself. The amount of sound that they hear around them and the realization that they are helping to produce it are also sources of pleasure. The fact that it happens relatively infrequently and that it contrasts with their regular, daily activity adds to the excitement. But beyond this is the singer's concern for the excellence of the performance—for the conscious application of controlled artistry, in order that the desired, carefully planned effects may have their fullest impact upon the audience. This could hardly be called the indulgence of emotions.

Now, let us consider the conductor. We can immediately abandon the idea that his heaving and jumping and fist-shaking—if he goes in for that sort of thing—indicate that he is going through a soul-searing emotional experience. The skills of the players in our leading professional orchestras are so great that they can play well entirely irrespective of the conductor's antics—which they in fact disregard.

A skilled orchestra that has been well rehearsed is presumably responsive to even the slightest gesture of the conductor. After all, one of the prime purposes of rehearsals is to inculcate just that sort of responsiveness. Therefore, when the conductor indulges in exaggerated motions during a concert, either he or she has not done a good job at rehearsals and must now try to coordinate the players, or else he or she is showing off for the audience—a by no means unheard-of weakness. If the conductor's interpretation of the *music is* a good one—as it often is—the reason is to be found in his or her musicianship as it manifested itself during the rehearsals. It has little to do with his or her antics on the podium during the concert.

Confining ourselves, then, to the feelings that a conductor genuinely experiences in the course of a performance, we can regard the act of conducting as partaking of the "emotional" only about the *performance* of the music. Of all the people in the concert hall—orchestra, chorus, soloists, and audience—the conductor is the *least* subject to the immediate emotional effects of the music. His task is to elicit from the performers that interpretation which will create the desired responses in the audience. Since he is the only one of all the performers who is concerned with the *total* effect, it is up to him to keep the balances adjusted. In effect, he must be an instantaneous critic. This requires the unceasing exercise of conscious judgment; it demands *control,* which is quite the opposite of emotional freedom.

The conductor's means of communication with his players are, of course, his hands, his facial expressions, and his body. Some of his gestures are standard, used by all conductors. Others, peculiar to the individual, are either carefully thought out or spontaneous. In any case, the conductor uses his facial expressions and his body in such a manner as to draw the proper interpretations from the performers. He tries to *look* and to *move* as he wishes the music to *sound,* and hopes that the performers will respond to his visually conveyed suggestions. If proof were needed that the conductor is not "responding to" the music, it lies in the fact that he must always be thinking *ahead* of the music, in order to plan his gestures.

His emotional satisfactions come, in the light of all this, not from the music, but from the successful *performance* of the music. His frustrations come from the failure of the performers to achieve what he had in mind, a phenomenon that draws from him some of his most anguished facial expressions. Thus, a particularly joyous and exhilarating portion of the music may find a troubled look on his face, because something—some subtlety—is not being properly realized. Similarly, a very somber passage that is being performed well may easily cause him to look joyful.

On those occasions when everything is going especially well (these are, of course, the sources of the conductor's greatest pleasure, regardless of the emotional coloration of the music), he may try something in the realm of interpretation that he had not attempted in rehearsal. Assuming that he succeeds in conveying his idea to the performers, and that they achieve what he had in mind, popular opinion would attribute it to his having "inspired" the orchestra. Actually, however, success is possible only when every player and singer has placed his skill entirely at the command of the conductor. That is, it is possible only when the conductor has complete control—the antithesis of an emotional, or self-expressive situation.

Turning now to another kind of performance, what about the emotional states of musicians who get together for the sake of playing music without an audience and without thought of public appearance—amateur chamber music players, professionals who sometimes play chamber music in their off-hours, and jazz musicians who get together for "jam sessions"?

The amateur chamber music player, like the amateur choral singer, comes close to being the ideal music lover. Since he is not concerned with preparing for public appearances, he is free to concentrate upon the music itself—and upon his pleasure in playing it—and for the most part he is not required to perform music he does not like.

Of what do his satisfactions consist? First, there is the fact that the activity is a form of recreation, of diverting his mind from the *genuine* emotional strains of everyday life. Regardless of the emotional temper of the music, regardless of the fact that the player is subject to the composer's dictates as to the succession of emotions, the entire activity is a pleasurable one. Nevertheless, in the matter of emotions, the discovery of a long-sought-for rare stamp might well create as great, or even greater emotion of joy in the philatelist, than would be created in the string player who takes part in the lighthearted finale of Mozart's G Minor Quintet. And a more genuine emotion of anger could easily be experienced by the weekend fisherman, from whom a big one got away after a long struggle, than by two pianists banging away at the turbulent portions of a four-hand arrangement of Tchaikovsky's *Romeo and Juliet*. There is a basic difference, then, between real emotions, as they are experienced in life, and the so-called emotions that occur in music and that may be re-created by its performers, and felt by those who listen to it.

Strictly speaking, the only true creative activity in music is composing. Because the notes that a composer writes do not become music until they are sounded, however, the performing of music is a kind of "re-creation." In a sense, every time one plays or sings a piece of music, one is in a kind of partnership with the composer, helping to bring his creation to life. This is as close as most people come to satisfying their creative urges in music.

It is true that the skilled musician can re-create music in his mind by reading the score, "hearing" the sounds of the instruments in his mind, as the result of his memory of previously heard music. But the emotional satisfaction in this is comparable to our recalling the sound of an actor's voice as he delivered a particular line, or our remembering the taste of a delicious steak. Regardless of how vivid such recollections may be, they cannot compare with the actuality of the sensuous experience itself. The amateur music-maker wants the sensuous pleasures that are afforded by the phenomenon not only of hearing sounds, but of producing them. He is therefore not satisfied with merely listening to a good recorded performance.

The fact that he enjoys playing or singing the same composition, even though he does it so much less well than the skilled professional on the recording, proves that part of the appeal of playing lies in the pleasures derived from the very activity of making the sounds. There is another attraction: the social element. Since a number of individuals have to work together toward the creation of the music, the task of *jointly* working out interpretations, of practicing and finally mastering difficult passages, produces its own satisfaction. Basically, however, this last satisfaction is no different from that experienced by a team of gymnasts who practice and master a trick requiring great coordination.

We have not yet mentioned one of the most important satisfactions of all music-making. It is the interest to be found in the *music* itself, in following for one's self the development and the interplay of the melodies, in tracing the changes, following the rhythms and harmonies, and, especially with regard to chamber music, in seeing how the themes are given first to one instrument, then to another. While the sensitive player will be alert to all the changes in mood that the composer creates, a much greater proportion of his pleasure will come from following the course of the various themes than from experiencing emotional thrills.

The popular conception—the general, unthinking acceptance of music as above all an emotional experience—tends to blind us to the fact that this process of following the course of the melodies forms a large part of our enjoyment of music. We readily grant that, in a play, we are interested in the exchange of ideas—in short, in the "intellectual development" of the playwright's thoughts; we do not expect a play to be *emotionally* stimulating at every moment. Moreover, no one recoils from the use of the term "intellectual development" in connection with the interplay of ideas in a play. But let the word "intellectual" be applied to music, and the layman tends to tremble, thinking that it means technicalities that are beyond him.

Actually, the meaning of "intellectual" as it applies to music is nothing more than the interest that the mind takes in following the manipulation of the five basic ingredients: rhythm, melody, harmony, tone color, and form. We hear a theme; we follow it to see what will happen to it. We respond to a rhythmic pattern and then respond again when it changes. We hear a melody, first with a particular harmonization and then as it reappears with a different harmonization. We hear how the composer breaks a melody into fragments, distributing certain of them among the various instruments or voices.

Now, let us consider the satisfactions obtained by the professional musician, who plays chamber music in his off hours. His situation, and his resulting motivation, give further proof of the point just made. First, let us acknowledge the extramusical reasons that impel a professional orchestral player to turn to chamber music for pleasure. There is the matter of ego-satisfaction—his freedom from the dictates of a conductor, and the fact that he is the only performer playing his particular part. Furthermore, the part itself may be more challenging to play, and there is less time spent merely counting measures while others play. But the significant difference is that the individual parts of a well-written chamber work are likely to contain more for the musical intelligence to dwell on than do the parts of an orchestral composition. This is why the player is willing to forsake the more obvious emotionalism of the massed sound, and chooses for his own satisfaction to play music of more limited emotional potentialities.

Thus, when we investigate the facts, we see that another widely accepted notion proves false, and that the truth is in fact the very opposite of the popularly held view. That is, the professional musician who plays chamber music in his off hours, with no thought of financial gain, does so not because he wants more emotional stimulation but because he seeks greater involvement for his musical intelligence. Again, everything points toward the conclusion that the true musical experience is not just the pure emotional release that the popular viewpoint supposes it to be; to a greater extent than is ordinarily realized, it consists of mental activity as well.

There remains to be considered the emotional satisfactions of the jazz musicians who get together for afterhour "jam sessions." To some extent, their motivations are the same as those of the other types of performers we have been discussing. They indulge in these sessions in order to escape from the restrictions placed upon them in their regular work. In addition, they do so for pleasure, rather than for financial gain. However, the similarity ends there, since these sessions assume the character of performances, even though the audiences may be relatively small.

The essential difference between these "jam sessions" and the chamber music readings just discussed lies in the basic fact that the jazz musician *makes his own music.* Being his own "composer," he is freed from the necessity to follow the succession of feelings as prescribed by the printed music. To that extent, he comes closer than any other performing musician to the idea of self-expression.

There is no doubt, also, that such music-making has a much more emotional coloration than has any of the other kinds that we have been discussing. It is characterized by an almost ritualistic dedication, in which emotionalism is paramount—as witness the facial expressions of both performers and hearers, the contorted bodily positions, and even the jargon that is used in discussing the music.

This kind of music-making, then, *is* a form of emotional release, to those who are susceptible to its influence. Even so, a good deal of the admiration that the players evoke stems from the inventiveness they display in embellishing a melody. In short, allowing for the obvious differences in musical style, they are doing essentially what Bach did when he improvised at the organ on some of the hymn tunes of his day, bringing intellectual capacity to the process of musical creation.

To summarize: the composer, as he writes music, does not experience an act of emotional catharsis. The performer—whether he be a soloist, a member of a small ensemble, large orchestra or chorus, or a conductor—is not indulging in an act of self-expression. The amateur player, or the professional orchestral or jazz musician who plays music in his off hours solely for his own satisfaction, does so in large measure for the genuine musical interest that the experience affords.

Everything about the creation and performance of music tends in a direction opposite to that of a purely emotional experience. Emotions are by nature without controlled shape. To exercise control over an emotion is to distort it or inhibit it. Music, on the other hand, is consciously controlled and shaped. The performer subjects himself to the discipline of the music, often in close coordination with many other performers. So long as he is not distracted by such considerations as consciousness of his lack of sufficient technique, fear of bad reviews, or boredom, he derives one overall feeling from the total experience, despite the fact that the music may have taken him through a wide variety of moods and "emotions." That over-all feeling is—pleasure.

CHAPTER 11

How Music Affects
Our Feelings

What about the emotional effects of music upon the listener? What about the tender, wistful feelings that we sometimes experience when we listen to a particularly haunting slow movement? A truly indescribable state can be induced in many of us by the soaring sound quality of massed violins. It is a combination of melancholy, nostalgia, and a semisweet sadness. While it defies accurate description, there can be no doubt that it exists. Again, what shall we say of the exhilaration that we feel at the conclusion of a large orchestral work, particularly when the ending is loud and rhythmic? And how shall we account for the appeal of certain melodies, or of certain portions of long works, which we regard as their "high spots?" All these effects upon us certainly seem to fall into the category of emotional reactions. They can be felt, to varying degrees, by even the casual listener; and they certainly do not require technical training to be appreciated.

In order to deal with these questions, let us first investigate the ways in which music affects our feelings.

We may grant, first, that music can affect our pulse rates and our respiration. If the sustained stillness of a quiet evening were suddenly to be broken by a single chord played *fortissimo* by a full orchestra, everybody within earshot would undoubtedly jump with fright.

Of course, *any* unexpected loud noise would produce a similar effect in us. Nevertheless, since music partakes of the realm of sound, this is evidence of one of its physiological effects. Moreover, our closeness to the source of the music, by affecting the degree of loudness with which the chord assailed our ears, would determine the extent of our reactions. Since the effect is a function of the loudness, we can see, by implication, how *dynamics*— that is, the degree of loudness— can influence our emotional reactions to music.

Incidentally, even though the example we gave above is oversimplified, its counterpart exists in music. Many unsuspecting listeners are taken unawares by an equivalent chord near the beginning of the *Oberon* overture of Weber, or by one in the first movement of Tchaikovsky's *Pathétique Symphony.*

Perhaps the most important of the physical effects in music *is rhythm.* It is the basis of much of the appeal of marches and dances; it is also the source of the utilitarian use of music in work songs and sea chanteys. In its more sophisticated forms, rhythm affects our feelings in practically all music.

In addition, *tempo* helps to shape our feelings, since fast music tends to excite us, while slow music makes for a feeling of restfulness. Here, too, it becomes apparent that combinations of different *tempi,* and the process of changing from one to another, can create many kinds of responses in us. Music, of course, exists in time, as we do. In any period during which we are actively listening to music, we are sharing that period of time with it, so that during that period, we tend to be carried along with the music.

Our minds and our physical beings accept the divisions of time (another way of saying "rhythm") as they are presented in the music. Changes in rhythm and in tempo seem to have us in their grip, so that we are at one with the music. We respond to it in much the same way as one electric fan that is running will cause another fan to turn, even though the second one is not connected to a source of electricity. It is just because music is shaped according to our own physiological and psychological responses that it can be compelling. In this regard, a composer is something of a psychologist; he understands the nature of our psychological and physiological responses and creates music that will act upon us.

A further physical aspect of music must be mentioned—the sensuous gratification that comes to us through the mere phenomenon of hearing musical sounds. It is the refinement of this sense that gives us our concern for details of orchestration. That the richness of the musical sound is a factor to be reckoned with is revealed in the preference of many people for the sound of an orchestra over that of a string quartet.

There is still another emotional response that music awakens in us. It comes from our tendency to identify ourselves with the rise and fall of a melody by our impulse to sing along with it. This can be demonstrated at its most obvious level by the empathy that we feel with a singer who is negotiating a passage that lies high for the voice. Part of our response to that passage is conditioned by the memory of our own attempts to sing, part by an identification with the singer at that moment. The sense of strain that shows on a singer's face is one of the ways of creating a comparable emotional state in the listener.

Because of this "remembered singing" there is a carryover of this process of identification when we listen to instrumental music, depending to a great extent on the instruments used. The tension that we feel as we follow an ascending passage is much greater in the case of wind and stringed instruments than it is in the case of a piano, harp, or organ. There is a sense of strain as the violinist progressively shortens the strings, and in the wind instruments the production of tone is physiologically comparable to the production of song.

These, then, are the sources of music's physical and physiological effects. They are a kind of stock in trade in every composer's storehouse. He is free to use them in any manner he wishes. In fact, no matter how he may treat these elements— regardless of the relative emphasis that he may give to them— he cannot escape them. These physical factors are indigenous to all music.

To the extent that we actually listen to a piece of music, there will be induced in us those moods and changes of moods that the composer has written into the piece. Through his knowledge of our physical and sensuous makeup, he can presumably compose such music as will induce in us the appropriate responses. This is done most obviously in the background music written for motion pictures and television dramas.

All of us are familiar with those brief bits of music. Indeed, they have become so stylized that many of us could probably guess the nature of the subject matter merely from the music alone: a love scene is accompanied by rhapsodic strings; a train wreck or similar disaster is introduced by ominous music; a political riot is accompanied by turbulent music. So conventionalized has this use of music become, in fact, that on those occasions when we arrive early and wait in the lobby for the start of the picture, we are always able to tell when the picture has ended, just from the music alone. There is almost invariably a "welling up" of the music as it attains a climactic feeling.

The fact that we are often able to identify the nature of the action from the music alone would seem to indicate that music *can* convey emotions. However, it is important to realize that all the given examples are, in essence, extreme in their emotional coloration. Further, the music accompanying them is never a fully developed composition, but a fragment, played only long enough to establish a mood. The most important point, though, is the fact that the nature of these musical fragments has been determined by usage.

Yet, obvious as these fragments are in their effect, and despite the fact that they are not complete, organized musical works, the process by which they achieve their effects gives us some insight into the ability of music to express emotions Their composers have seized upon the most obvious and extreme attributes of music's physical appeals. These same attributes, in more subtle form, are the source of the emotionalism of more extended and sophisticated compositions. The mysterious passage that connects the scherzo of Beethoven's Fifth Symphony with the finale—with its ominous drum beats, and its gradual increase in loudness—achieves its emotional effects in essentially the same way as that by which the tremolo of the strings heightens the suspense in a mystery movie. And the lightness of feeling that we get from a Mendelssohn scherzo stems from the same source as that which produces the lightheartedness in those inconsequential musical snippets that introduce the fashion shows or the caperings of animals.

However, as the music becomes more extended, more complex, and more developed—in other words, as we move beyond the brief mood pieces with their one obvious emotional coloration—we realize that a single composition may contain a great variety of feelings. Moreover, as the compositions become more sophisticated—as the composer gives himself over to the process of "thinking musically"— we realize that there are an increasing number of places in which it is impossible to determine exactly what emotion is being expressed, or if indeed any emotion is being expressed at all.

It is here that the layman is justifiably mystified by the familiar claim that music is the language of the emotions. As long as any piece of music has physical qualities that make the more obvious emotional states apparent, such as the climactic moments in a symphony or a concerto, the listener is on safe ground. But what, he asks himself, is he to feel during those many passages which have no immediately apparent emotional coloration?

At this point, the limitations of music's ability to express emotions should be apparent. Do we, in actuality, experience "emotions"—love, hate, anger, jealousy, sadness, joy, and fear— when we hear a piece of music? Emotions, by definition, are always accompanied by some physical manifestation; there is usually some marked change in our respiration and in our pulse rate. Our complexions become noticeably paler when we experience fear. Our faces become flushed and we clench our teeth when we experience the emotions of hate, anger, or jealousy. Even during so minor a form of emotion as embarrassment, we blush. Has any piece of music by itself ever caused any of these reactions in you or in any of your friends? (It goes without saying, of course, that for the moment we are not speaking of music with words, or music that accompanies a drama. We are considering the effects of *music* alone.)

It is evident that music does not cause in us these obvious physiological changes that accompany emotions. This is demonstrated by the fact that concert audiences can sit still for long periods of time, without any apparent changes in their physiological states; they do not become flushed, even in the most excited passages, and we may doubt that anybody experiences any difficulty in breathing.

Now, in order to be accurate, we must grant that even so minor a physical manifestation as the desire to tap one's foot or to bob one's head in time to the music is, technically speaking, an emotional reaction. By the same measuring rod, the response to the tone of a violin, to the degree that it creates even a pleasant sensation in us, must be regarded as an emotional reaction. Similarly, the phenomenon of a long held dissonance finally resolving to a consonance, in so far as it creates in us even an imperceptible and not consciously thought-out feeling of progressing from tension to relaxation (that is, from "pain to pleasure"), falls under the category of an emotional response.

But notice how slight all these effects are, in comparison with those that accompany real emotions. Let one individual in a concert hall dare to follow his natural inclinations and tap his foot, or even to breathe heavily, and he is subjected to immediate complaints from those seated around him. This, in spite of the fact that the nineteenth-century composer, in his symphonies or tone poems, is usually assumed to be laying his very soul bare before us. The accepted way to listen to a symphony most effectively is to sit motionless, perhaps with eyes closed, or with the head resting in the hand. This is hardly the attitude of a person undergoing a true emotional experience.

The difference between the extent of our reactions to music and the extent of our reactions to real-life emotions is so great that music must be regarded as an extremely small scaled reflection of our emotional life. Some writers have attempted to account for the gap between the musical expression of emotions and real-life experience by saying that music deals with the *memory* of emotions. Despite the fact that we must, on technical grounds, refer to our reactions to music as emotions, what we really get from music is momentary *feelings*, rather than emotions, in the generally accepted meaning of the term.

A good deal of the source of the confusion lies in a semantic misunderstanding. The word "emotions," as it is commonly used, has strong connotations. Its widespread use in connection with music, and its consequent unthinking acceptance, has led many music lovers to expect the wrong things from music. If we could substitute the word *feelings*, and if we could realize that, for a great portion of our listening experience, those feelings are of a relatively slight order, we should arrive at a more accurate insight into the actual state of affairs.

Let us look further into the actual nature of our reactions to music. Curiously, in spite of the great emotional powers that have been ascribed to music, the effects of even the most over-powering work are actually so slight as to leave us untouched or annoyed, unless we are in a receptive mood when we hear it. The emotional effects of music last only while we are hearing it, or, at most, for only the briefest time after the music has ceased. Otherwise, how shall we account for the fact that audiences almost invariably applaud—breaking the mood left by the music—immediately upon the conclusion of a work? In fact, in many instances, they do not even wait for the final measures. This is especially true when a singer has finished an operatic aria. In this case, when a glamorous performer is being applauded, the listener's emotional involvement in the music itself must be slight indeed. The point that applause is a form of release for the listener's pent-up feelings of admiration for the performer is tenable; it does not, however, negate the fact that the music's emotional hold is of a very slight order, once the music has ended.

Record manufacturers have adopted a standard length of time for the silences between different works on a disc, and between movements of the same work. It is six seconds. There is general agreement that a longer pause will cause the listener to become restless! Here is sufficient indication of the strength of the emotions that any piece of music may provoke, and of the length of time that the emotions remain with us.

CHAPTER 12

Can Music Express Emotions?

As "natural" and "inevitable" as we may consider our Western music to be, it is still created within a contrived system. Its content—its message—can be as arbitrary and as meaningless to, let us say, an East Indian, as his music is to us. What we consider an extremely emotional moment in our music may very well, as we saw in an earlier chapter, have no significance whatsoever for him, and vice versa.*

The fact that our music systems are formalized can perhaps be made clear by returning to the example given earlier—the hypothetical situation in which the stillness is broken by a sudden loud chord played by a full orchestra. Let us suppose that the sound were to be heard by an African tribesman and a Westerner, sitting side by side. Both might be equally startled by the purely physical effect of the loudness and the unexpectedness of the sound. But the Westerner—assuming that he is familiar with the Western system of music—would in addition recognize that the components of the sound made up the musical entity that we know as a chord. Suppose the chord were a dissonance, requiring resolution to a consonance. To the African tribesman, this consideration would be entirely without significance; the only effect upon him would be the shock value of the sudden noise. The Westerner, on the other hand, having been brought up within the conventional usages of our music, would (after he had recovered from his shock) not only recognize the sound as a chord, but would also expect another chord to follow!

As simplified as this example is, what are its implications? Within a formalized, ethnically determined system of music, a single chord can set up a feeling of expectancy—an "emotion." Not only are our emotional responses to music shaped by ethnic and cultural considerations; within a single culture, they vary with the customs of the time and the locality. Compare, for example, the emotional temper of eighteenth-century French orchestral music with that of late nineteenth-century Germany—say, of the music of Wagner and Strauss. From our vantage point in the twentieth century, the later music would be considered far more "emotional," while, by comparison, we should be inclined to look upon the early French music as merely courtly, almost lacking in emotional quality. Yet, to judge from the testimony of eighteenth-century writers, the

---

* Occidental listeners who claim to appreciate East Indian (or any other oriental music) are really responding only to its exotic qualities. These music systems are actually organized in extremely complex ways, the true appreciation of which would take a lifetime of study on the part of anyone not brought up where these systems are the norm.

music of their time abounded in the vivid expression of the passions.

The difference in emotional temper stems, of course, from several sources. The later composers' musical vocabulary embraced the innovations that had accrued in the intervening decades, including an expanded harmonic palette, a greatly enlarged orchestra, and the improved technical qualities of the instruments. In addition, there are contained in the two schools the influences of their respective national characteristics.

To consider a specific example, Monteverdi's *"Lasciatemi morire"* (or "Arianna's Lament") was, in the period of its composition, considered one of the most moving pieces of music ever written. It was said to have brought tears to an audience of a thousand people. Yet, to our ears, accustomed as we are to the relatively unbridled emotionalism of nineteenth-century Italian opera, Monteverdi's lament sounds rather restrained.

Here is another example of formalized emotionalism. The Greeks codified the various modes (scales) of their music, according to their presumed emotional effects. Soldiers were not to hear the languorous mode before going forth to battle, and so on. Yet despite the widely different emotional effects that the Greeks ascribed to their musical modes, the average listener of today would, in all likelihood, be unable even to tell one from the other!

The mere fact that the musical means of conveying emotional states varies from one era to another, and from one locality to another, demonstrates that there is nothing absolute about our emotional responses to music. This, despite the fact that the basic physiological and psychological makeup of people has remained essentially unchanged during the entire period from which we have drawn our examples.

Our emotional responses to music are largely learned reactions, shaped by usage, convention, and association. Here is the source of the view that music can convey patriotic feelings. What actually happens, of course, is that *any* melody chosen for a national anthem becomes a *symbol* of patriotism in its particular country. The words help to give it its specific emotional coloration, just as they do in the case of a school song, or a song adopted by a children's camp. It is these associations, ingrained as a result of numerous repetitions, that then make the melody, even when it is played without the words, an evocation of patriotic feelings. By itself, the *music* cannot create patriotic feelings except in those who are already familiar with the arbitrarily assigned associations.

If music by itself—unaided by words or by any nationalistic or folk associations—were really capable of creating patriotic sentiments, then it should be possible to write a single piece that, played to an audience of mixed nationalities, would evoke patriotic feelings in every listener, for his *own* country. Obviously, such a piece of music does not and cannot exist. Moreover, by the same token, it should be possible to write a tyrannous or seditious piece of music. This, too, is manifestly out of the question.

To a greater extent than we might think, our emotional responses to music are the result of social sanction, and, by extension, of socially imposed restraints. Consider the markedly different, but expected, behaviors of jazz audiences and performers and those of concert audiences and players. Notice, also, that our social mores permit a much greater degree of freedom at sporting events than at concerts. Contrast the shouting and the body movement of spectators at a baseball or football game with the decorum shown by concert audiences, and you will realize that the emotional response experienced by the listener to music is of a very specialized and severely limited type.

The influence of social custom may again be seen in the differences of audience behavior in different countries while listening to the same music—for example, Italian opera. American audiences remain quiet during the famous arias, reserving their outbursts of approval until the end; Italian audiences sometimes sing along with the singers!

Further indication of the fact that our emotional reactions to music are largely learned lies in the lack of responsiveness on the part of, let us say, the average rock'n'-roll enthusiast to the emotionalism inherent in socalled classical or serious music. Even within the same culture and the same period, a sensitivity to the emotional expressiveness of certain types of music has to be nurtured and developed. If music were actually capable of conveying definable emotions, it would speak directly to everyone within its cultural orbit. We know, from the relative lack of interest in serious music on the part of the public at large, that this is quite far from being the case.

Many of us, taking for granted the supposed emotional effects of music, have difficulty in accepting the thesis that our reactions are largely shaped by tradition. An analogy from another field—motion pictures—may help to make the point clearer. Many years ago, near the end of her career, Sarah Bernhardt starred in a film as Queen Elizabeth of England. In keeping with what was then regarded as the most valid means of expressing emotions, this greatest actress of her time indulged in wide-eyed stares and exaggerated gestures, complete with the back of the clenched fist pressed to the forehead. This was undoubtedly a very serious, moving, emotional experience to the audiences of her day; from the modern audience, it evokes nothing but gales of laughter.

Notice that the difference in effect is not just a matter of degree, of a greater or lesser emotional involvement. Even with the specific dramatic implications of a story to direct its feelings—a situation that, as we have seen, is lacking in music—the audience still could not become involved. The basic human emotion of anguish has not changed since that film was made; the *style*—the manner in which that emotion is formalized and presented to audiences—has changed.

Whether we consider the ethnic and social forces that help to shape our attitudes toward emotional expression in music generally, or in individual pieces of music, or even the emotional effects of certain moments in music, the element of formalization or stylization remains crucial. Let us see how it affects the forms of individual pieces of music. Because of our previous experience, the word "symphony" has certain connotations; it predisposes us to approach such a composition with a particular attitude. We expect an orchestral composition in four movements, each of which will be characterized, for the most part, by an individual emotional coloration. The very division into four movements conditions our psychological attitudes. However, our experience causes us to recognize differences within the category of the symphony, depending upon the composer's name and the style in which he wrote.

The anticipation of hearing a symphony by Haydn or Mozart brings with it one kind of expectation. If, however, the composer is Beethoven, or Mahler, we immediately expect, first, a longer work, and second, a greater degree of emotionalism. Experience also tells us that we are usually safe in assuming that the final movement of a symphony will end with mounting excitement, making for an exhilarating finish.

Now, what of the formalization that takes place within an individual movement? The slow movement of Beethoven's *Eroica Symphony is* one of the most affecting funeral marches in the entire literature of music. The popular assumption is that we experience the emotion of sorrow as we listen to it. But in the middle of the movement, Beethoven gives us a lengthy section whose mood, while serious, would be singularly inappropriate to the emotions usually associated with a funeral. Technically, it is a *fugato*—that is, a relatively "intellectual" treatment, in which one of the motives reappears successively in different instruments, making for a complex texture. Then, with a sense of proportion and balance, Beethoven returns to the opening music of the funeral march for the conclusion of the movement.

Those who maintain that we are, or should be, moved to deep sorrow by this movement conveniently overlook the presence of the middle section. The words "funeral march" are all that they need to open the floodgates. But is it likely that the emotions we experience during a sad occasion like a funeral would occur in this balanced, three-part form? Would our emotional state then permit us to take time out for an "intellectual" consideration of the elements that go to make up our feelings? Yet Beethoven's funeral march does those very things.

Obviously, our emotions do not occur in three-part forms or four-movement forms. Yet everything about music tends toward a heightening of form. Not only are the over-all shapes of compositions and movements of compositions organized, sections within the movements are also carefully balanced against one another. Even individual phrases are given a form. While we may not be aware of it, since we have been conditioned by exposure to take such things for granted, the very fact that we can recognize and enjoy any musical phrase stems from its having been given a form or "shape."

At this point it would be well for us to consider another important way in which music differs from emotions. In real life, our emotions stem from actual situations. They are the outcome of the interactions of many factors: the objective situation, chance, a certain amount of self-determination, and our physiological and psychological state. At any one moment, our emotional reactions are the result of all these forces and influences.

A composer, on the other hand, sets to work, not with facts or situations, but with one or more musical ideas. If we can say that the emotional tones of those ideas can mirror our varying emotional states, then we see that the composer starts with the *effects,* since his music cannot specify the causes. Thus, there is nothing in the music that determines the order in which the emotions, feelings, or moods must occur.

It is customary, for example, for the opening movement of a symphony or a sonata to be lively, with the emotional tone that a fast tempo gives; yet Beethoven's *Moonlight Sonata* begins with the slow movement. Moreover, four of Beethoven's nine symphonies have slow introductions, as do many (but by no means all) of the symphonies of Haydn and Mozart.

Ordinarily, the scherzo movement is placed third, in order to contrast with the slow second movement. However, Beethoven, in his Ninth Symphony, and Mendelssohn, in his Third *(Scotch)* Symphony, place the scherzo second, and the slow movement third. Such deviations from the conventional sequence occur throughout the literature.

Within an individual movement, also, there is nothing that predetermines the succession of feelings. One mood or emotional tone may be quickly replaced by another. Now, if we were actually emotionally affected by the music at any one moment, we would require time for one emotion to run its course before we could go on to the next. The opposite is the case: we accept these sudden changes in mood with no difficulty.

(Throughout this discussion, by the way, we have been considering only instrumental music, since in vocal music, the words can determine the emotional coloration at any one moment, and the rapid succession of emotions, as in an opera plot. Yet much vocal music, too, conforms to the conditions we are discussing.)

Now, these two facts—the lack of any prescribed succession of emotions in music, and the rapidity with which they can replace one another—are a further indication that music does not simply concern itself with expressing emotions, as we ordinarily construe the phrase. By a process of elimination—since we see that the emotions alone do *not* govern the course of a musical work—we may conclude that a musical composition follows its own laws. Even granting that there is often a certain correspondence between sections of a composition and our own emotional states, we are still faced with the fact that the composition has its own life, that its shape is dictated by considerations that have nothing to do with the course of our emotions.

With this, we return to the factor referred to earlier, the purely *musical* interest that a composition can hold for us. Many listeners have been so conditioned to think of music as only an outpouring of emotions, that it becomes difficult to convince them that there can be anything else in music. The idea that a piece of music can have "logic"— that it is possible to *think* in music—has to fight for its existence in the mind of the average listener. Yet, the realization that there is such a thing as *musical thought* supplies a means of understanding those portions of a work that lack an immediately identifiable emotional import. In other words, the extended sections before and after the obvious emotional climaxes are not necessarily just padding; they are most often part of the very substance of the development of the work.

Now, to the extent that it can be demonstrated that the basic materials that composers use in music stem from human emotions, we can agree that our emotions figure in music. We have already noted the elements of music that share a physiological basis with our emotions—rhythm, tempo, dynamics, the sensuous qualities of sounds, and the rise and fall of melodies. At a more subtle level, we can grant that the shape of our sighs may sometimes be imbedded in the shape of a melody, perhaps consciously, perhaps by an unconscious process of association in the composer's mind. A sudden, brief pause during the course of even an instrumental melody can draw from us memories of our gasps, and thus create an emotional coloration.

One of the techniques in vogue during the twelfth and thirteenth centuries was the *hocket* the sudden interruption of the vocal part. Its purpose was to lend a feeling of greater emotionalism to the music, by suggesting a gasp. A similar effect is to be found in many of the more dramatic moments of nineteenth-century Italian opera. And, to offer an example of a purely instrumental work, the great emotionalism of the slow movement of Schubert's C Major Quintet derives, in large measure, from the fact that the first violin part is punctuated by *hocket*-like pauses.

Certain madrigals of Claudio Monteverdi go a step further: they achieve their emotional qualities as the result of what almost amounts to an imitation of sobs and anguished cries. But it is important to realize that, in order for these devices to be accepted into the realm of music, they had to be *formalized*. Neither the gasp itself, nor the sob, nor the actual anguished cry, was admitted.* Instead, their physical properties were adapted to the rigorously controlled system of carefully selected sounds that we call music.

A similar formalization holds for all musical effects that stem from the patterns of our emotional life. The most turbulent moments in a dramatic orchestral climax still consist of carefully planned manipulations of *musical* ideas—melodies or fragments of melodies, harmonies, rhythms.

Consider the difference between the actual sounds called forth by our emotions and those used in music. Nobody has ever described a gasp of fear or a hysterical laugh or a sob of grief as an artistic sound; we are not at all concerned with whether such audible manifestations of true emotions are sensuously pleasing or not. But notice how quickly we condemn the soprano whose singing is even momentarily shrill, or the violinist whose tone becomes slightly harsh.

At first thought, music would seem to be an ideal vehicle for the emotions, since it uses sounds—the very medium that we so often use in expressing our emotions. Yet, from the few points we have considered, it should be clear that even the "raw materials" of our emotions—the sounds that we utter—have little correspondence to the raw materials of music.

To the extent that the emotional element is present in a composition, it has undergone a conscious formalization at the hands of the composer. We are now in the presence not of the emotion itself (if there was one), but of an *esthetic experience,* something that may stem from an emotion, but has been distilled and crystallized. Carried beyond the formless emotion itself, we are confronted with a new phenomenon—the music. It is this fact, among others, that permits us to anticipate

---

* There are moments in operas, of course, in which singers use actual gasps and sighs, but these fall into the realm of dramatic, rather than musical, devices.

hearing Beethoven's "Funeral March" with an attitude of pleasure rather than of sorrow or pain.

The all too frequent, uncritical acceptance of a descriptive
verbal phrase about a composition tends to blind many listeners to the true nature of music, and to the infinite variety of
emotional tones that music can give them. It is possible to characterize the over-all emotional tone of a single short piece of
music by means of words such as "powerful," "gay," or "gentle." Appropriate words can also be found to characterize the
various moods of the different movements of a longer composition, or the changing sections of an extended single movement.
But—as we have already pointed out—it is impossible to convey the actual effect of music by means of words alone.

One may use the word *savage* in describing portions of
Stravinsky's *The Rite of Spring;* but it might be applied with
equal validity to sections of the "March to the Gallows" in
Berlioz's *Fantastic Symphony.* Even descriptions of the greater
rhythmic freedom of the Stravinsky work, or of the ways in
which Berlioz uses the orchestral instruments, and the differences in their harmonic coloring, while these might help us to
tell the two works apart, would still not convey the particular
emotional impact that each work has when heard by a receptive
listener.

It is completely beyond the power of words to duplicate the
musical experience contained in even the simplest progression
of chords, such as the familiar "Amen" sequence. In
Beethoven's *Pastoral Symphony,* the transition from the third
movement (the scherzo) to the fourth movement (the "Storm")
is effected by means of a sudden change in key. The emotional
quality of this change is remarkable. Yet words are unable to
convey it; we are limited to exclamations over the fact that it
exists. We can be so specific as to say that it is a progression to
an unexpected key, and this progression, known to any student
of harmony as a "deceptive cadence," can even be called to
mind at will. Nevertheless, we still have no words to convey
just what happens within us when we *hear* that progression.

Then add the factor of the orchestration, which gives
another source of emotionalism. We can say that the chords in
the full orchestra are followed only by the basses and the cellos
at the moment when the key is changed. That still does not
convey the emotional effect that that orchestration has upon

us. Add the element of dynamics, another very important source of emotionalism. Say that the chords in the full orchestra are loud, that they seem to call forth a final, loud chord, and that, instead, we suddenly hear nothing but a quiet rumble in the basses and cellos. True, this description might be enough to recall the music to someone who knows the work well. But to the person who has never heard it before, or who is only slightly familiar with it, the description cannot possibly convey the particular emotional effect of that passage. There is one and *only* one way to have that precise emotional experience: it is by listening to the music.

It should now be clear that the emotional effects of music exist in a different realm from the emotional effects of words. (We are discussing here, not words set to music, but the ability of words to describe music.) There is another popular misconception that we must examine, to the effect that, as a means of emotional expression, "Music begins where words leave off." This implies that one is the continuation of the other. But that is not the real case. The two arts can both affect our feelings at every level of emotional intensity, but they do so in completely different ways. The sooner the listener realizes that the emotional effects of music *cannot be put into words,* but are simply to be *felt* by him, in his own way, the sooner will he come to a true appreciation of music.

Although we talk and think about our emotions in the medium of language, we do not *experience* our emotions linguistically. When we say, "I am feeling sad," that statement, in its shapes and sounds, has nothing in common with the way we actually feel when experiencing the emotion of sadness. Perhaps the point becomes clearer when we realize that, just by a change of one word, and only a slight change of its sound, we change the entire emotional significance of the statement: "I am feeling glad." The means and form of expression of the thought have hardly changed, yet the way we actually *feel,* if this is a true account of our inner condition, is at the opposite pole of the emotional scale.

In a sense, therefore, we might say that our emotions have aspects that words are inadequate to express. Despite the possible differences in their interpretation and the subtleties of their meanings, words, as we know, have been given specific, discrete significances. Our emotions have no such significances; we can-

not "think" with our emotions as we can "think" with words—
a process that depends upon the fact that words have been
endowed with these specific meanings. The "shapes" or "forms"
of emotions have little in common with the forms of language,
despite the fact that, through years of practice in thinking linguistically, we may make the mistake of thinking that a verbal
description of an emotion is synonymous with the emotion.

Music, on the other hand, has certain dynamic properties in
common with our feelings and emotions, such as the increasing
and relaxation of tensions. Moreover, just *because* music has no
vocabulary of discrete significances as words do, it is better able
to match the changing course—the flow—of our feelings. In
other words, what might be thought to be one of music's disad-
vantages—its inability to be "about" anything specific—is the
very source of its ability to match our emotional states.
Therefore, music can be—within certain limits—a more accurate expression of our emotions than can words. Music *sounds*
the way our emotions *feel.* When we hear a person say in a language that we do not understand, "I feel happy," we have no
idea of what he is talking about, and consequently, no idea of
how he feels. But if this person were a composer, his music
might well give us an insight into the emotional state that he
wished to convey.

Moreover, by making changes in any or all of the elements
that go to make up his music—the melodies, tempo, dynamics,
rhythms, harmonies, orchestration—the composer can change
our understanding of the conveyed emotional states. But we
must recognize one important limitation as we follow the subtle involutions of feelings that a composer sets forth in his
music. We must forgo all hope of being able to discover *specific*
feelings that we can name. We can experience even the subtlest,
most evanescent aspects of the emotional states that a composer sets forth, but we cannot do so by means of verbalization.
Once we accept this limitation of music, we are open to its
unique communications.

Going back to the person who says to us in an unknown language, "I feel happy," it is obviously possible that the sensitive
listener will get some idea of the prevailing emotional tone
from the speaker's intonation. Yet his words, if written down,
would leave us entirely in the dark. Notice that the factors that
make it possible for us to recognize the emotional tone when

the words are spoken are exactly those that are true of music—intonation, speed, intensity; or, in musical terms, pitch, tempo, and dynamics. Composers employ these elements in such a manner as to make us aware of their music's emotional tone.

It is to this extent, and to this extent *only,* that there is any justification for the idealistic, wishful statement that music is a universal language. Its universality stems only from the fact that, dealing in sounds that have no specific verbal significances, music transcends linguistics and addresses itself directly to our feelings.

It is important for the listener to be on guard against the idea that music is merely a translation of the emotions. We find that what actually takes place within a musical composition may have little or no correlation with our emotional lives.

The succession of harmonies to be found in, let us say, the opening chords of Tchaikovsky's famous First Piano Concerto have no equivalent in our real-life emotions. Or take the matter of rhythm, which forms such a large part of our emotional responses to music. Consider such a rhythmic piece as the last movement of Beethoven's Seventh Symphony. There is nothing in our emotional life that has that particular rhythm. The only characteristic of our emotional life that the music reflects is its vitality, drive, and exuberance. But even so obviously exciting a work is not "about" any *specific* emotion. One might say that it is "about" exuberance and vitality and excitement.* But these are not emotions; they are some of the *qualities* of emotions. Therefore, music reflects not the emotions themselves, but the *conditions* of the emotions.

This explains why the same music has often been thought of as "expressing" opposite emotions. Since sadness and joy can share the same conditions, some listeners feel that the slow movement of Beethoven's Seventh Symphony is "sad"; others call it "serenely happy." The slow movements of any of Mozart's violin concertos, or of Beethoven's Violin Concerto, can convey either sadness or quiet joy, or mere calmness—depending upon the listener's orientation. "Tenderness" in music is often nothing more than an absence of vigor.

---

* The final movements of Beethoven's Third and Fifth Symphonies are equally "about" exuberance, vitality, and excitement. Thus, since these emotional qualities are common to all three works, by a process of elimination we realize that each work is really "about" its respective themes, with their own characteristic musical rhythms—none of which has any counterpart in our emotional lives.

Notice the scope that this approach affords. Most of us would probably agree that an extremely loud and fast composition creates a feeling of excitement. If that same piece were made more dissonant in its harmonies, convention might cause many of us to feel that the music represented anger. The question is: what degree of dissonance is necessary to cause each of us to change his or her emotional interpretation from "excitement" to "anger"? Obviously, the degree varies. Let us be grateful for the fact that there are no absolutes of emotional expressiveness in music. Its indeterminate quality not only allows each of us to have his or her own reactions; it permits us to return again and again to a given piece, and to have a different response each time.

Furthermore, music is supreme in its ability to effect *changes* in our feelings—tension and relaxation, expectancy and fulfillment, welling up and subsiding. But all of these, too, are *conditions:* music cannot specify what *caused* the tension or relaxation, welling up or subsiding, or what may be expected as a result of the feeling of expectancy that it creates. But, as we have seen, genuine emotions always have a cause, an object, real or implied. They are the result of the interaction of forces. In some cases, the forces work in opposition to one another, causing frustration and its concomitant emotions. In other cases, when the forces work in the same direction—when the expectancy is satisfied—we experience pleasurable emotions.

However, since no musical idea—a melody with its rhythm, harmony, and orchestration—is capable of taking a stand or of expressing a viewpoint, music is unable to supply those forces and those oppositions that are necessary to the creation of what we know as a real emotion. Pit one melody against another, and what do you have? Counterpoint. Wagner, toward the end of the Prelude to *Die Meistersinger,* has three distinct melodies going at the same time. This fact contributes not one whit to the creation of any specific emotional state in us, other than admiration for the mind that could carry out such a musical feat. To be sure, we can experience a feeling of exuberance, of excitement, and of climax, thanks to the cumulative effect of the dynamic qualities of the music up to that point, and thanks, also, to the realization of the *musical* fact that the three separate melodies are being heard simultaneously. But we cannot make those melodies fight one another—that is, work in opposition.

Nor can they set up any emotional state—in the sense in which we construe emotions in real life—solely as a result of their relative positions.

Thus, despite all that has been written and said about music's ability to express hate, love, jealousy, fear, and anger, we see that it lacks the ability to juxtapose ideas in the way that is indispensable for the creation of these genuine emotions.

Many of us are greatly influenced by what we are told about individual works. Thus, large numbers of listeners believe that the *Liebestod* from Wagner's *Tristan and Isolde* is an expression of love in music, solely because it has been dinned into them, as the result of the association of the music with the story. Granted that the music is extremely appropriate in emotional tone, it is much more importantly a highly organized structure, treating several formalized musical themes. It is impossible to point to a single phrase of the piece and prove that it expresses the emotion of love. We may say that the "surgings" of the music reflect our yearnings when we are in love. We may also go so far as to say that the constantly mounting tension and the ultimate relaxation in the work as a whole mirror one's physical state in the act of love. But all of these things are still only the *dynamic aspects* of the feelings; they are not the feelings themselves.

It is only through usage and convention— stylization— that we attribute to music of this kind the ability to "express" the emotion of love. Remember, however, that it is attributed only by us in the Western tradition. Listeners of other cultures share many of our responses in the emotion of love, and they certainly share our physiological reactions in the act of love. Yet, as we have already pointed out, what we would regard as the most impassioned moments of the *Liebestod* would be meaningless to anyone not familiar with the conventions of Western music.

This conditioning, then, is one of the main sources of the romantic feelings that may be created in us when the entire violin section of an orchestra plays a broad, sweeping melody. It also accounts for our tender, wistful feelings when we hear a particularly haunting slow movement, or the sentimental feelings that may well up in us in response to a romantically played violin solo.

Suggestion and context play a crucial role. Witness the fact that so many people immediately equate the *Liebestod* with love, because of its association with the story, while comparatively few, if any, think of love in connection with the slow movement of Schumann's Second Symphony, or the climactic moment in the slow movement of Brahms's First Symphony. Both of those works, in varying degrees, contain treatments of romantic melodies that, in their "surging" and "yearning" qualities, are similar to the treatments to be found in the *Liebestod.* Disregarding the stylistic differences among the works, the similarities in the ways in which the melodies are handled are so marked as to prove that the ascription of the emotion of love to one and not to the others is the result only of extramusical suggestion.

Let us realize that we do not go to music for real emotions. We go, instead, for an *esthetic* experience—or, for what we might term "esthetic emotions." Each time we listen to a piece of music, we enter into an implied contract with the composer, whereby we agree to expose ourselves to what he has to say, within a formalized musical system that is actually a way of thinking unto itself. We voluntarily place ourselves in an attitude of receptivity, knowing that what we experience will not be a re-creation of redemption, profane love, or what-have-you, but will consist of following his methods of organizing sounds into abstract patterns.

The sounds themselves will be carefully chosen; the forms, the patterns, the treatment of the sounds will sometimes bear a resemblance, in their dynamic aspects, to the dynamic aspects of our feelings. Large forms will be built— symphonies, sonatas, fugues, rondos—that bear little or no resemblance to the forms of our actual emotions. They will house the interplay of musical ideas, in such a way that the emotional climaxes are planned, and placed in positions relative to each other, in a manner that we would never experience in real life. Rhythms *not* drawn from our actual emotions will also be subjected to conscious manipulation. Harmony will lend tensions to these formulations; the orchestration will supply sensuous variety.

By our acquired acceptance of the musical conventions, we will interpret the resultant music as conveying greater or lesser degrees of emotionalism. Sometimes, as a result of our associations, the music will recall to us feelings of poignancy, the memory of which can bring tears to our eyes. A kind of communication with the composer may then take place, at a level that we may term "emotional."

PART TWO

The Materials and Forms of Music

CHAPTER 13

Musical Textures, Keys, Major and Minor

As preparation for our discussion of musical forms, it is advisable for us first to establish a few basic facts about the nature of music. First, let us consider the matter of musical *texture,* since it constitutes what might be termed the "fabric" of music. There are three types of texture: monophonic, homophonic, and polyphonic.

When music consists of a single line of melody presented without accompaniment, its texture is said to be *monophonic.* Gregorian chant, mentioned earlier, is a good example. The fact that the melody is sung in unison by a number of singers does not alter the monophonic texture. An unaccompanied melody played by a flute would also exemplify the monophonic texture, which would remain unchanged even if, say, an oboe, clarinet, violin, or voice were to be added—provided that the added instruments or voice played the identical notes at the same time.

When a melody is accompanied by chords, the texture is said to be *homophonic.* A folk song with guitar or piano accompaniment exemplifies this texture. The music is in homophonic style when one melody predominates, while everything else is essentially accompaniment. This is the case even if the accompaniment is played by a full orchestra, with the melody, say, given to all the violins. Nor is this texture changed if the melody is given to the cellos and double basses, with the accompaniment in the higher instruments.

Polyphonic texture is typified by the familiar round *Three Blind Mice*. By contrast with the monophonic style of writing, in which everything is subordinated to one melody, here the interest is equally divided among all the voices, or parts. (The word polyphonic means "many-voiced.") The second and third voices are as important as the first. For a full appreciation of this sort of texture, the ear must forsake its tendency to listen to only the top melody, and concentrate on all parts simultaneously. For this reason, polyphonic listening is the most demanding kind. Note that the harmonies in polyphonic music are the *incidental* result of the simultaneous sounding of the various strands of melody at any one point, rather than the result of a succession of chords as such.

Another term for the simultaneous sounding of two or more melodic strands, or parts, is "counterpoint," from the medieval concept of a note as a "point." Thus "counterpoint" may be regarded as synonymous with "polyphony," and "contrapuntal" as the equivalent of "polyphonic."

The example given, *Three Blind Mice*, presents only one melody. However, there is nothing to prevent a composer from presenting two or more different melodies simultaneously. A popular ballad with the melody given to the singer, while a trumpet weaves an independent line around it, is, technically speaking, an example of *polyphony*. When *Swanee River* and Dvořák's *Humoresque* are sung or played simultaneously, polyphony is the result.

It is important to realize that the three basic textures just described are frequently mixed in any extended composition. It is only a very short piece of music, such as a simple folk song, or a round like *Frère Jacques,* in which the texture can be expected to remain consistent throughout. J. S. Bach is often described as the outstanding master of the polyphonic manner of writing, yet there are numerous works of his—and many portions of his essentially polyphonic works— that are clearly homophonic. The symphony, as a form, has its main historic roots in the homophonic texture, yet there is hardly a symphony that does not contain some contrapuntal writing.

An easily accessible example of the mixture of textures is to be found in the second movement of Beethoven's Seventh Symphony. The opening is clearly homophonic, with the quiet melody in the violas accompanied by chords in the cellos and basses. Shortly thereafter, as the melody is repeated in the violins, the violas and cellos intone another melody at the same time. Thus, in music that began quite homophonically, we find a clear suggestion of polyphony. Later on, about two-thirds of the way through the movement, the texture becomes unmistakably polyphonic, at the point at which the first and second violins present the main melody in combination with another, so-called "counter melody."

Not only is it true that the textures are often mixed; it is also frequently difficult to determine whether any given passage is in one texture or another. In one sense, a hymn may be said to be polyphonic in texture, since the soprano, alto, tenor, and bass sing different parts at the same time. Yet the ear tends to hear the hymn homophonically, with the melody in the soprano as the center of interest, and the other three parts as mainly accompaniment. It is only when one of the three textures clearly predominates that we can say that the music is written "in" that texture. But such a classification is for the most part an academic matter. Clearly, for the listener, it is the mixture of textures—and the shifting from one to another— that is of interest.

Let us move on to the matter of "keys," since this often seems to present problems to the listener who cannot read music, and finds himself confronted with the statement— seemingly of considerable importance—that a certain symphony is "in the key of E Flat."

The concept of key can perhaps best be conveyed to the beginner by suggesting that he sing the final line of any familiar song or national anthem, or the ending of almost any melody. The tendency to come to rest on one "home" note—the note without which the melody would be incomplete—demonstrates the concept of "tonality." Generically, that "home" note—no matter what it may be—is called the "tonic." The specific letter designation ("C," "D," "E," "F." "G." etc.) of that note determines the "key" of the music. Thus, if the home note or tonic happens to be the note "C," the music is said to be "in the key of C." If the tonic is G Flat, the work is "in the key of G Flat."

Any listener familiar with our system of music *feels* the concept of tonality. As proof, note the effect if a radio is turned off just before the final chord of a composition is reached. But the identification of a key cannot be made by a listener without the written music at hand, unless one happens to have what is known as "absolute pitch," or "perfect pitch"— the ability to recognize the letter designation of any note, without the aid of an instrument on which to check one's accuracy. This is a rare ability, even among musicians. The point of all this is that a listener need not give any conscious attention to the matter of key as he or she listens to music.

Since the effects of key, and key changes, are *felt,* it is possible to enjoy thoroughly a symphony—or any other work, for that matter—without the knowledge that it is "in" G Minor or F Major. Notice that program notes never specify the key of a song, an opera, or an oratorio. There, the title serves to identify the work. However, in the case of titleless forms, such as symphonies, concertos, sonatas, quartets, and so forth, the key designation can be regarded merely as another means of identifying the work. Masses, too, since they use basically the same text, tend to be identified by their keys.

Here, it might be advisable to fortify the reader against the possibility of being told, or reading, that one must be concerned with keys because, after all, many composers chose specific keys for the expression of certain kinds of feelings. We learn, for example, that Mozart often chose the key of G Minor for his more dramatic utterances, and that Beethoven preferred the key of C Minor for the expression of his more powerful sentiments. Nevertheless, the mere fact that the chosen key differs for each composer proves that there is nothing in them that has universal applicability. They are, rather, personal preferences on the parts of composers and, therefore, we as listeners need not feel we are missing a point of fundamental significance if we fail to appreciate the *aural* distinction between, say, C Minor and C Sharp Minor.

Further, anyone who holds to the view that a specific key imparts a specific emotional coloration overlooks an important historical fact. The pitch of all music was lower in Beethoven's time, so that the orchestra which originally played his Symphony in D Minor—his Ninth Symphony—was playing it, by the pitch measurements of today, in the key of D *Flat* Minor, a half-tone lower! Incidentally, this made the vocal parts sound less strained than they do in present-day performances, since the singers were not required to sing quite so high.)

In order to see to what extent the concept of key *does* figure

124 HOW WE EXPERIENCE MUSIC

in our understanding of music, let us return to the melody that you chose to sing a few paragraphs back. Notice that you can begin it on any note. Notice also that, regardless of the note on which you start, the relationships among the various notes of the melody remain the same, as does the feeling of the *tonality.* However, with each change in the starting note, you have changed the *key.* (In changing the key, you have performed the technical act known as "transposition.")

We realize from this that a number of different keys are available to a composer. If he were to allow his composition to remain in any one key for an extended period of time, there is a real likelihood that the listener would feel the onset of boredom. After any starting key has been established, a change of key suggests unrest, an increase of tension. Thus, in the course of a composition, a composer takes us through several different keys, the number depending upon the length of the work and its intended emotional intensity. (The process of moving from one key to another in the course of a movement is called "modulation.") The degree of ingenuity that the composer shows in the handling of keys determines, in part, the degree of interest and emotional excitement that we derive from a work.

It is important to realize that even a brief, simple melody, as it is accompanied by *different* chords during its unfolding, suggests a different key with each chord. Those moments at which it seems to be "up in the air" are the moments at which it ventures into a different key or keys; the reason for the strong sense of finality at the end is the fact that the melody has returned to the starting key. This sense of inconclusiveness during the course of a melody, and the sense of satisfaction at the end of it, are *felt* by the listener, regardless of his or her lack of ability to name the key or to analyze the chord structure.

It is the composer's duty to carry the listener along with him; he does this by technical means that we must *feel* first and analyze later—if our interest in the music warrants it. Moreover, while a symphony, or any other large work, almost invariably begins and ends in the same key, it is nevertheless the fact that, during the course of its duration— lasting anywhere from twenty minutes to over an hour—the number of keys through which we will have been taken is so great that, except for the relatively few who have absolute pitch, hardly anyone will be able to remember the key in which the work began.

As is well known, the seven notes of our ascending scale, besides being identified by their position numbers, have been given the names "do," "re," "mi," "fa," "sol," "la," and "ti," respectively. (The eighth note, or the "octave," being essentially the same as the first, has the same name as the first.) These are generic names, applicable in all keys. In our system of music, it is possible to build a chord on each note, or, as it is technically called, each "degree" of the scale. The progression from one of these chords to another brings with it certain emotional implications, whose intensity is determined by the imagination with which the composer chooses the succession of chords. (These effects are separate from those caused by melody, rhythm, tempo, dynamics, and the tone colors of the performing instruments.)

In the course of centuries of musical practice, it has been found that, after the chord built upon the first degree, the strongest chord is the one built upon the fifth degree, "sol." (In a scale consisting of eight degrees, or eight notes, five notes is the farthest distance that it is possible to venture from the tonic.) The note, and the chord built upon it, are called the "dominant." Many melodies, being in essence brief musical "compositions" in themselves, progress from the tonic to the dominant and back again to the tonic, thus supplying a feeling of departure, with its subsequent inconclusiveness, and a gratifying return to the starting point.

The progression from the dominant chord to the tonic chord is one of the most familiar in all of Western music. You have heard it so many thousands of times that you literally take it for granted. It occurs at the end of the great majority of individual movements of all our music, both classical and romantic. It is presented vigorously at the end of almost any Haydn, Mozart, or Beethoven symphony or concerto. At the end of almost every overture by Rossini, and other nineteenth-century composers, the timpanist can be heard pounding out two notes. These are the dominant and the tonic, with the tonic heard last. This final, clinching progression from dominant to tonic is called the "perfect cadence."

Another widely used progression—perhaps the next in order of frequency of occurrence—is from the chord built on the fourth degree of the scale, to the chord built on the tonic— that is, from "fa" to "do." The name given to the fourth degree, and to the chord built on it, is "subdominant," and the progression from subdominant to tonic (called the "plagal cadence"), is the familiar "amen" sequence.

Now, these two elementary progressions possess important implications. Extended and elaborated, they figure in the creation of the larger musical forms. Let us suppose that a composer wishes to build a composition out of three themes, or melodies, of varying moods. The variety of emotional states that results from their being in different moods can be heightened by their being presented in different keys, as well. The first theme, by definition, is in the key of the tonic; the second theme, in most classical works, is likely to be in the key of the dominant, while the third theme might well be in the key of the subdominant. The first theme might reappear after each of the other themes, bringing with it its return to the tonic.*

For each period in which either the dominant key or the subdominant key predominates, the ear will feel a tendency to return to the tonic key for a feeling of rest and resolution, just as one anticipates—in a more immediate sense—the final chord, the progression from dominant to tonic, at the end of a Beethoven symphony. Thus, another source of both emotional and intellectual interest in music is the way in which the composer juxtaposes keys.

Needless to say, there are many more relationships of keys than the ones just described. These were chosen not only because they are among the most frequently encountered in the classical and romantic literature, but because they exemplify the principle of key relationships.

An explanation, now, of the meaning of major and minor. While it has become the custom to say that a work is "in the key of C minor," it would be more correct to say that it is "in the key of C," and "in the minor mode." Both "C major" and "C minor" have the note "C" as their starting point, and only a slight difference in the relationships among the rest of the notes determines whether the scale and its chords will be major or minor. In order to see what this difference is, let us refer to the diagram, representing one octave—from "C" to the next higher "C"—on a piano. The "C" can be located easily, because it is the white note just below—or to the left of— any group of *two* black notes.

* This, in fact, is the outline of the "Rondo" form, to be discussed later.

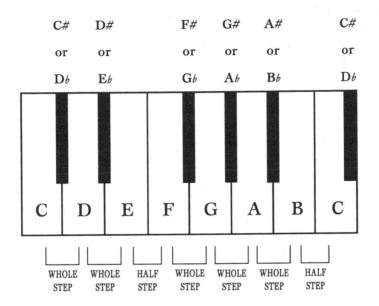

Anyone can produce our ordinary ascending scale by playing, in succession, all the white notes on the piano between any "C" and the next higher "C." This is our familiar "do," "re," "mi," "fa," "sol," "la," "ti," "do." While the sequence is applicable to any key, for this example we have chosen to make "C" the "do," or tonic.

When any note in our scale is altered by being raised, it is said to be "sharped." The black note just to the *right* of the note "C" is called "C Sharp." The musical symbol for "sharp" is #. If a note is lowered, it is said to be "flatted." The black note just to the *left* of "D" is called "D Flat." The musical symbol for "flat" is ♭.

The space between any two notes is called an "interval." It is determined by counting the number of degrees—or letter names, disregarding the sharps and flats—in the scale, between the two notes. In the case of the interval "C" to "E," "C" is counted as 1, "D" is 2, and "E" is 3. Thus, the interval "C" to "E" is a "third." The interval "C" to "G" by the same process, is a "fifth," since "G" is five degrees away from "C," in the scale.

Our ordinary scale consists of an arrangement of whole

steps and half steps. The interval from "do" to "re" in any key ("C" to "D" in our diagram) is a whole step. Notice that it consists of two half steps, since the "C Sharp"—a raised version of "C"—exists between "C" and "D." Similarly, from "re" to "mi" ("D" to "E") is a whole step. But the interval from "mi" to "fa" ("E" to "F") is only a half step, and so is the interval from "ti" to "do" ("B" to "C").

Now, chords are built by the simultaneous sounding of certain specific notes of the scale. In the common chord, made up of three notes (a "triad"), the notes are the tonic, the third note of the scale, and the fifth note. This is the well-known "do," "mi," "sol," made doubly familiar because it is so often used as a practice device by singers. In our chosen key of "C" the notes are "C," "E," and "G." Suppose that we alter this chord slightly, by lowering the middle note, "E," one half step to "E Flat." This is done by playing the black note immediately below the "E." We have thus made the interval of the third, "C" to "E," smaller. The original interval, "C" to "E," being the larger one, is called a "major third." The interval "C" to "E Flat," being smaller, is called a "minor third." The triad "C," "E," "G" is a major chord. The triad "C," "E Flat," "G" is a minor chord.

It is one of the phenomena of our reactions to music that a minor chord by itself suggests sadness, while a major chord seems to sound cheerful. We still do not have a completely satisfactory explanation for this. However, it is certainly not an invariable effect, and such factors as tempo, instrumentation, and dynamics serve to shape the total impression. Generally, the beginning listener all too readily accepts the idea that minor means sad and major means happy. But if a composition in the minor were played quickly and lightly, the effect would be a gay one. While there is no denying the fact that the combination of the minor mode, slow tempos subdued dynamics, and the use of instruments in the lower part of their range can make for a somber feeling, we would do well to remember that one of the saddest of all melodies— "Taps," played at military funerals— is in the major mode.

Just as it is unlikely that a musical work will remain in one key throughout its length, so it is unlikely that a composition will remain in one mode. There are many minor chords and passages in any composition said to be in the major, and vice versa. The change of mode is another means by which composers impart variety to their music. To say that a composition is "in the minor" usually refers only to its beginning. In Bach's time, it was the custom to end a composition in the minor mode with a major chord, and most eighteenth- and nineteenth-century works that are supposedly in the minor mode actually end in the major.

Rounding out this discussion of scales and keys, here are a few smaller points that trouble some untrained listeners.

The letter designations—"C," "D," "E," "F," "G," "A," "B"—of the notes of the scale are completely arbitrary. There is nothing "C-ish" about the note "C," or the key of "C," and there is nothing about, say, the note "G" that has anything in common with the letter "G" as it occurs in verbal communications. The French, in fact, use "Ut" for the note we call "C," and the Germans employ the letter "H" for the note that we designate as "B." Moreover, while it might ordinarily be expected that. in any field, the simplest example would be identified by the letter "A," with "B" and "C" reserved for examples of increasing complexity, this is not the case in music. It happens that the simplest key in music—the only one in which a major scale can be played by using only the white notes of the piano—is the key whose first degree is the note designated by the letter "C."

It is of course possible to construct a major scale beginning on *any* note, using the same pattern of whole and half steps that we examined in the case of the "C Major" scale. On the piano, this necessitates using one or more of the black notes. As can be readily seen, the writing down of each different scale or key will require a number of sharps or flats—called "accidentals"—in order to make the succession of notes conform to the basic pattern. Rather than place the sharp or flat before a note every time it occurs, the custom is to group the required accidentals at the beginning of a work (or of a section, should the key change for an extended period of time during the course of a composition). This grouping of accidental signs is the so-called "key signature," which, for the musician, identifies the key.

Another point often referred to is the matter of "equal temperament." Measured scientifically, the note C Sharp is actually slightly higher in pitch than the note D Flat. However, the piano, which is something of a compromise instrument, produces both pitches by means of the same note. The half step up and the half step down have arbitrarily been made equidistant from the notes C and D, and in fact all the half steps on the keyboard are made equidistant from one another. As a consequence, all scales on the piano are equally in tune (or equally out of tune, according to acoustical considerations). Incidentally, the fact that in equal temperament one key sounds exactly like another reinforces our earlier point that there is no such thing as a "dramatic key of G Minor" as opposed, say, to a "tragic C Minor." Such attributions reflect either a composer's individual key preferences or a commentator's faulty generalization.

The system of equal temperament for keyboard instruments came into use in the middle of the seventeenth century. In order to demonstrate its merits, J. S. Bach wrote a series of preludes and fugues progressing systematically through all the keys, in both major and minor. This is the collection we know today as the "Well-Tempered Clavier."

About two and a half centuries after its adoption, equal temperament permitted the birth of the theoretical system known as "atonality," which achieves an eradication of the sense of tonality by means of certain carefully worked out procedures. Arnold Schönberg, its creator, argued that all the notes available within the octave—twelve—should be given equal stature and made independent of one another. The note C Sharp, for example, would no longer be regarded as an alteration of the note C, but would become an independent entity. The application of this procedure completely altered our ideas of keys and harmony as practiced for the last three or four centuries.

The composer Paul Hindemith has concluded, however, that music cannot do without a tonal center. He has likened the need for it to such an immutable law of nature as the force of gravity. Aaron Copland, who has occasionally written in the atonal system, has commented that all atonal compositions tend to have a family resemblance. The fact that, after more than half a century, so few works of Schönberg and his numerous disciples have attained any genuine acceptance from the music-loving public suggests that the need for a tonal center is deeply rooted within those of us who are brought up in the Western system of music.

CHAPTER 14

The Purposes of Musical Form

You have just placed on your CD player a recording of Tchaikovsky's *Pathétique Symphony*. You notice that the back of the booklet accompanying the CD reads:

> First movement: Adagio-Allegro non troppo.
> Second movement: Allegro con grazia.
> Third movement: Allegro molto vivace.
> Finale: Adagio lamentoso.

You have read similar listings of movements in concert programs; you have heard them read, also, by radio and television announcers.

In all likelihood, the following questions have occurred to you at one point or another:

1. What is the reason for this division of large musical works into movements, and how is the number of movements determined?

2. What relationship does one movement have to another? Are they part of an organic whole that admits of no change?

To answer the first part of the first question, we need only to think of a play with its customary division into acts. We take for granted the limitations of our attention span; there is a point beyond which we are not able to concentrate without an intermission of some sort.

However, there is more to this division than merely the playwright's or the composer's desire to avoid overtaxing us. In a play, an act will end at the moment at which a situation has been made clear to the audience, or at the point at which the relationships among the characters have been developed. In a symphony, a movement ends after the themes, or melodies, have been developed. Here we come to one of the basic differences between music and drama.

It is not unusual for an act of a play to end with the sudden introduction of a new character or an unexpected situation. In fact, the second act often ends with the problem of the play "wide open," waiting to be resolved in the third act. Music does not lend itself to that kind of treatment. Since music deals with abstract melodies rather than with concrete situations, we find it more satisfying for each movement of a work to give us a sense of completion and of resolution. (This does not rule out the possibility that a theme from one movement may reappear in a later movement, but more about that when we reach the answer to our second question.)

It is because of this completeness that we are able to enjoy hearing a single movement from a large work when it is presented alone, for example, the so-called "Air for the G String," which is in fact the second movement of Bach's *Suite Number Three.* The essential difference between music and the drama is again pointed up by the fact that a comparable excerpt from a play—a single act, let us say—would be likely to leave us unsatisfied. We might be pleased by the acting, or absorbed by the emotions portrayed, but our understanding and satisfaction would be limited by our lack of knowledge of the underlying situation, or of its ultimate resolution.

By and large, however, making allowance for the differences among the arts, we might regard the movements of a large musical work as roughly comparable to the acts of a play or the chapters of a novel.

To the best of my knowledge, no one nowadays extols the artistic excellence of the three-act play, and there is little comment, if any, about the number of chapters in current novels. Yet in music, we are repeatedly led to the belief that there is some great significance to the four-movement form. True, the large majority of extended works—symphonies, sonatas, quartets—are written in four movements, but surely there is no greater significance in that fact than there is in the three acts of the average play.

If we are to admit that this four-movement form is the best of all forms—if it really merits all the praise that has been heaped upon it—then how are we to regard one of the acknowledged masterpieces: Schubert's *Unfinished Symphony,* which has only two movements; or César Franck's *Symphony,* which is in three movements; or Beethoven's *Pastoral Symphony,* which is in five movements (of which the last three are joined to create one continuous movement in three sections)? And if we are to bend the knee in admiration for Beethoven's use of the four-movement form in most of his larger works, how are we to react when we discover that one of his last masterpieces, the string quartet, Opus 131, is in seven movements?

Now, since the composer has obviously exercised his choice as to the number of movements in which he has cast a work, must this number have some significance for us? In other words, when the radio announcer says, "The symphony is written in four movements: *Allegro con brio, Adagio lamentoso,*" and so on, does this mean that in order to appreciate the work we have to regard it in a different manner from that in which we would anticipate, let us say, a six-movement work? Generally speaking, No—any more than the occasional play in two acts or four acts calls for a different approach on our parts, other than to anticipate fewer or more intermissions and longer or shorter attention spans.

It is probably apparent by now that the number of movements in any work—symphonic, instrumental, or choral—is determined by the purpose and content of that work. Bach's *Mass in B Minor,* a setting of the text of the Mass, is in twenty-four separate sections. Strauss's tone poem *A Hero's Life is* in one gigantic movement; Berlioz's *Fantastic Symphony* is in five movements; Mozart wrote his numerous divertimentos in as many as eight brief movements. Brahms cast all his four symphonies in four movements, each of which is fairly long. He felt that the thematic material he had chosen was sufficiently important to warrant the longer movements. Putting it another way, what he had to say about his melodies was important enough, in his mind, to justify his asking us to listen for a longer time at a stretch. It is the *content,* then, that determines the length and number of the movements.

From the fact that we can find successful compositions in almost any number of movements that we might name, we can conclude that there is nothing inevitable about the four movement form. Its widespread use for symphonies and chamber works indicates only that many composers have found it a convenient framework for their thoughts, in view of the kind and the amount of musical material they are dealing with, and considering the need for contrast and variety.

The answer to our second question, "What relationship does one movement have to another?" is: "Sometimes there is a relationship; sometimes there is none." If it were possible (and worthwhile) to make a survey of all the multimovement compositions ever written, it is a safe bet that the overwhelming majority of them would turn up in the column headed "No Connection." I confess that if some conductor were to switch the minuet movements in two of Haydn's symphonies, I might be unaware of the substitution. The fact is, nobody can really prove that each of the minuets of Haydn's one hundred and four symphonies must belong only to its particular symphony and to no other. Moreover, I am certain that Haydn himself could not have correctly identified each one of them. This is not mere conjecture; it is borne out by the fact that Haydn once confessed that he could not tell whether or not certain compositions were his own.

Much the same point might be made about most of the minuets or other movements of Mozart's forty-one symphonies, and of the thousands of trios, quartets, quintets, sonatas, and divertimentos that were turned out by Mozart, Haydn, and their many contemporaries and predecessors. In a similarly realistic vein, we may note the lack of relationship between movements in the sonatas and suites of Bach, in the *concerti grossi* of Handel, and in the numerous concertos of Vivaldi. The movements are separate entities, each with its own themes. With certain exceptions, to be dealt with in a moment, we can also say that there is no relationship between the movements of the symphonies by such composers as Schubert, Beethoven, or Brahms.

Of course, we must not jump to the wrong conclusion and assume that any extended composition is merely a collection of movements chosen at random. The "suites" of the period of Bach and Handel were collections of dances of contrasting character, all in the same key, in any one work. For this reason, obviously, a certain relationship may be said to exist among their movements. But even so, without altering the cumulative effect, one gigue or sarabande might have done as well as another, provided it were in the proper key.

Similarly, certain relationships may be found among the keys of the different movements of a symphony. Yet we know that when a movement is said to be in a certain key, this means only that it begins in that key and returns to it at the end. Since it is not likely that any large movement will remain in the same key throughout its length, any connection among the movements that stems only from considerations of key relationships is a tenuous one. A good deal is made of it in program notes and the like, but it remains largely a technical point that holds little or no interest for the average listener.

A more important kind of relationship stems from the style and the over-all feeling of the various movements of a work. When I suggested that it might be possible to interchange the minuets of any number of Haydn's or Mozart's symphonies without anyone being the wiser, I should have gone on to say that it would be impossible to make the minuet from Mozart's late G Minor Symphony seem at home in one of his early symphonies. His later style had become so mature, so much more complex and sophisticated, that the discrepancy would be noticed immediately. Again, we could not very well substitute the relatively light scherzo movement of Beethoven's First Symphony for the dramatic scherzo of his Ninth Symphony. The difference in the composer's style—his way of dealing with his material—had become so great by the time he composed his Ninth Symphony that the two movements seem like the work of two different composers.

Yet even consistency of style does not of itself mean that there is any direct relationship among the movements of a symphony. Had Beethoven written, as the scherzo of his Ninth Symphony, not the specific movement that he left us, but one equally good although entirely different, that would not have made the symphony one whit less remarkable or less cohesive.

Now we come to the actual, definite kinds of relationships that exist among the movements of certain works. Occasionally, a composer will join two or more movements of a composition. Sometimes the link connecting movements is hardly noticeable, perhaps consisting of no more than the direction *attacca subito,* meaning "go on to the next movement without pause." The opening movement of Mendelssohn's Violin Concerto is connected to the second movement by means of a single sustained bassoon note, but to judge by the fact that concert audiences invariably applaud at the end of the first movement, Mendelssohn's attempt to join the two movements fails. Beethoven joins the third, fourth, and fifth movements of his *Pastoral Symphony,* yet there is no thematic connection among them. They are in actuality three distinct movements, each with its own melodies, but joined by means of musical bridges. The first of the three movements supposedly depicts the gathering of the country people, the second suggests a storm, and the third is called a song of thanksgiving after the storm. It was Beethoven's desire for dramatic contrast that caused him to connect the three movements.

This type of connection may be called purely mechanical. It increases the sense of continuity, but it has nothing to do with the musical content of the individual movements. Regardless of the connection, they do not have any musical ideas in common.

However, in Beethoven's Fifth Symphony, we find a definite relationship between two of the movements. Out of the third movement, the scherzo, there emerges a long, mysterious bridge passage that leads without a break into the finale. The bridge passage is itself an outgrowth of the themes of the scherzo; moreover, after the fourth movement is well under way, there is a return to the music of the scherzo. It is apparent that we are here dealing with a work in which there *is* a specific, easily heard relationship between two movements.

Other composers have imparted a similar effect of unification, by repeating, as Beethoven does, a melody or theme from one movement in a later movement. The *Symphony* by César Franck embraces this principle, as does the Fourth Symphony of Robert Schumann, and the *New World Symphony* of Dvořák. Brahms ends his Third Symphony with a recollection of the opening melody of the first movement. Prokofieff does the same thing in his First Violin Concerto. While these examples by no means exhaust the list, they serve to show that certain well-known works display movements that are thematically related.

One more example, although it is not typical. Beethoven begins the final movement of his Ninth Symphony with brief quotations, one after the other, from the three previous movements. This must certainly be regarded as a connection among the movements, but since the melodies do not reappear during the remainder of the finale, the relationship is only a momentary one, dictated by dramatic considerations.

From all this it is apparent that there is considerable variety in the number of movements in any work, and in the degree of relationship among the movements. It is equally apparent that the composer is not bound by any particular rule in the matter of the order of the movements—fast or slow, dramatic or playful. It might be well for us to realize that, despite the tremendous amount of specialized skill required for the creation of an extended symphonic work, the final product must appeal to the listener.

It is the need for unity, and, above all, for contrast and variety, that determines the number and the order of the movements. A brief piece for the piano may exploit only one mood and sustain itself without contrast- not so an extended composition, in which we look for a variety of moods. With this in mind, a wag once summed up the typical four-movement form thus: "In the first movement [the serious one] the composer shows how erudite he can be. In the second movement [usually the slow one] the composer shows how deeply he feels. In the third one [ordinarily the jocose "scherzo"] he shows how funny he can be. And in the fourth movement [usually quite lively] he shows how glad he is that it is all over."

Despite its irreverence, this description gives us an insight into some of our basic esthetic needs—our desire for variety, contrast, and balance. These needs express themselves at every level—in choosing a necktie to go with a particular suit, in watching a humorous television show after a strenuous day's work, or in deciding at what angle to place a chair in our living room. A composer must see to it that the different movements of his work sustain a variety of moods, and that there is the proper balance among them—all this for the purpose of supplying us with a satisfying experience. If he can produce that feeling in us, it makes no difference how he arranges the individual movements.

Beethoven chose to make the scherzo of his Ninth Symphony the second movement, giving it the place customarily reserved for the slow movement. This has the effect of placing two tense, exciting movements together, the first and second. But with over-all balance in mind, and realizing that the fourth and final movement would be tremendously long and employed a chorus and vocal soloists as well, he set it off by placing the tender slow movement immediately before it. The needs of the individual composition determine the order of its movements.

Tchaikovsky, in his *Pathétique Symphony,* saves the slow movement until the end. This is an unusual and extremely dramatic device. As a result of this change, the movement that ordinarily would have been the finale becomes the third movement. Probably many listeners are not consciously aware that they have not as yet heard a slow movement. They have had a dramatic, rather long first movement, a lighter second movement, and a tremendously exciting third movement, closing with a definite feeling of finality. There is nothing at this point that makes a slow movement inevitable. As a result, from the purely musical standpoint, it comes as a rather anticlimactic surprise. Its placement out of its usual position is justified only by Tchaikovksy's desire to end the work gloomily.

To sum up, we might say that, since the creation of a large multimovement form is an art rather than a science, there is no absolute rule that must be followed. In other words, there is nothing inherent in any first movement that will inevitably call forth one specific type of second movement and no other. Nor can the number of movements be predicted from the nature of the opening movement. It is the composer's task to create a total form that will satisfy the listener.

If you are unaware of even the larger form when you listen to a composition, you should still be able to appreciate the music. At the same time, when you enjoy listening to a symphony or a concerto, it is well to be aware that you are appreciating—no matter to what degree—some of the most complex musical forms in existence.

CHAPTER 15

The Elusiveness of Musical Form

Here, in order to avoid any possible misunderstanding, it would be well to refine our conception of the term "form" by realizing that in music it has two applications. In the context in which we have been discussing it so far, it refers to the over-all structure of a multimovement work, as in the case of a symphony. But the term also refers to the structure of in dividual movements—whether they are part of a larger work, or are independent compositions.

Of the five basic elements that we learn to respond to in our appreciation of music, the last to be understood and made a source of pleasure, quite clearly, is form. We are much more susceptible to music's immediate charms—to a melody, a rhythmic figure, a progression of chords, or their emotional appeal—than we are to the structure. A loud, exciting passage in which the full orchestra overwhelms us with sound and rhythm is likely to be immediately appealing, simply because of its momentary and obvious satisfactions. To relate this same passage, however, to another passage that may have occurred ten minutes earlier in the same movement requires a different kind of listening.

It calls for not merely an immediate sensuous, rhythmic, or emotional response, but also the ability to remember a theme and to recognize it in a later appearance, even though it may reappear considerably changed. Moreover, it demands that the listener retain an awareness of the position that the theme occupies in relation to the other themes. Position is one of the elements of form in music.

To consider this in another way, imagine two enthusiastic music lovers comparing their favorite moments in a particular work. They might point out an appealing melody or an exciting climax, but it is unlikely that they would exclaim over the way in which the composer extended the codetta of the exposition, or delayed the return of the subordinate theme in the recapitulation. Although the composer might well have done these things (in spite of the technical terminology, there is nothing unusual about either example), they are not apt to concern the average listener; nor should they. To recognize them for what they are requires a great deal of purely technical training.

It is for this reason that form, for most listeners, is the least appreciated musical element. In spite of all the emphasis that is placed on form in concert program notes, record liner dissertations, and the like, it would seem that, except for the occasional student who happens to be listening with analytical ears—performing a kind of aural vivisection—the percentage of listeners who are actively aware of form as they listen is exceedingly small.

Many listeners who genuinely enjoy music and derive tremendous satisfaction from it could not, if asked to, describe the form of even a relatively simple musical work. To study conscientiously all the technicalities of musical form would be the equivalent of studying engineering before we undertake to enjoy the beauties of architecture. In the case of architecture, we immediately see the absurdity; in music, we persist in the unwarranted assumption that our appreciation must hinge on purely technical considerations.

There is no doubt, of course, that the trained architect, by virtue of his technical knowledge, is capable of a more complete understanding of a building's design than is the layman. Similarly, the trained composer will be aware of more of the formal subtleties in music than will the average music lover. But since the demands of living do not permit all of us the luxury of becoming experts in every field, it is wrong to hope or expect the layman to be in possession of all the technical details. In music, this common expectation is especially harmful, because it adds unnecessarily to the layman's feeling of inadequacy. This, in turn, keeps him or her from gaining what might otherwise be a healthy appreciation of the art.

Let us consider a typical example of the explanations intended to assist the music lover who attends a concert or plays a CD:

The chief and romantic theme is sung by the English horn over a soft accompaniment of strings. The development is extended. After the theme is sung by two muted horns, there is a change to C sharp minor (*Un poco più mosso*). A short transitional passage on a contrasting theme leads to the second theme in the woodwinds over a bass in counterpoint and pizzicato.

From even the closest study of this passage it is impossible to derive any conception of the music it describes. It happens to be a portion of the slow movement of Dvořák's *New World Symphony*. Granted that every one of the statements is true; has our understanding or appreciation of the music been helped in the slightest by this listing of facts? Yet, this is the sort of thing that is continually presented to the layman, supposedly in order to "unlock the door" of music to him.

George Bernard Shaw demonstrated beautifully how unrelated these purely technical analyses are to any real appreciation of music. Applying the typical music commentator's method to Hamlet's soliloquy "To be or not to be," he wrote:

Shakespeare, dispensing with the customary exordium, announces his subject at once in the infinitive, in which mood it is presently repeated after a short connecting passage in which, brief as it is, we recognize

the alternative and negative forms on which so much of the significance of repetition depends. Here we reach a colon: and a pointed pos-
itory phrase, in which the accent falls decisively on the relative
pronoun, brings us to the first full stop.

A law requiring music analysts and commentators to com-
mit these lines to memory before they embark on their mis-
sions of enlightenment might have a salutary effect.

Of what possible use are such "analyses"? To read them
before the music is played is useless; they contain far too many
details for the mind to retain. To read them during the performance would keep anyone from listening to the music as such.
We would be so concerned with finding the "short transitional
passage on a contrasting theme," that the process of listening
would become akin to puzzle-solving. This is not the way to
music appreciation.

The truth is, a large part of this inadequate approach to
music is based on merely *naming* things. To be able to name
something has become confused with the appreciation of it. But
merely to be able to identify and name a progression of chords
is no guarantee that we are sensitive to their artistic import.
Nor will knowing at what moment a development section ends
and the recapitulation begins have anything but technical significance for us, if we cannot *feel* the effect of the change.

The question now arises: Since form is an important basic
element in music, how much must be understood about it by
the layman for the appreciation of music? There is no cut and
dried answer. Ideally, we might say that the more comprehen-
sive the listener's knowledge of form is, the better will he or she
be able to understand music. Yet, as we have already seen, a
complete awareness of all the intricacies of form in a large
musical work is possible only for a highly trained musician—
and even in his case, the question might be raised as to whether
he really brings all his knowledge to bear every time he listens
to a piece of music for his own enjoyment, or whether this
knowledge is mainly his teaching or composing stock in trade.

The theoreticians would be the first to admit that form in
music is, above all, a means for providing esthetic satisfaction.
The sense of having had an entire, self-contained artistic experience is, after all, what we are seeking. But that is something
which—if it is to be valid—must be *felt*. One cannot merely be
told that one is having, or should be having, an artistic experi-

ence. And why should one be advised that the form of a movement has some unusual characteristic if one does not become aware of it merely by listening? Such knowledge can in that case have only a historic interest. If the only way in which the listener can become aware of the particular form of a given movement is by reading a description of it, the composer has failed in his purpose.

The purpose of form in music, as we have just seen, is to give the listener a sense of completeness. It imparts an overall unifying shape to the various disparate elements. However, because of the flexibility of music, the composer has considerable latitude in the means by which he attains a feeling of completeness. There is nothing inherent in any theme or in any set of themes that dictates that only one arrangement of them is possible. This is a basic fact of music. Unlike arithmetic, in which two people given the same problem must finally arrive at the same answer, two composers, starting with the same theme or the same set of themes, will produce entirely different musical works. To carry the illustration further, a composer may return to a theme that he has already used and derive from it a second, completely different composition.

In the light of this, once the large design of a movement is perceived by the listener—and even this in itself is a difficult task, if we mean conscious, verbalized perception—it is of only academic interest for him or her to know what lesser formal characteristics the movement contains. Yet it is precisely these insignificant formal characteristics that are so often expounded to us, as listeners, in the confident hope that they will increase our appreciation.

In a sense, music itself is its own greatest deterrent to an appreciation of form. Its immediate sensuous and emotional appeals are so satisfying that the average listener is not impelled to look further. It is both music's strength and its weakness that it can please us at almost any moment, even if we are listening in only the most casual fashion. If, as is often the case, we use music merely as an accompaniment to our reveries, there is hardly any incentive for us to be concerned with whether it is a passacaglia or a rondo, a sonata or a suite.

The person who carries on some such activity as reading a book while listening to music is even less concerned with its form. The only thing required is that the music continue to supply pleasant sounds, and that it not unduly attract the conscious mind. Realistically, these are probably the levels of listening indulged in by many people, perhaps even in concert halls. Music is not a matter of vital concern for them; it is mainly an escape. The usual comment of such a listener is, "I listen to music for relaxation and pleasure; I don't want to have to think about it." But if we demanded as little continuity and sense of form in the drama as many listeners seem to feel they need or want in music, our plays could be nothing but a succession of pleasant-sounding words quiet babble.

Even for the more attentive listener, however, musical form is, as we have already seen, one of the most difficult things to comprehend, and perhaps the last musical element to be appreciated. This is understandable for two reasons: first, the materials of music are by nature abstract; second, a musical work exists in time only. Comparisons with other art forms will make these points clear. In the case of a play, the materials are concrete thoughts and ideas, human problems with which most of us have something in common—if not actually, then vicariously. In any case, the drama deals with the interplay of specific ideas that appeal to our understanding, and our sense of form is satisfied at the point at which the problem or situation is resolved. It is for this reason that we are able to take issue with a play, and maintain, perhaps, that "it should have ended differently."

In music, however, the basic material consists of melodies—themes—essentially abstract series of sounds. While these are subject to a certain amount of logic in the ways in which they are handled, and while there can be important interrelationships between them, it is obvious that musical themes permit of a greater amount of freedom in their handling than do dramatic themes. Their lack of concrete "idea content" in any specific literary sense makes them much less answerable to the demands of ordinary logic. Because of this abstract nature of melodies, what the composer does with them—which is, after all, what produces the form—is apt to be a more elusive matter to the listener.

Now, the second point: that music exists in time only. When we look at a painting, we are able to take in the entire canvas at one glance. The relationships among the various parts are immediately apparent. True, one can argue that it takes a certain amount of time for the eye to follow the course of a line, and that the more time we spend examining a painting, the more we are likely to find in it. But by comparison with music, we can maintain that the over-all form and content of a painting can be grasped almost instantaneously. Not so in music. It is impossible to get an idea of the form or "shape" of the opening movement of Beethoven's Ninth Symphony without listening for the full sixteen minutes or so that its performance requires. There is no short cut. To abridge the movement, or to get through it sooner by playing it faster, is to change the music.

Time being the dimension in which music moves, it is obvious that as we listen to some of the longer movements, it becomes increasingly difficult to grasp the over-all formal structure and at the same time to retain the various parts in the mind. The first movement of Beethoven's Violin Concerto, for instance, requires an attention span of no less than twenty-three minutes, and the first movement of Mahler's Tenth Symphony over half an hour. An awareness and appreciation of the form of such works may sometimes be difficult to attain.

Contradictory as this may sound, form is not a structure superimposed on the other musical elements, but the very *content* of the music. It is an utter impossibility to have music without form. To prove this quickly, think of the "noodling" indulged in by orchestra players during the few minutes before the conductor appears in order to begin the concert. As the players warm up, it is quite probable that, in the aggregate, they will play most of the notes that will be used in some complex orchestral work—and with beautiful tone as well. Yet, obviously, this is not music. It is a jumble of notes, without organization.

The ingredients of music, then, are meaningless without some plan, some guiding principle that unifies them and, so to say, propels them forward in time. Someone whistling the simplest of melodies—*Swanee River,* let us say—is producing *music,* because the sounds are organized—in this particular example, chiefly by means of their rhythm and repetitions. On the other hand, the sounds produced during an orchestra's warming-up period, no matter how beautiful and varied they may be as individual sounds, lack the vital element that makes them music—form.

CHAPTER 16

Musical Forms and How They Are Shaped

The smallest structural unit in any musical form is the single note, which could be said to correspond to the single word of the written language, or perhaps to the individual letter, depending upon how far we carry our analogy. But just as, in reading, we are rarely conscious of single letters or even of single words in a sentence, so we are seldom aware of the individual notes in music. We tend to hear music in terms of phrases. Discussions of literature do not concern themselves with single letters, and seldom even spend time upon the way in which an author uses a single word. It is no more fitting for music appreciation to be approached from the standpoint of the smallest musical unit. Here, we will therefore deal with the *phrase* as the simplest unit.

Phrases

Musical phrases are roughly comparable in length to those we encounter in speech and in writing. Their length is governed by two simple considerations—namely, the length of our attention span, and human lung capacity. Obviously, singers can sustain a musical line only as long as their breath holds out. This applies as well to the players of wind instruments. Therefore, a natural limit is placed on the length of the musical phrase.

It is true that players of stringed instruments and of the piano are under no such limitations. The violinist's training includes development of the ability to change the direction of motion of the bow, so that there is no perceptible break in the tone. Obviously, the pianist is also completely free of all dependence upon the length of the breath. Yet so accustomed are we to thinking in "breath-determined" phrases, that pianists and string players "phrase"—that is—break up the music into reasonably short segments, in spite of the fact that they are capable of playing continuous lines.

Here enters the other consideration: the limitations of our attention span. Just as the phrases of our spoken and written languages cannot exceed certain lengths without becoming incomprehensible, since we lose the sense of the relationships among the parts, so—and for the very same reason—we are limited as to the length of the musical phrases that we can absorb.

In music, there are many small units, or segments, separated in some cases by the merest suggestion of a stopping place, if not by an actual break. Of course, in the process of listening to music, we are not ordinarily aware of phrases, at the conscious level. We take them for granted, just as we do when we listen to a speaker. Sometimes we feel the pressure when a speaker tries to complete a sentence before he runs out of breath. As we listen to a singer or to the player of a wind instrument, we may well feel a similar identification with the performer. A long, slow, unbroken phrase tends to carry us along with it. We are affected by its "long-breathed" quality, as well as by the rise and fall of the notes themselves. That is one of the means by which a composer creates a mood. On the other hand, a series of short, staccato phrases coming in rapid succession will produce the opposite effect in us, because we tend to breathe with the music.*

It is by adding one phrase to another that a composer constructs a melody. Within the limits that have been discussed, there is of course no set length of a musical phrase; nor is there any set rule governing the relationships between the lengths of the phrases that go to make up a melody. It is up to the composer to create the most appealing entity. He may do this by combining phrases of various lengths; or, he may keep his phrase lengths perfectly balanced. Which he does depends on the effect that he wishes to create.

Of course, melodies are subject in turn to the same limitations of our attention span as those that govern our reactions to their component phrases. There is a limit beyond which we lose our ability to grasp the relationships among the various parts. If a melody is too long, we may come to regard it as a

---

* An interesting speculation: what sort of music would we be listening to today if human beings were born with lungs of twice their present capacity?

series of more or less connected phrases, but in so doing we would lose our sense of it as a complete entity: we could no longer tell when it began and ended. Therefore, if we advance to the next higher level of organization and regard the complete melody as the smallest basic element in the form of a movement, it is apparent that there is a practical limit to its length.

Binary and ternary forms

Once the composer has created his melodies—of whatever length they may be—how does he go about creating a complete composition out of them?

Technically speaking, a melody itself can be regarded as a miniature composition. The melody of *Yankee Doodle* consists of two distinct and equal parts, the first part ending very clearly at the words: ". . . and called it Macaroni." The entire "composition" consists of no more than a single melody; yet that melody in turn displays a clearly defined form. In fact, so definite is that form that it has been given a name; because of its division into two parts, it is called the "binary form."

Now, to grasp the next level of complexity of form, let us investigate the melody of "Believe me, if all those endearing young charms," which is so familiar that it can be recalled by means of the words alone. The notes to which the words of the first line are set ("Believe me if all those endearing young charms, Which I gaze on so fondly today") constitute the "theme" (it consists of two clearly marked phrases), in the very same sense in which the famous melody of Schubert's *Unfinished Symphony is* one of its themes. Notice that the end of the first line leaves us with a feeling of unrest. We cannot stop the piece there; it has a feeling of being "up in the air." Whether we realize it or not, it is our feeling for the harmony that gives us this sense of unrest. The piece must move on to a state of rest.

In the second line ("Were to change by tomorrow, and fleet in my arms, Like fairy gifts fading away,") the "theme" is repeated, at least through the first phrase. This is an example of the principle of repetition, whose purpose is to familiarize us with the thematic material. As simple as this example is, it is none the less evidence of organization. Notice, though, that the second half of the melody—the second phrase ("Like fairy gifts fading away,")—brings us this time to a state of rest. Instead of the "up in the air" feeling that we had at the end of the first line, we now have a sense of completion, thanks to the return to the starting key. The first part of the form has been "rounded out." Notice, also, that each line is the same length. Thus we are left with a sense of balance, from the standpoint of the division of elapsed time. So far, we have had a complete, although very small, form. Since the composer wanted to extend his piece, however, to write in a larger form, he goes on.

In line three ("Thou woulds't still be adored as this moment thou art, Let thy loveliness fade as it will,") we have in essence a "second theme"—another musical "idea." Its purpose is to provide contrast. Yet note that it is somehow related to the opening melody, if only in its "feeling." It cannot be demonstrated that this is the *only* melody that could go with the opening theme; yet it has both enough similarity of mood to satisfy our desire for continuity, and enough contrast to fulfill our need for variety. Notice also that, at the word "adored," we come upon the highest note in the song: the "climax."

Yet again, at the end of this third line, we are left with a feeling of incompleteness. This comes from two sources: first, the fact that the note itself is left "up in the air," and second, the lack of balance among the parts, in the time sense. Thus, we need one more complete line of music to balance the two lines that comprised the first half of the song. Line four ("And around the dear ruin, each wish of my heart Would entwine itself verdantly still!") is a return to the opening theme. However, in order to convey the sense of finality, its ending is similar to the end of line two rather than to that of line one.

To summarize: the work consists of the statement of a theme, leaving us with an unsettled feeling at the end of the first line: then, a repetition of the theme, but this time with a sense of completion. This is followed by a contrasting idea, which brings us to the climax, but also leaves us with a sense of incompleteness. The piece ends with a return to the first idea, and a return to the starting key.

This is the ground plan of the so-called "song form," or "ternary form," because of its division into three parts. (The second line, being largely a repetition of the first, is not regarded as a new part. It merely supplies us with an opportunity to become more familiar with the first "theme.") It is the form of such familiar songs as *Drink to Me Only with Thine Eyes, Swanee River,* and Dvořák's *Humoresque.*

As a convenient means of specifying forms, it has become the custom to represent each section of a song by a letter. In the binary form, the two parts are designated as "a" and "b." In the ternary form, since the second line is largely a repetition, it is identified, like the first, as "a." The third line, the new musical idea, is called "b." The form of the most simple songs, accordingly, can be indicated thus: a a b a. This ternary form has been found to be an ideal method of combining two musical ideas for variety of interest, and yet readily achieving a sense of continuity.

Many large compositions are, in essence, nothing more than expansions of these simple binary and ternary forms. Suppose we were to enlarge all the elements of one of these basic forms, so that the "a" section consisted, not of a single phrase, or even of a single melody, but rather, of a group or "family" of melodies. Suppose, also, that the "b" section contained another group of melodies, contrasting with the "a" melodies. Here we would have the genesis of a large composition—a movement of a symphony, for example. To carry the possibilities further: any or all of the individual melodies in this larger scheme could be cast in either binary or ternary form. A long movement may thus be made up of forms within forms.

The binary form was very popular among composers of the short pieces that appeared in such profusion during the seventeenth and eighteenth centuries. Most of the so-called keyboard "sonatas" by Domenico Scarlatti, for example, were cast in this two-part mold, with, of course, the sections considerably extended. ("Sonata," as used in this case, meant simply "sound-piece," and the term should not be confused with the "sonata" or "sonata-allegro form" that we shall examine in Chapter Eighteen.)

The dance movements of the eighteenth century—allemande, courante, sarabande, gigue, bourree, gavotte, and minuet—while they differ greatly in rhythm and tempo, are usually excellent examples of the two-part form. The beginning of the second part is easily heard, and each half of the composition is customarily repeated.

The three-part form is the ground plan of any number of independent, single-movement pieces that are known by various names. Among them are the nocturne, ballade, capriccio, impromptu, berceuse, intermezzo, prelude, etude, and romance—these names being applied more or less at the fancy of the composer. A berceuse and a nocturne, as their titles imply, are likely to be in slow tempo, but no set rule governs the mood or tempo of the others. While there is no guarantee that a piece with one of these titles will be in three-part form, the chances are fairly good that it will be.

The ternary form also supplies the ground plan not only of almost all of the minuets in the symphonies of Haydn and Mozart (as distinct from the minuet in the eighteenth-century dance suite, which is in binary form), but also of nearly all the scherzo movements of the symphonies of Beethoven, Schubert, and Brahms. It also applies to most of the minuets and scherzos in the same composers' many quartets, trios, and sonatas.

The rondo

Suppose, now, that a composer has three contrasting themes or melodies with which he or she wishes to write a movement. Assuming that the first theme is the most interesting one, the composer might wish to repeat it, by alternating it with the two other themes. In this way, we have the variety offered by each new melody, as well as the sense of recognition resulting from each reappearance of the first theme. The ground plan of such an arrangement would be a b a c a. This is the familiar form called the "rondo," whose distinguishing characteristic is the return to the first theme, after each digression.

The rondo is the form most often used for the lighthearted, fast, closing movement of a large work, such as a concerto, but it is also found in slow movements. Form, as we see from this, is an element that exists independently of tempo. The rondo form permits any degree of elaboration. For example, should the composer wish to extend it, using only three themes, he might arrange them in the following variant of the rondo form: a b a c a b a. It is also possible for a fourth, or "d," theme to be incorporated into the design, thus: a b a c a d a. Notice that, in the first case, the movement has perfect symmetry in the distribution of the various sections. It might be viewed as two a b a's, separated by c. It is the "a" theme that binds the movement together.

Repetition and free forms: rhapsody and fantasy

The simplest way to create a musical form is through the use of the principle of repetition, as we saw in the first two lines of "Believe me if all those endearing young charms." Many simple nursery songs and folk songs are built this way. The method is especially useful when a story is to be told, as in the case of *Clementine.* Here, obviously, the purpose of the music is merely to act as a vehicle for the many verses, so that it makes little difference that the "composition" consists of seemingly endless repetitions of the same brief melody. Obviously, however, if it were not for the words, such a composition would not satisfy us, on purely musical grounds. As important as repetition is as a *principle,* mere repetition of the same brief melody is not sufficient to hold our interest for any considerable length of time. Along with our desire for a sense of continuity, we also crave variety.

Many of the songs of Schubert are built on the idea of repetition, in so far as the same music is used for several verses. In such instances, however, the music that is repeated, instead of consisting of only a brief melody, is in itself a complete composition, with several contrasting sections that are capable of holding our attention. It must be admitted, nevertheless, that certain of these songs can become somewhat wearing, once the sensation of repetition predominates over the effect of variety.

Ravel's *Bolero is* essentially nothing more than a series of repetitions of the same melody. The popularity of the work would seem to negate the contention that mere repetition will not make an interesting composition. Ravel's piece is a *tour de force* that makes its appeal just because of the seeming endlessness of its repetitions and the cumulative effect of its incessant rhythms. It is a "one-of-a-kind" composition; another work written on the same principle would immediately be branded as an imitation. Then, too, Ravel's work does not consist of literal repetitions. With each reappearance of the theme, there is a distinct and imaginative change of orchestration. The composer seems to have deliberately chosen to use a single melody in order to concentrate the listener's attention on the extraordinary variety of his instrumental coloration.

Theoretically, one could go to the other extreme, and create a composition by merely "tacking together" a series of melodies, one after the other. Such a composition would obviously have variety, but at a certain point we would begin to lose our sense of unity. Somewhat the same effect would be created if a speaker were merely to announce an endless series of topics, and never return to any one of them, in order to enlarge upon it. In music, each melody, or theme, may be likened to a "topic," and in a sense must be treated like one, if we are to follow its course. Melodies, as it happens, are often called "subjects."

As a matter of fact, certain very popular compositions consist of loosely linked subjects. This form is known as the "Rhapsody," or "Fantasy." Two of the best known examples are the *Hungarian Rhapsody Number Two* of Liszt, and the *Roumanian Rhapsody Number One,* by Enesco. While both works consist essentially of a series of different melodies, both composers are careful to see that their pieces are of limited length, in order not to present us with too many themes. A successful rhapsody, therefore, takes into account our tendency to become confused by too great a profusion of musical ideas. A rhapsody of the length of a Beethoven symphony would quickly lose the listener's attention.

Rachmaninoff's *Rhapsody on a Theme by Paganini is* a long work, taking over twenty minutes to perform; yet it in no way refutes this point, since the work is essentially devoted to exploring the possibilities inherent in a single melody, with a few additional melodies introduced for contrast. Rather than a rhapsody, it might more properly be called a set of variations on a theme, like Ravel's *Bolero.*

To return to the rhapsodies of Liszt and Enesco: if their form consists basically of a number of melodies strung together, how does the music manage to hold our interest? First, of course, there is the appeal of the individual melodies. Most of them have a folk quality, or are in dance rhythms. To the native Hungarian or Roumanian, the melodies may have sentimental associations; to the nonnative, the folk cast of the melodies gives the music an attractive exotic quality. Then there is the variety of tone colors resulting from the instrumentation; the sound of a full orchestra playing in a captivating dance rhythm can be very exciting. Both of these factors are what might be termed the "immediate" appeals of music. We can enjoy a melody or the sheer sound of an orchestra even if we happen to turn on our radios while the music is already in progress.

Yet even in such a relatively free musical form as a rhapsody, we find that part of our enjoyment stems from something that might be considered a purely formal consideration. There is a tendency on the part of the composer to linger over one melody before going on to the next, so that the rhapsody is not merely a stringing on of a new melody or a new theme every few bars. One may "expand" on a melody by repeating it, perhaps with a different instrument or with a different sort of accompaniment. (This is the case especially with the opening melody of Enesco's *Roumanian Rhapsody.*) Or one may repeat portions of the melody—perhaps only its final phrase. Then too, one may take a short but characteristic part of the theme—a "motive"—and play it at a higher or lower pitch level with each repetition—a technique known as a "sequence." Or if the next new melody is to be a loud, exciting dance, the composer may give us a sense of continuity by "working up" a small portion of the previous theme—playing it successively faster, higher, and louder, with an increasing number of instruments. In this way, when the new theme finally appears, it seems to be a logical climax to what came before.

It appears, then, that the "joints" between themes ("bridge passages" is the technical term) play an important part in establishing a sense of continuity. Even in as relatively simple and straightforward a form as the rhapsody, the composer is constantly concerned with the two concepts of unity and variety. The problem is to give the work enough variety to hold the attention, and at the same time, enough continuity so that it seems to be "all of a piece."

Music lovers sometimes speak of the sense of inevitability that they find in certain great symphonies. It is as if the *music "had* to be that way," they say. Realistically speaking, this feeling comes in part from their familiarity with the specific piece. The more we hear a work, the more do we become accustomed to the succession of its parts. But to a large extent, this sense of inevitability is the result of the quality we have been discussing—the composer's ability to impart so great a sense of unity to the different elements of a work that we get the feeling it could never have been composed otherwise.

Musical growth and development: the variation form

In our discussion of what may happen to a single melody in two such relatively "free" compositions as the rhapsodies of Liszt and Enesco, we arrived at an extremely important concept: that of "development"—the process by which a melody can be made to grow. It is important for two reasons: first, development can show us what to look for during a given portion of a piece of music—it is the "text" of the music at that point; second, it plays an important part in the most advanced of musical forms, the sonata form.

Let us return for a moment to the opening of Enesco's *Roumanian Rhapsody Number One.* Notice that the opening melody (which consists of several short phrases, with repetitions) is repeated as a whole several times. Each reiteration of the entire melody, however, is presented in a slightly different way: the instrumentation is varied, so that the melody, first heard as a clarinet solo, is finally presented by the full string section. The accompaniment becomes fuller, and there is even a slight change in the melody itself, since Enesco "decorates" it at one point.

What we have here, in essence, is the concept of variation, or one of the ways in which a musical idea is made to develop. Consider the possibilities that it opens up. Think of the myriad ways in which a melody can be varied, and its instrumental coloration varied. Furthermore, it is possible to present a musical idea in new ways by changing its tempo—that is, by having it played faster or slower. Variety can be obtained at a more subtle level by changing the harmonies, or by changing the type of accompaniment. Notes can be added, to make a simple melody more interesting. Or the rhythm of the melody can be changed—which makes for another source of variety.

The variation concept is so important that it is used as the basis of a complete form, known as "Theme and Variations." The concept of variation can be applied to themes of different character, whether slow or fast. In addition, the emotional implications of the original melody (or melodies) as well as of the variations are in no way limited by the fact that they are part of a Theme and Variations form. The slow movement of Beethoven's Ninth Symphony—a set of variations—is often called one of the most "ethereal" and "sublime" utterances in all of music, yet it is at its most sublime at just those points at which Beethoven is merely embroidering one of his melodies.

Variation, not only as a form, but as a manner of "thinking" in music, is basic to our understanding of the ways in which a piece of music grows. It may seem rather odd that the word "development" was mentioned in connection with that form in which development is least to be expected. After all, a rhapsody, by definition, is essentially little more than a series of melodies. Such "development" as that which we find in either of the two rhapsodies referred to is relatively slight; it represents hardly more than the "germ" of the idea. But it was intentionally mentioned in relation to this form, in order to bring home more dramatically the point that *some* degree of development must go into any extended piece of music, no matter how slight it is.

Let us take stock for a moment of the kinds of form that have been dealt with, so far. Note that they differ in one basic and very important respect. The binary and ternary forms—the minuet or scherzo (a b a), and the rondo (a b a c a)—are based essentially upon the relative *positions* of various themes. They are large ground plans, designed to accommodate movements that are based on several ideas. Recall that we might even have a rondo containing four themes, thus: a b a c a d a. The rhapsody can go even further in the number of ideas it contains; it is one of the "free forms"—so free as to be hardly a "form" at all. But observe that, by contrast, the Theme and Variations is a form that depends upon the *growth* of one or two ideas.

In one set of forms, it is the contrasting of several different ideas that determines the large design. In the case of the Theme and Variations, however, the over-all design of the movement is somewhat subordinated to our concern for "what happens" to one or two ideas. It is more than likely that a Theme and Variations will be merely sectional in form, with one variation following another. Yet there is still a difference in *kind* between these two types of form. One, being based upon the alternating *positions* of themes, is essentially static; the other, since it is based on the *growth* of one or more melodies, is dynamic. (Of course there is a measure of oversimplification here, in order to bring out a principle. No minuet or rondo is likely to be so lacking in development as to be completely static; furthermore, the Theme and Variations form is by no means the extreme of the concept of development and growth.)

CHAPTER 17

Polyphony and
Polyphonic Forms

All the forms presented so far may be described as "sectional."
That is, they have their being mainly as a result of the relationships among the contrasting sections of a piece of music.

Let us now investigate the other family of musical forms—
those arising directly out of the polyphonic or contrapuntal
musical texture. The most important of these are the canon,
round, fugue, madrigal, motet, concerto grosso, passacaglia, and
chaconne.

The technique of imitation—such as we find in a round like
Frère Jacques—is basic to many of the polyphonic, or contrapuntal forms, from the simplest round to an involved fugue. At
the outset, therefore, it would be advisable for the reader to
realize that the essence of a fugue is found—in rudimentary
form, of course—in a simple round, such as *Frère Jacques*.

"Canon" is the name given to a more elaborate species of
imitation, in which the imitation is continued from the start of
the piece to the end. The successive voices, or parts, may enter
with the melody at the same pitch, in which case it is called
"canon at the unison," or an octave higher or lower, in which
case it is called "canon at the octave." In more complex canons,
however, the successive voices may enter at an interval other
than the unison or the octave. Suppose the second voice were to
present the melody, say, five scale notes higher than the original
melody. This is termed "canon at the fifth." Note the possibilities for sophistication and complexity of musical thought that
are opened up by the principle of voices entering at different
pitch intervals.

The "round," we now see, is actually a simple polyphonic
form, based upon the technique of "canonic imitation."
As soon as any voice has completed the melody, it starts again.

A moment's thought will reveal the fact that the round is potentially infinite. In order to end it, one must decide arbitrarily upon the number of times that the melody shall be repeated.

Several techniques are available to the composer, in order to increase the interest and sophistication in polyphonic writing. While one voice presents the melody in its original form, another may present it upside down, or in "inversion," as it is technically called. That is, where the notes of the original melody went up, in the inverted version they would go down.

Another technique frequently encountered in polyphonic or contrapuntal writing is that of "augmentation"—having a melody played in note values of longer time duration, so that, in effect, it is slowed down. The opposite process—shortening the time values of the notes—is called "diminution." To the ear, the result is that the melody seems to be played faster. Each of these devices can be employed by the composer for its specific emotional effects.

Still another contrapuntal technique is to play the melody backward. This is known as "retrograde motion," or *cancrizans* ("crab motion"). There is nothing to prevent the composer from presenting his melody in both retrograde motion and inversion, simultaneously.*

The most involved and sophisticated of the contrapuntal forms is the "fugue," which means "flight." The form of the fugue is subject to so many individual differences, and can become so complex, that only the basic principles will be presented here. First, it should be realized that a fugue can be written for any number of instruments or voices, and in any combination. Most fugues are written for from three to five voices, or parts, although there are some for more than five voices.

Despite the latitude that exists in the form, all fugues begin with what is known as the "exposition"—the presentation to the listener of the main melody, called the "subject." This is usually of well-defined character, both rhythmically and melodically and is presented as a single line in some one voice—

*It might be mentioned that the composers who have adopted what Arnold Schönberg called his "method of composing with the twelve tones" make frequent use of elaborate contrapuntal devices.

soprano, alto, tenor, or bass. (These generic terms are used, even if the fugue is for instruments only.) Upon the completion of the subject in the first voice, it is then presented in one of the other voices, higher or lower than the original presentation, at the discretion of the composer.

During this second presentation, called the "answer," the first voice does not stop, but continues with new music, called the "countersubject." After the completion of the answer in the second voice, the third voice enters with the subject, the second voice going on to the countersubject, while the first voice, having completed both the subject and the countersubject, continues with further new music as a "free voice." At the moment at which all the voices (three, four, five, or more) have presented the subject and the answer, the exposition of the fugue is considered to be completed. In some fugues, the exposition is now repeated, but with the order of entry of the various voices changed, for variety.

From this point on, there is considerable freedom in the form. However, the basic idea is to explore the fugue's subject, so that it is presented in a variety of interesting ways. Any or all of the contrapuntal techniques described above may be used—imitation, inversion, augmentation, diminution, retrograde motion. However, because the texture of a fugue may become extremely complex, the composer often presents sections, called "episodes," which supply periods of relaxation. These episodes are usually made up of contrapuntally treated portions of the subject or the countersubject. There is no rule governing the number or placement of the episodes.

Generally, the emotional temper of any fugue tends to mount toward the end, as the result of the cumulative effect of the exploration of the subject. (There are lighthearted and gay fugues. Bach's *Fugue a la Gigue* and the Fugue from Jaromir Weinberger's *Schwanda* are examples. But even they end in powerful fashion.) The device of diminution, described earlier, adds to the feeling of excitement, because of the implied increase in tempo. Conversely, augmentation, by drawing out the melody, can lend an effect of majesty and grandeur to the subject. Augmentation, combined with an increase in loudness, is usually reserved for the end of the fugue, where the greatest emotional climax is desired. Still another technique that may be used by the composer, in an attempt to add to the excitement of the climax, is the *"stretto,"* in which the subject enters in various voices at very short time intervals, thus giving the effect of the voices "piling up" on themselves.

The interest in listening to a fugue comes from following the ways in which a composer presents and develops the subject. Without question, the fugue is one of the most demanding forms to listen to attentively, since it requires that the ear follow simultaneously the various contrapuntal strands. Because of this, fugues are in general of limited length. But, as if the original form were not complex enough, we might add that there are "double fugues" and "triple fugues," in which the composer exploits the possibilities of not one, but two or three subjects.

Another essentially polyphonic form is the "concerto grosso." This is a form that flourished during the first half of the eighteenth century. It should not be confused with the nineteenth-century concerto, which is a virtuoso piece for a solo instrumentalist with orchestral accompaniment. The concerto grosso had its origins in the fascination that the seventeenth-century composer found in contrasting a small body of solo instruments with a large body of accompanying instruments. The small group was called the "concertino," and might consist of any combination of instruments chosen by the composer—typically, two violins and a cello. The larger group was called the *"ripieno"* (meaning "filling-in" instruments). The texture was most often polyphonic, sometimes fugal. Among the best-known *concerti grossi* today are the twelve for string orchestra by Handel, and the six *Brandenburg Concerti* by Bach. In the latter set, the make-up of the *concertino* varies greatly.

Human voices by their very nature lend themselves to polyphonic treatment. The vocal polyphonic forms that should be mentioned are the madrigal and the motet. Both are for groups of unaccompanied voices, ranging from two to eight or more parts, the standard being four or five. When the text is secular, the work is called a madrigal; when the text is on a sacred or liturgical subject, the work is called a motet. Both forms use the same polyphonic devices. However, it is to be expected that the motet, having a text on a religious subject, will be more sedate, while the madrigal is likely to be livelier and more joyful. Considerable drama is possible in both forms. It should be added that madrigals run the emotional gamut from the most frivolous kind of expression to deeply moving works. (The listener should bear in mind the fact that, even in these essentially polyphonic forms, it is not unusual to find sections of clearly homophonic texture.)

One essentially polyphonic device—and the forms that derive from it—should also be mentioned here. It is the "ground bass," a melody or motive that is repeated over and over in the bass. It is also referred to as a *"basso ostinato,"* or "obstinate bass." Above the repeated bass, the composer is free to weave any sort of melody or melodies. Curiously enough, this form, which would seem to be restricting, because of the necessity for repeating the one strain over and over again, has given rise to some of the most emotional music ever written. There is no better way to become familiar with its effect than to listen to any of the following compositions, all of which are built on a ground bass: the *"Crucifixus"* of Bach's *Mass in B Minor* has a four-part chorus over the ground bass in the orchestra; the slow movement of the same composer's *Violin Concerto Number Two* gives a rhapsodic part to the solo violin, while the orchestral cellos and basses play the ground bass; in *"Dido's Lament,"* from Henry Purcell's opera *Dido and Aeneas* a solo voice soars movingly above the repeated figure in the bass; *"The Plaint,"* from the same composer's equally beautiful, though less-known work, *The Fairy Queen,* has a soprano voice and a violin interweaving in most moving fashion, above the ground bass. Brahms, in the closing portions of his *Variations on a Theme by Haydn,* introduces the *basso ostinato,* and in the twentieth century, Stravinsky, in the second movement of his humorous *L'Histoire du Soldat,* employs this device.

The concept of the *basso ostinato* has given rise to two forms, the "passacaglia" and the "chaconne." Both have the following characteristics: they are based on a slow melody, usually eight bars long, in triple meter (that is, three beats to the bar). In the passacaglia, the theme is first presented in the bass, unharmonized—that is, as a single line of melody. In the chaconne, the first presentation of the theme is accompanied by chords. Each form is a series of variations over the ground bass, with additional musical material superimposed upon it, usually increasing in complexity and in emotional temper. The bass melody itself may be brought into the higher registers.

In the ordinary Theme and Variations form, there is often a pause after each variation, since each is a complete entity in itself. In the passacaglia and chaconne, however, there are no such pauses, since the various sections are joined to one another. This technique is known as "continuous variation." The best-known example of the passacaglia is Bach's *Passacaglia and Fugue in C Minor,* for organ. (Incidentally, the subject of the fugue is the first half of the passacaglia melody. It is presented simultaneously with another subject, and thus the work is an example of the "double fugue" mentioned earlier.) The best-known example of the chaconne (even though the ground bass is frequently only implied) occurs in Bach's *Partita Number Two in D Minor* for unaccompanied violin. Another familiar chaconne is the final movement of Brahms's Fourth Symphony.

CHAPTER 18

Sonata–Allegro Form

The slow movement of the typical symphony, concerto, string quartet, or sonata—it is usually the second movement—will often be written in the expanded song form, or in the form of Theme and Variations. The quicker minuet or scherzo movement (normally the third movement) is likely to be in the A B A form. (It is customary to refer to the large sections of a complete musical form as "A," "B," "C," and so forth, to differentiate them from the smaller "a," "b," "c," which indicate merely themes or melodies.) The final, more rapid movement is often in the rondo form. Exceptions to all these practices will spring to the mind of any experienced listener, but it should certainly be clear by now that there are no hard and fast rules governing a composer's choice of forms, or the manipulation of the musical material within the forms. What we have described here is the typical scheme of a symphony or other multimovement work.

We can now take up the first movement—ordinarily the most complex of the four. Typically, it will be written in what is called "sonata form," or "sonata-allegro form." But first, let us clear up the various meanings of the word "sonata." Its many different meanings result from the accumulation of several centuries of different usages, since the same term has been used in different periods to denote different forms.

The word "sonata" comes from the Italian *suonata*, which, centuries ago, referred to any instrumental "soundpiece," as distinct from a *cantata*, which was a vocal work. Therefore, it is used as the title for numerous instrumental pieces of the seventeenth century. It subsequently came to be applied to the harpsichord works of Domenico Scarlatti, which were relatively brief, single-movement pieces, usually in binary form. The sonatas of other composers of the late Baroque period—Bach, Handel, Vivaldi, and others—are usually in four movements, alternating between slow and fast. The forms of the individual movements were not standardized. This "baroque sonata" was likely to be in polyphonic texture.

In the time of Haydn, Mozart, and Beethoven, the term took on a third, and entirely different meaning, the one that it still has today. It referred to a relatively extended instrumental work in several movements—usually, though not necessarily, four—*regardless of the instrumentation*. It is important to realize at the outset that the typical sonata played by a pianist, say, is not a form that is peculiar to the piano alone. In this case it is merely a sonata that was written for the piano. A symphony may be considered a *sonata for orchestra;* technically, it is nothing more. Were a piano sonata to be orchestrated, it would become a symphony. A string quartet, which is also ordinarily a sonata by another name, if it were orchestrated would also turn out to be a symphony.

There is one specific requirement, however, that makes any multimovement work, technically, a "sonata." At least *one* of the movements must be in the "sonata form." This brings us to the fourth meaning of the term sonata: the specific descriptive term for a single-movement form, rather than a complete composition. It is also sometimes referred to as the "first movement form," since, as we have seen, it is most often the opening movement of a work that is in sonata form. Since it is also called the "sonata-allegro form," the word "allegro," which is the Italian designation for "fast," would seem to imply that the sonata-allegro form is always a fast movement. This is not the case; slow movements can be described as written in sonata-allegro form. (The terminology of music is beset with misnomers. The intelligent listener learns to live with them!)

Over centuries of usage, the sonata form has become the ideal vehicle for the presentation of several contrasting musical ideas in a cohesive manner. (From this point on, the term "sonata form" will mean the "sonata-allegro form" or "first movement form.") Yet, in addition to being the most intellectually complex of forms, it is also one of the most satisfying for the expression of drama and emotions, in purely musical terms. The first movements of Tchaikovsky's *Pathétique Symphony,* Schubert's *Unfinished,* and Beethoven's Fifth Symphony are all in sonata form and, by common agreement, these are among the most exciting, emotional, and generally satisfying of all movements in the entire musical literature. Thus, the complexity of the sonata form is not a matter of mere intellectual complication, in spite of the fact that it does permit the greatest scope for the exercise of the musical intellect.

Every time you listen to the opening movement of a symphony or concerto by Haydn, Mozart, Beethoven, Schubert, Mendelssohn, Brahms, or Tchaikovsky, you are hearing an example of sonata form. When you consider how far removed some of these composers are from one another—chronologically, temperamentally, and stylistically—it becomes apparent that the sonata form must be an extremely satisfying means of conveying both the intellectual and emotional messages of music. Incidentally, if the composer wishes to do so, there is nothing to prevent him from casting any or all four movements of a work in the sonata-allegro form. (Mendelssohn's Third Symphony—the so-called *Scotch Symphony*—is an example.)

Let us begin an examination of the form with the thought that a composer wishes to write an extended movement, on a number of musical ideas. He feels that the ideas—themes, melodies, or subjects—are so important and full of possibilities for development, that a form that depends upon mere alternation of position-—for example, the rondo—will not allow him to make the most of them. True, the rondo would supply a means of obtaining contrast, but he is interested in creating music that will allow for greater emotional in intensity. In other words, he will not be satisfied with merely stating the themes, one after another, and then returning to one or more of them for a sense of continuity. Instead, he wants to treat his ideas "in depth"—to seek out the inherent drama and emotional excitement the themes presumably contain. It is in the opportunities that it offers for this sort of intense emotionalism that the sonata form is supreme.

First, of course, the composer must state the themes, or ideas, just as a playwright introduces the characters. The opening section of the sonata form corresponds, therefore, to the first act of a play. Then, having introduced his ideas, the composer will proceed to explore them, and to bring them into interesting relationships with one another. This portion of the sonata form corresponds, roughly, to the second act of a play, in which, as we say, "the plot thickens." Finally, in the third and concluding section, the composer will recall the ideas, more or less as they were presented originally, and more or less in the order in which they were first heard. This section, loosely speaking, corresponds to the resolution that we find in the third act of a play. We cannot carry the analogy any further, however, since the final act of a play is not likely to be a review of the first act—another demonstration of the fundamental difference between music and literary art forms.

This tripartite structure is the very essence of the sonata form. So basic is it, in fact, that the three sections are given their own names. The opening section, in which the themes are first presented, or Exposed, is called, logically enough, the "exposition." The middle section, in which the melodies are brought to emotional heights not reached before, is called the "development." The concluding section, which brings with it the sense of resolution as well as the recollection of the original themes, is called the "recapitulation" (or "restatement").

In the classical sonata or symphony of the eighteenth and nineteenth centuries, the composer indicates that the entire exposition is to be repeated, note for note, before the development is begun. (Recall the satisfactory effect obtained by repeating the first line of "Believe me if all those endearing young charms.") The purpose of the repetition is to familiarize the listener with all the musical ideas, before they are brought into more complex relationship with each other. In recent times, as the understanding of the classical musical vocabulary has increased, performers and conductors have generally deemed the repetition of the exposition unnecessary. In recorded performances, the repeat was omitted until the advent of the long-playing record, with its increased playing time, made it feasible. The repeat of the exposition, or A section, will be heard in some, but not in all modern recordings. When the repetition is played, in accordance with the classical concept, the over-all form may be synopsized as our already familiar A A B A, with B standing for the development section. Even though the A section may contain many themes and occupy several minutes of playing time, and the B section may be even longer, the sonata form, with its A A B A, shows its derivation from the song form. In dealing with abstract musical ideas, both composers and listeners appear to find the greatest satisfaction in the basic three-part concept of "presentation of ideas, digression (or development), and return." The plan suits our needs on both the small scale of *Swanee River,* and the large scale of the opening movement of a Beethoven symphony.

As we go further into our examination of the sonata form, we must adjust our thinking to the larger scale. We will be listening to movements that may continue for as long as twenty-five minutes or more. In such cases, it is obvious that even the smaller subdivisions of the form will be fairly large. The first practical significance of this thought comes when we realize that the term "theme" will now refer not to a single melody, but to a group or family of melodies. When we speak of the "first theme" or the "second theme" in the sonata form, we are referring to several melodies in each case. More properly, our term should be "first theme group." Remember that the sonata form is a means of handling a movement that contains *many* ideas. Some of the ideas will inevitably be more arresting than others, and therefore more prominent. It is the complete grouping of a main melody with its "hangers-on" that we have in mind, when we speak of a "first theme" or a "second theme."

What are these themes that comprise a family, or group? Perhaps the easiest way to become aware of them is to listen to the opening movement of a Haydn or Mozart symphony. For the moment, disregard the slow introduction—in the event that there is one—since it is not an essential part of the sonata form. (We will come back to these slow introductions a little later.) Begin your listening at the *Allegro,* or fast portion. In all likelihood, the very first melody will have a distinctive quality, making it fairly easy to remember and to recognize when it recurs. This first melody will probably be followed by other melodies which, though they may add to the feeling of excitement, will be less distinctive. They may have the quality of a fanfare, with the trumpets and drums featured in a rhythmic pattern, or they may consist of fast, running passages in the strings.

The possibilities are limitless; in any case, these passages will be somewhat less memorable, less immediately recognizable, perhaps less singable than the main melody, and serve essentially as foils to it. These are the "other" melodies that go to make up the "first theme group." (In sonata movements by such later composers as Beethoven and Brahms, some of these lesser themes will have become the kind of melody, like the principal one, that we want to hum or whistle whenever we think of that particular movement.)

One of the most important concepts in the sonata form is the contrast between the first main theme and the second main theme. It is the custom for the first theme to be forceful and assertive. The second theme, by contrast, is usually more lyrical and expressive*. This contrast of character is one of the sources of the drama to follow in the development section.

A word about the term "second theme" in the sonata form—which is also called the "subordinate theme" or "subsidiary theme." These are technical names, referring only to the relative *position* of the theme. They have nothing whatsoever to do with the actual importance of the second theme. To demonstrate this fact, you need do no more than recall the most memorable theme of Schubert's *Unfinished Symphony.* You will in all likelihood be thinking of the subordinate theme, since that is the position occupied by the famous melody. The most appealing melody of the first movement of Tchaikovsky's *Pathétique Symphony is,* likewise, the subordinate theme.

Now, let us examine the simplest possible layout of the sonata form.

---

* Moreover, the first theme is always in the tonic key—the main key of the work—while the second theme is most often in the dominant key. The key relationships, to be summarized later, are at this point not a necessary part of our understanding of the form.

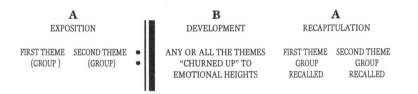

| **A** | **B** | **A** |
| EXPOSITION | DEVELOPMENT | RECAPITULATION |

FIRST THEME	SECOND THEME	ANY OR ALL THE THEMES	FIRST THEME	SECOND THEME
(GROUP)	(GROUP)	"CHURNED UP" TO	GROUP	GROUP
		EMOTIONAL HEIGHTS	RECALLED	RECALLED

The symbol separating the exposition from the development, the "double bar," indicates that the exposition is to be repeated. Note that it might be rather awkward if the vigorous, assertive first theme were to be followed immediately by the gentle second theme. The natural sense of timing of events, which we all share to some degree, dictates that a suitable space separate the two contrasting themes in a large work. The lesser themes of the first group, besides supplying their own immediate delights, also perform the structural function of acting as a transition to the second theme. So important is this function, in fact, that the intermediate melody (or melodies) is called a "bridge." To be fully correct, therefore, the diagram of the exposition presented above should contain the word "bridge," between the first theme group and second theme group.

Theoreticians sometimes disagree over when one of the themes in the first theme group ceases to be an actual member of the family, and becomes a bridge. The distinction is far too subtle for the layman to be concerned with. It is sufficient for our purposes to be aware of the fact that there is a bridge, or a transition from one theme to another. Often, in the symphonies of Haydn and Mozart, the bridge theme makes it easy to locate the appearance of the second theme: it may end abruptly in a flurry of excitement, so that the more lyrical mood of the second theme stands out in greater relief.

Now, recall the natural impulse that most of us have to end things, as we say, "with a flourish." It manifests itself, for example, in the tendency that people have to follow their signatures with a flamboyant line, or decoration. Obviously, such flourishes add nothing to the legibility of the signature; they are simply a manifestation of an esthetic impulse to give some slight extra prominence to an ending. In music, the outcome of this impulse takes its place as an integral part of form. It is more than possible that the sense of excitement you feel at the conclusion of a symphony, or at the close of a movement, is the result of the composer's having written that "extra push" at the end. It may be nothing more than a brief flourish, or it may be an extended section lasting several minutes. Regardless of its extent, this section, an appendage to the A A B A structure, is known by the Italian word *coda* ("tail").

A coda may be appended to many forms. It may be found at the end of a complete work, as in the case of a symphony or a concerto. It may also be found at the end of a movement, such as a theme and variations or a minuet. In the sonata form, it is possible to find a coda not only at the end of the movement, but at the end of a section, such as the exposition. Naturally, a coda that occurs *within* a movement is not likely to be as extended as the one which *concludes* the movement. The name for the smaller coda, *codetta,* suggests its less ambitious scope.

The composer may build the coda or codetta out of some of the melodies previously introduced. In that case, it becomes a "summing up"—a last musical glance at the ideas. Further—a coda or codetta may be based on new ideas. In that case, the codetta, following the second theme group, becomes essentially a "third theme," or "third theme group."

Just as it is possible for the composer to append new material at the end, so it is also possible to start the first movement with a slow introduction. This introduction may be nothing more than a brief "attention-getter," as it sometimes is in the symphonies of Haydn and Mozart. On the other hand, it may be a lengthy section, which not only sets the mood, but which presents a foretaste of some of the ideas to be presented in the exposition. In other words, the presence of an introduction, its length, and the degree to which it is related to what follows are all at the discretion of the composer—as are, after all, all the features that make the sonata form a vehicle for dramatic musical expression.

To see at a glance the relationship of all the parts we have discussed, let us look at an expanded diagram of the form. At the top, the A B A sections show the form at its simplest. Reading down, we come to the elaborations that we have just studied. At the bottom appear the key relationships. Note that the exposition is characterized by a shift from the tonic to the dominant—that is, from the home key to a key that creates a state of unrest. The development, presenting its material in "foreign" keys? emphasizes and extends the feeling of unrest. The recapitulation reaffirms the return to the tonic key, bringing with it a sense of rest and satisfaction.

Note also that this diagram in no way represents the amount of time or emphasis that is given to each section by the composer. This is merely a schematic representation of the sequence of events in the standard sonata form. We shall go further into the individual sections of the sonata form in Chapters Twenty and Twenty-one.

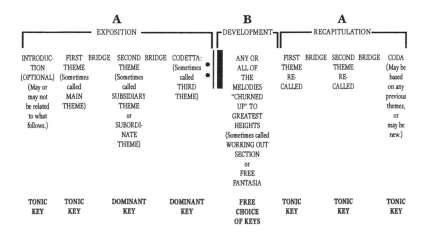

A EXPOSITION					**B** DEVELOPMENT	**A** RECAPITULATION			
INTRODUC- TION (OPTIONAL) (May or may not be related to what follows.)	FIRST THEME (Sometimes called MAIN THEME)	BRIDGE	SECOND THEME (Sometimes called SUBSIDIARY THEME or SUBORDI- NATE THEME)	BRIDGE	CODETTA: (Sometimes called THIRD THEME)	ANY OR ALL OF THE MELODIES "CHURNED UP" TO GREATEST HEIGHTS (Sometimes called WORKING OUT SECTION or FREE FANTASIA	FIRST THEME RE- CALLED	BRIDGE	SECOND THEME RE- CALLED	BRIDGE	CODA (May be based on any previous themes, or may be new.)
TONIC KEY	TONIC KEY		DOMINANT KEY		DOMINANT KEY	FREE CHOICE OF KEYS	TONIC KEY		TONIC KEY		TONIC KEY

PART THREE

Your Approach to the Understanding and Enjoyment of Music

CHAPTER 19

Listening for Sensuous Pleasure

It seems to be the custom for treatises on music appreciation to warn the reader about the evils of letting oneself revel in the sounds of music for their own sake. I wish to endorse the opposite view—which is that the sensuous qualities of the sounds themselves are an extremely important part of our enjoyment of music. If this were not the case, why should composers be so concerned with the art of orchestration—the differentiation of sounds by means of specific tone colors? Moreover, is it not the sensuous satisfaction to be derived from sounds that is at the core of the justifiable assertion that no recording or broadcast can truly replace a "live" performance?

Certainly, in the first hearing of an unfamiliar work, you are entitled to simply let the sounds sweep over you, and to enjoy the music for its immediate sensuous and physical satisfactions. (This suggestion is based, of course, on the assumption that the work is available in recording, and so can be heard again at will.)

As you listen to the sounds, themselves a potential source of immediate pleasure, associations will certainly be awakened in your mind. This process will take place without any conscious effort on your part. (During subsequent hearings of the work, after the sensuous appeals of the music have made their impact, you can begin to look for the subtleties of construction—along the lines explained in Part Two and in the chapter following this one.)

Many of our associations, and their attendant responses, take place, of course, at the unconscious level. But the fact that we may not be able to account for some of these associations should not lead us to rule out the pleasurable responses that they bring. This approach, incidentally, might bring us closer to the enjoyment of some ultramodern works, in which composers have begun to make use of sounds for their own sake—for their "evocative" powers. What is this evocativeness but another exploitation of the concept of association?

Association will be an important factor at every level of the listening experience. Our ethnic and national and social backgrounds can make us more partial to one kind of music than to another. Witness, for example, the sentimental glow that comes over a group of expatriates who are hearing the folk music of their homeland. This nostalgia for the familiar would certainly enter into their appreciation of.a piece of music in which that folk influence was present.

Even the sentimental association that results from the fortuitous hearing of a piece of music at the same time that we have had some emotionally charged personal experience can -influence our subsequent reactions to similar music. Granted that this is hardly the basis upon which to build an esthetic theory, since the sentimental associations are usually the result of an accidental juxtaposition of the music with the event. Still, is this not the source of the "our song" concept that we find in the more romantic motion pictures? The implications of this practice are perhaps more far-reaching than we might expect. The music chosen for such situations is almost invariably of the lush, romantic kind; the melodies of Tchaikovsky and Rachmaninoff are the prototypes. Once these associations have been made, can we possibly hear any music in that same style without having some recollection of the sentiment affect our reactions?

Now, to what extent does our liking for or our dislike of any particular musical instrument or family of instruments, or any type of human voice, reflect the preferences that each of us has for various types of sounds? To what extent is our reaction to any particular type of musical sound partly the result of deep-seated associations, whose origins we perhaps cannot even trace?

What we call the "tone color" of each instrument is a source of the sensuous pleasure that that instrument gives us (whether or not we are able to name the instrument without error as an oboe or a clarinet, or whatever the case may be). This tone color is also subject to certain particular associations for each one of us. An obvious example is the saxophone, whose tone color, associated for the most part with jazz, makes it an infrequent member of the symphony orchestra. When it is used in symphonic music, it cannot help bringing with it its associations.

The texture of the sound that impinges upon our ears is one of the sources of our emotional response to music. We all recognize the fact that we respond differently to the different speaking voices of various people. In the same way, the sounds of the various instruments affect each individual differently, and make for greater or lesser degrees of emotionalism, depending upon the sensuous pleasure that they afford.

Certain voices are pleasant to listen to, regardless of what the speaker is saying, just because of the attractiveness of the voice itself. When we disregard the content, or the sense of the words, and enjoy only the texture of the sounds, we may be said to be listening to the "sensuous" or the "musical" qualities of the voice. By extension, is it not true that the sense or the intellectual content of a spoken statement can be made more appealing by virtue of the sensuous attractiveness of the voice?

Political views can be made more appealing—within limits, of course—by the qualities of the voice that is uttering them. It is a known fact that voters are more likely to be swayed by the personality of a candidate than by a careful examination and consideration of his or her views and qualifications. Hence, the attention given to those aspects of speech and appearance that will make the personality more appealing. It goes without saying, of course, that the total personality, including physical appearance and facial expressions, must be considered. But when we are able to say of a candidate, "He or she sounds so sincere," notice to what extent our statement is the result of speech mannerisms, and of vocal tone color.

A good deal of the emotional appeal of music is based upon this sensuous attraction of sounds, and the different reactions that the sounds of various instruments create in us. Along with the "sense," the sensuous or "sensation" assumes great importance in music. To return to the analogy with speech: the intellectual *content* of any talk can be conveyed to us, irrespective of the beauty of the speaker's voice. If the content or the "sense" of what a speaker has to say is important enough or sufficiently impelling, we will listen, regardless of the vocal qualities. In music, however, the "sensation," the gratification that we derive from just hearing the sounds, is always of great importance.

This, as we noted earlier, is the basis of the art of orchestration. Composers are careful to present their "ideas," their themes or melodies—the "sense" of the music—in such a way that they are embodied in the most appealing "sensation," or instrumental coloration. Not only does the idea become more appealing by virtue of the sound of the particular instrument that utters it, but the variety, contrast, and cumulative effect of the sensations provided by the various Instruments supply another source of emotional gratification.

Here we might make a simple analogy. Suppose that the different sentences in a short story were to be printed in a variety of colored inks, with the colors ranging from cool to hot in order to heighten the emotional appeal of the respective thoughts. We should then have a form of "orchestration." The thought, the "sense," would remain inherent in the words themselves, of course; but the "sensation" of the colors—with their associations in the mind of the reader—would add another source of emotionalism.

The appeal of sensation as opposed to sense can be very easily demonstrated in another way. The sense of the following suggestion is readily apparent: "Think of the sound of chalk scraping on a blackboard." Now, try to disregard the sense, the meaning of those words, and their unpleasant implications. Instead, imagine the sentence spoken by an actor who pronounces the hard consonants in an especially crisp and pleasing way. Notice the physical pleasure to be derived from just the *sensation of* hearing the "k" in the word "think," the "d" in the word sound," the "k" in "chalk," and so forth. To the extent that you derived pleasure from this reading, you would be having an experience that partakes of the "musical."

As a further demonstration, we know that young children will often seize upon a word or phrase that they have heard, and repeat it endlessly, apparently for the sheer delectation that the sounds afford, with their particular rhythm, as well as for the pleasure to be derived from the activity of making those sounds, entirely irrespective of the sense. This is part of the stuff of which music is made.

In music, it is impossible to have the sense without the sensation. Think of any melody that may come to you—a familiar one, or even one that you make up. Notice that, if you sing it aloud, it has the sensuous embodiment of your own voice. If, on the other hand, you merely imagine it, you cannot avoid "hearing" it with some tonal coloration. You may purposely resolve that you will not hear it as played by a violin or by a trumpet or even by electronically produced tones. Yet, if you actually imagine the melody at all, you cannot avoid imagining it with *some* tonal embodiment. Moreover, buried in your imagination are your memories of all the musical instruments and voices you have ever heard.

Similarly, a composer is unable to express his musical ideas except in some sensuous embodiment. It is possible to retell the story of a dramatic poem in prose. Nothing comparable can be done with music. Musical content is contained in its sensuous embodiment. The two cannot be separated, for the simple reason that they are one and the same.

Now, to carry our experiment a step further: imagine a simple melody played by a flute; then imagine the same melody played by a violin. No matter how slightly, you have changed the *content* of the music. Granted that the melody—the sense—of the music remains unchanged. The fact nevertheless remains that the setting originally given to those notes by you (or by the composer, if you are dealing with an actual melody), with whatever sensuous qualities and emotional associations the sound of the flute may have, is a definite part of the content of the music. Besides being "about" the notes, or the melody, the music at that point is also "about" the sound of the flute.

A great deal of music is, of course, recast for instruments other than those for which it was composed. Symphonies, for example, are arranged for the piano for study purposes, and in order to afford people the pleasure of playing these orchestral works at home. Such piano reductions are the equivalents of black-and-white reproductions of oil paintings: they preserve the lines (the melodies); they reveal the draftsmanship (the form); but by reducing all the sounds to the single sound of the piano, they deny us the sensuous and emotional pleasures that the various instrumental colors afford. Of course, they do provide the tone of the piano, with its own particular coloration and its own emotional implications; but, in essence, the music's content has been changed. (I suspect that most people who play piano arrangements of orchestral works with which they are familiar probably "hear" the orchestral version in their mind's ear.)

Now, what of the possible delights to be found in musical sounds themselves? First, there are the myriad sensations to be had from the very tone of an instrument, just as we enjoy the texture of someone's speaking voice. Merely go down the list of instruments that we have in an orchestra, and there is an inventory of sensuous delights. Then, further sensuous, coloristic pleasures await us in the ways in which composers combine and contrast various instrumental timbres.

Just as the hard "k" of "chalk" can be a source of aural pleasure, so particular aspects of musical tone can be pleasing. The sound of the individual notes, in addition to the melody, in the piano music of Mozart, is a source of special pleasure. In the slow movements of his concertos, Mozart sometimes has a quiet passage in which the pianist is called upon to play, with one hand, a single line of melody, unharmonized. The exquisiteness of those moments stems in part from the contrast with the liveliness of the preceding movement, in part from the beauty of the melody itself, with its subdued orchestral accompaniment, and in part from the "ping" of the sound, as the individual hammers hit the strings. The dreamy nocturnes of Chopin also present the piano tone in this light, with their long-drawn-out melodies in the right hand.

The ramifications of this approach, and the possible sources of gratification it affords, are endless. There is a spine-tingling delight in the evenness of a quickly executed run on the piano—again, stemming not only from the shape of the melody itself, but also from the bell-like percussiveness of the sound of the piano. But listen to the very different sound of the piano in, let us say, Brahms's Second Piano Concerto. Here, the massiveness of the chords, the "thickness" of the sound, supplies a completely different kind of sensuous pleasure, drawing on who knows what deep-seated emotional overtones in each one of us.

Other typical sources of sensuous pleasure include the sound of a violin as it plays a series of notes very rapidly, with each note bowed separately. The fact that the resined hairs of the bow tend to stick to the strings imparts an almost percussive character to each separate note, which can be sensuously pleasing, and can heighten the emotional tension or excitement. Also, the sound as the violin bow "bites" the string at the beginning of a sustained, deep-throated, low note can have its emotional overtones. These contrasting qualities, of course, are to be found and enjoyed throughout the family of stringed instruments.

Also providing for this sensuous pleasure are the tones of the woodwind instruments (flute, oboe, clarinet, bassoon), when the notes are "tongued," that is, played with separate bursts of air, instead of *"legato,"* which would demand that many notes be played, rapidly or slowly, during one breath. Notice that the two different methods of producing the notes in the wind instruments create completely different effects in us. Imagine, also, the infinite variety of emotional effects that can be created by the planned combination of the two methods.

There is a still further pleasure to be had from the sounds of two or more solo voices or instruments—for example, two sopranos or two violins—when they are performing different parts. The blending of the voices or instruments produces a sensuous effect, at times, that is in fact more than the sum of the parts.

Sensuous pleasures and associations—how can we determine where one begins and the other leaves off, or how much of any so-called "pleasure" may be made up of associations whose origin we cannot trace? What hidden memories of feelings of physical warmth and security may be bound up with the general preference for rich, lush, "romantic" music? What physical parallels do we unconsciously draw between the pleasant tactile feeling of fur or velvet, and what we call the "velvety" sound of a large group of strings? Can we possibly hear a wind instrument being played without experiencing (perhaps not even consciously) some feeling of empathy with the player, since we recognize from the nature of the sound that he must use his breath, just as we do in talking and singing, and that the longer the melody, the greater the demands on his breath control?

What memories of our infantile crying, with the attendant quaver in our voices, are bound up with our interpretation of the "vibrato" as signifying emotionalism? We tend to regard the violin as being more emotional, more personal than the flute, because it lends itself more readily to the use of the vibrato. The tone of the flute is usually considered to be somewhat "cooler" in its emotional import.

To what extent did hunting horns evoke the feeling of the outdoors, when those instruments were first admitted into an indoor orchestra? And to what extent do we, today, upon hearing French horns in a modern work, still hear evocations of the outdoors? Is it not possible that when a composer gives a melody to the viola or the cello, in a high register, some of the impassioned quality that we may feel stems from our identification with the difficulty that the instrument has in playing unusually high? And can an unaccompanied chorus, singing in a large hall with much echo, fail to suggest "religious" music to us, regardless of what text it may actually be singing?

When a composer prescribes that all the violins are to play a passage with only the tip of the bow, what hidden association with our own vocalizations gives us a feeling of tentativeness as we hear that effect? Or would some of us feel that it is more properly a "floating" feeling? On what grounds?

Is there not a kind of physical identification with a chord in the massed strings, played by all the bows going in the same downward direction—even though we may never have held a stringed instrument in our hand? Do we not have enough responsive identification with the production of vocal sound, so that we can tell the difference—*feel* the difference, in fact—between a tone that is sung softly, and one that is sung loudly, but is coming from a great distance? We are not likely to confuse the different emotional implications of the two sounds.

These are just a few of the possible sources of emotional pleasure that we can derive from music. At every level, they stem from the two sources of sensuous pleasure and association.

The true appreciation of a piece of music, of course, requires detailed understanding, which involves conscious listening and attention. But once we have responded to the physical and sensuous appeals of the music—its emotional appeals—we are better able to embark upon the exploration of its other sources of interest.

CHAPTER 20

Listening for
Intellectual Pleasure

What we have termed the "intellectual pleasure" of music is at bottom a consciousness of the relationships among the parts of a piece of music. This embraces both the ability to discern the relationships among the sections of a movement—which is form—and—even more important—the ability to follow the ways in which a musical idea is transformed and developed. We shall explore each in turn.

How shall we go about listening to music to determine its form? Shall we approach each new piece of music with analytical ears and furrowed brow? Definitely not. If you are hearing a work for the first time, I recommend that you give no conscious thought to its form as such. Rather, enjoy the music's melodies, harmonies, rhythms, instrumental colors, and emotional effects. The first and most important step in getting to know any composition is to become familiar with it in these respects. Above all, become familiar with the melodies. Only then might it be advisable to listen to a piece whose form is announced in its title—a *Theme and Variations,* a *Minuet,* or a *Rondo*—and to try to follow its over-all form.

Theme and variations, minuet, scherzo, and rondo

The Theme and Variations can be a particularly rewarding form to begin with. In addition, it can serve our purpose as *a* way of becoming familiar with the techniques used by composers for transforming their melodies. To follow the changes in a theme sharpens our ability to follow a development. The Theme and Variations can be approached by starting with some of the simpler examples. The slow movement of Haydn's *Surprise Symphony* (the movement containing the loud chord

178

that gives the symphony its nickname) is excellent for this purpose. The same composer's variations on *Gott, erhalte, Franz den Kaiser* (or, as it was later known, *Deutschland über Alles)* in his so-called *"Emperor"* Quartet should also present no problems. Two brief, and very easy-to-follow, popular examples of the Theme and Variations form are the "Russian Sailors' Dance" from *The Red Poppy,* by Glière, and the Prelude to Bizet's *L'Arlesienne* Suite Number One.

Mozart's Piano Sonata in A Major (K.331) opens with a Theme and Variations; the concluding movement of his String Quartet in D Minor (K.421) is another easy example to follow.

Two of Schubert's best-known chamber works contain variations that should make rewarding listening for the beginner. They occur in his so-called *Trout Quintet* (the fourth movement), and in the String Quartet in D Minor, subtitled *Death and the Maiden* (the second movement). The latter variations contain some extremely dramatic music.

The second movement of Beethoven's Fifth Symphony is in the variation form, as are also the concluding movement of his Third Symphony, and the slow movements of his Seventh Symphony and Violin Concerto. His Piano Sonata Opus 26 opens with a set of variations that is fairly easy to follow, and the second movement of the *Appassionata Sonata* for piano (Opus 57) also should present no great problems. Note, however, that, since these are all extended movements, Beethoven sometimes writes variations on more than one melody. Thus, in the second movement of his Fifth Symphony, he varies two themes alternately. At other times, *both* themes may be presented simultaneously, as, for example, in the Finale of the Third Symphony, where the first theme shows up as an accompaniment to the second theme!

Should you wish to try something more complex and subtle in the way of variations, you might listen to the slow movement, and to the choral Finale of Beethoven's Ninth Symphony. From the point at which the famous "Ode to Joy" theme is introduced by the orchestral cellos and basses playing softly, the closing movement is essentially a huge Theme and Variations for orchestra, vocal soloists, and chorus.

In his *Variations on a Nursery Song,* for piano and orchestra, Ernst von Dohnanyi puts the familiar *Twinkle, Twinkle, Little Star* (also known as *Ah, vous dirai-je Maman)* through its paces. A word of warning, however: do not be taken in by the exceedingly dramatic, portentous introduction by the orchestra. Its intent is a humorous one, since it merely leads you to the entrance of the solo piano, playing the nursery tune in a *one-finger* version!

Prokofieff, in the second movement of his Third Piano Concerto, has written a delightful set of variations. After the orchestra has played the theme at the opening of the movement with a suggestion of eighteenth-century courtliness, watch for the first entrance of the piano, which suddenly presents the theme in an unexpected key. Besides being a piquant moment in itself, this demonstrates one of the ways in which composers achieve variety.

At this point the reader should be warned that composers have sometimes written variations whose connection with the original theme may be very tenuous. Brahms, in his orchestral *Variations on a Theme by Haydn,* and in his piano *Variations and Fugue on a Theme by Handel,* writes what might be considered "variations on variations." As the compositions progress, the music may seem to wander far from the original melody. The same may be said of the closing movement of his Fourth Symphony (a chaconne, as mentioned earlier), in which it is sometimes impossible to find the original theme without seeking it out, note by note, in the printed score. In such instances, we can appreciate the music for all its other appeals This should be borne in mind, too, at those moments in Elgar's orchestral *Enigma Variations* or Franck's *Symphonic Variations* for piano and orchestra, when you feel yourself getting lost. Repeated hearings of the music may finally make clear a relationship of any section with the theme, that at first seemed elusive.

Let us now see how to go about appreciating the formal structure of most minuets or scherzos—in symphonies, sonatas, quartets, and the like The over-all aspect to be aware of is the tripartite structure: the statement of a theme or group of themes, the digression into a contrasting section, the return to the first section. Listen to the minuet movement of almost any symphony by Haydn or Mozart. The over-all form will be ternary: the "A" section, called the minuet proper; the "B" section, called the "trio," which is a second minuet of somewhat more relaxed character; finally, a repetition of the first minuet.

The B section will usually be clearly discernible, both because it begins after the decisive ending of the A section, and because its melodies will generally be in sharp contrast to those already heard.

However, in listening to one of these minuets for the first time, you may fail to find the beginning of the B section. Your natural tendency, at first, will be to expect it each time you hear a "cadence"—which will sound like a more or less definite ending. (A "cadence," which is nothing more than a close, or an ending, is comparable to the dropping of the voice at the end of a sentence. It occurs at the end of a movement, at the end of a section, and at the end of most melodies. The "half-cadence," a less decisive ending, may be likened to the effect of a comma in a spoken sentence.)

As you encounter cadences, while still awaiting the beginning of the B section, remember that their presence indicates the presence of smaller "forms within forms." The minuet proper consists of several melodies, which, as already pointed out, are themselves likely to be in binary form. The repetitions of these melodies, which are prescribed in the score, increase the number of cadences that you will hear, before the B section is reached.

You will find that Mozart and Haydn often help you to identify the B section—the trio—when it comes along. The chances are that, in their desire to create a sense of contrast, they Ovid have changed the instrumentation in the trio. If the melody was given mainly to the strings in the minuet proper, it may be the wind instruments that are featured during the B section. In the trio, as in the minuet, watch for the music to break into smaller binary forms, with cadences and with repetitions.

When the trio has been concluded and there is a return to the A section, you will notice that this entire concluding section is shorter than it was at its first hearing. This is not an aural illusion. It is the result of the fact that the repetitions within the A section are not being played. It is assumed that the repetitions during the first hearing of the minuet were sufficient to familiarize you with the melodies. To hear them twice on their return would be too much of a good thing.

A word of warning: occasionally, Haydn or Mozart may impart a sense of unity to their minuets by carrying some idea over from the end of the A section into the beginning of the B section. It may be an accompanying figure, or it may be some characteristic part of a melody that occurs near the end of the first section. This makes the recognition of the start of the second section a little more difficult, but the difficulty may not last too long. In all likelihood, the B section will shortly present a completely different mood. The same carrying over of an idea may also happen upon the return to the A section.

It is well to remember that in the works of Beethoven and the later nineteenth-century composers, any of the sections of the scherzo can be considerably extended, so as to continue for a fairly long time. A good example of this expanded form is the scherzo of Beethoven s Third Symphony (the *Eroica*). Despite its length, however, the division into three parts is still apparent, with the beginning of the B section, or trio, clearly discernible at the entrance of the three French horns. In the *scherzi* of his Seventh and Ninth Symphonies, Beethoven further extends the form, by introducing the trio more than once. Schubert, in the scherzo of his Seventh Symphony, so elaborates the form that the A section is itself in the sonata-allegro form.

The rondo, although it involves a number of melodies, is a form that makes little intellectual demand upon the listener; as we have seen, it consists mainly of the alternation of one theme with others. The slow second movement of Beethoven's *Pathétique Sonata* for piano is in rondo form. It is an especially easy example to follow, since the themes are very clearly separated, in spite of the fact that they are all in a similar tranquil mood.

The final movement of the same composers Violin Concerto is also a rondo, and has three themes, presented in the following order: A B A C A B A. If you listen for the form of this movement for the first time, notice the constant reappearance of the lively opening theme. Remember, however, that the cadenza (the extended virtuosic passage for the unaccompanied violin, occurring just before the final reappearance of the A theme) was not composed by Beethoven, and is not a part of the form. Other examples of the rondo form occur as the final movement in many of Mozart s piano concertos.

Sonata-allegro form

Going on from the Theme and Variations, the minuet, scherzo, and rondo, how shall you listen to the more complicated sonata form? Some of the answer can perhaps be suggested if I recount an experience that I had when I was first becoming seriously interested in music. This was before the era of long-playing records, cassettes, or CDs, when a complete symphony occupied as many as eight or ten records. At an odd-lot sale, I happened to buy a single disc containing only the first four minutes of the opening movement of Brahms's Second Symphony, a work then unknown to me. For quite some time, my knowledge of the symphony was confined to the exposition of the first movement—that is, the statement of all the themes that Brahms was to use throughout that movement.

At the time, however, I was not aware that any of these themes might reappear. Later, when I heard the complete first movement for the first time, I had a remarkable musical experience. Here was music that was not only as appealing as that which I had found in the first four minutes of the movement, but which rose to heights of lyricism, excitement, and drama. The most interesting part of it was that, being familiar with the themes, I was able to recognize each one as it reappeared, and to follow its transformations. Without consciously realizing it, I was responding to musical development.

Now, was I also aware of the movements *sonata form?* If we mean a conscious awareness—with the ability to name the sections that I was hearing—then the answer is No. I was not in the least concerned with the exposition, development, and recapitulation that the textbooks emphasized. But the emotional *implications* of this standard form had their full effect, and the form, as I game to understand it, was merely the over-all shape in which Brahms had presented his material in order to make it as emotionally meaningful as possible. My complete familiarity with the opening four minutes—the exposition—by enabling me to recognize all the melodies, wherever they occurred, and however they were transformed and varied, gave me the insight into what it was that unified the movement. This is the crux of the matter of the understanding of sonata form—or, for that matter, of all form. If the means of unification are apparent to us, then the form will have its full effect.

Now, once having familiarized yourself with the melodies of the opening movement of a symphony, especially as they are presented in the exposition, the most important thing to be aware of is the development of those melodies. Recall the other names by which the development section is known—the working-out section and the free fantasia. The first sounds rather matter-of-fact, while the second is more poetic-sounding; both, however, describe what takes place.

It is here that the composers creativeness has the freest range; he is held in by nothing but the limits of his imagination and inventiveness. No rules govern the succession of the various elements, such as those that we find in the exposition. Anybody can invent themes (try it sometime; notice that it is relatively easy to imagine a melody with a Mozartian quality). Following the ground plan, it is possible to create a correct, if not necessarily inspired, exposition. But to write an exciting development is a more difficult matter, just because of the freedom that it entails.

In a sense, the development section of the sonata form should appeal to those who have a more romantic or poetic approach to music. All the elements of drama, conflict, and excitement—in short, all the emotionalism that the composer can find in the themes—are exploited here. As you listen to the development, do not try to anticipate what the composer will do. He may, if he wishes, use all the themes of the exposition, but he or she has equal freedom to base most or all of the development on some relatively obscure fragment of what may have seemed an unimportant bridge passage. Mozart, in fact, does that very thing in the opening movement of his *Jupiter Symphony* (Number Forty-one), developing a fragment from the codetta of the exposition.

There is no technique, no device that is denied the composer in the development. One may use the technique of variation, applying it to one or more ideas. One may use some of the contrapuntal devices discussed in an earlier chapter, such as augmentation—setting forth the melodies more slowly, which will make them sound more impressive. The opposite process—diminution—gives the melodies a more excited quality. One may present two melodies simultaneously. In this last case, notice how skillfully the melodies must be constructed, so that they will be interesting when heard separately, and yet will admit of being played simultaneously. It is also very possible that the composer will present one or more themes, or portions of them, in what sounds for a time like a fugue. A passage making use of the technique of fugal imitations is called a *"fugato"*—the Italian for "in fugue style."

Along with the rest of his artistic freedom in the development, the composer has complete freedom in the choice of keys. Typically, he will modulate through quite a range of keys in order to exploit the sense of drama through contrast. This is the portion in which one travels farthest from the home key of the movement—the tonic key—so that, when one does return to it, at the beginning of the recapitulation, there will be a definite sense of homecoming.

In short, the composer's main purpose in the development section is to be interesting: to show new facets of the themes, to present them in ways, in combinations, and in keys that we had not expected before, and to rise to great heights of emotionalism.

To guide you in your listening, it is well to bear in mind the fact that there is no set limit of length for the development. In the compositions (symphonies, quartets, sonatas) of Haydn and Mozart, the development sections are *relatively* short, usually occupying nowhere nearly so long a time as the expositions. It was Beethoven who increased the length of the development section until it became the center of gravity of the sonata form. Rather than regarding such a statement as merely a dry, historical fact, suppose we look at it from another angle.

We know that Beethoven's name is associated with the heights of self-expression in music, and we are often reminded of his daring, of his having advanced the frontiers of music. This is undeniably true. But it was his desire for greater emotional expression that led to his expanding the forms. In the course of giving greater scope to the emotional element in his music, he inevitably enlarged the development section, both in its length and in the power and drama with which he suffused it. Thus, it was *expressive* compulsions, and not *theoretical* considerations, that determined his expansions of the sonata form.

Beethoven's music, of all the music generally known, best exemplifies the concept of development, and the result is one of the chief sources of his greatness and of his popularity with listeners. It is just because of the excitement and drama of Beethoven's developments that the average, untrained listener finds his music so compelling, whether or not he realizes, consciously, that he is listening to a "development" as such.

Our discussion of listening to developments brings us to an extremely important principle in music, one that is too often overlooked in the conventional, romantic approach toward music appreciation. According to that approach, it is customary to speak of the "inspired melodies" of the great composers, as if those melodies alone were the reason for the composers' greatness. This viewpoint puts the emphasis in the wrong place. Naturally, it takes a great gift to be able to create melodies such as those we find, say, in the works of Schubert and Tchaikovsky. The origin of such melodies will always be a source of wonder to us.

The true greatness of a composer, however, lies not so much in his melodies as in what he *does* with them. Liszt's *Hungarian Rhapsody* and Enesco's *Roumanian Rhapsody,* which we discussed in Chapter Sixteen, both contain many appealing melodies, but relatively little "happens" to them. Consequently, these compositions, and others like them, do not compare in greatness with the first movement of Beethoven's Fifth Symphony, which stems for the most part from a brief, four-note figure that can almost be described as "*un*melodious." The Liszt and Enesco works might be likened to a beauty contest, in which a succession of beautiful girls parades by. But one would hardly look for "drama" in such an instance. The opening movement of Beethoven's Fifth Symphony, on the other hand, can be compared with a play, based on no more than two or three characters. The physical beauty of the characters is less important than the emotion that is generated by exploring each one of them in depth.

Some of the very greatest among composers—Mozart and Beethoven, for example—were not outstanding as melodists, in the conventional sense. To be sure, they could create some magnificent melodies; but just as often, they would use as their starting points seemingly unpromising motives, based on simple scale passages or chord patterns.* It is their ability to make

---

*At a gathering during which several pianists were rivaling one another at improvising, Beethoven, as he strode to the piano, is said to have picked up the cello part of a work that had been played earlier placed the music upside down on the piano rack, and used the arbitrary result as the theme of his improvisation.

exciting, compelling music out of almost nothing—the capacity for sustained thought—that makes them creative geniuses.

Proceeding now to the third section of the sonata form, how shall we listen to the recapitulation—the return to the beginning? Again, let us view the form, not as an academic following of rules, but rather as the means of supplying our need for emotional expression. Imagine, for a moment, that we have just listened to a turbulent development section. Using any or all of the devices that are available, the composer has taken us far afield, has increased the tension, by hurling the themes back and forth among the instruments, and by taking us into many different keys. Then, at the moment of climax, or perhaps just past it, we hear again the first theme—the main melody of the movement—proclaimed in its original form and in its original key. It is the point of greatest affirmation, the moment when the main theme is presented to us in a bright, clear light, after the darker harmonies that accompanied it during the development. It is, with the possible exception of the very end of the movement, the place where the theme is heard with its greatest effect.

This will be the case even if the first theme is presented softly, rather than dramatically—which is exactly what happens in the first movement of Mozart's *Symphony Number Forty*, the G Minor. After creating a certain amount of turbulence in the development, Mozart ends that section with a brief passage that quietly merges with the beginning of the recapitulation. However, so strong is the sense of returning to the home key, that you will have no trouble discovering the moment at which the recapitulation begins.

Remember, first, that it occurs about two-thirds of the way through the movement; second, that you will have listened to the entire development section, which will be the stormiest part of the movement, with (in this symphony) the first three notes of the opening theme exploited at length, very vigorously and turbulently; then remember the brief, quiet passage that ends the development. It is played by the woodwinds. It will seem to be a transition; its constantly descending fragments of melody will tend to carry you along. Your mind will follow the descending harmonies, seeking a place of rest, just as a gently falling leaf tends toward a place of rest on the ground. Yet, after taking us through these descending harmonies, at the very moment at which Mozart reaches the home key—the point of rest that we have been seeking—he reintroduces the first theme.

The purpose of the recapitulation, as mentioned earlier, is to recall the themes of the exposition, to emphasize the feeling of return after the excursion into other realms, just as the final line of a song is often a repetition of the opening line. While the composer may recapitulate all the themes of the exposition, he is not required to do so. A sense of proportion will dictate how much emphasis is to be placed on the various themes, and which, if any, to omit or change. One may even develop the themes further during the recapitulation, or even later, during the coda. Beethoven blazed the way for this use of continuing development in the sonata form.

Even the most literal sort of recapitulation serves a specific emotional purpose. The reason is not hard to discover. First, you were exposed to the themes (for the moment, let us call them the characters of the drama); then, in the development section, we might say that you witnessed the unfolding of the plot. The recapitulation is then a recollection of the themes, more or less as they were before the drama was wrung from them. Your outlook toward them is now colored by your knowledge of what has happened to them.

The return to the beginning is, therefore, a rounding out of a larger emotional experience. To drive home this point, we might consider the effect of the recapitulation on a listener who arrives late at a concert, and hears only the third section of the movement. Since he or she will have missed the drama of the development section, the themes of the recapitulation will not possess for him or her the emotional implications that they have for you. This, then, demonstrates in another way that form is determined in large measure by our emotional needs.

CHAPTER 21

Some Additional
Suggestions for Listening

Perhaps the most important factor in your listening is not the possible complexity of the music, but your attitude. Since your purpose in being concerned with form in music is to increase the amount of enjoyment and satisfaction that you derive from listening, you should not let your attempt to learn more about the form of any piece of music cause you to lose track of the immediate rewards of the music. Furthermore, you should not try to identify every small detail.

In many cases, your *feelings* about the music will be your best guide to the larger, more important divisions. For example, in listening to the first movements of many symphonies and concertos, you may discover a point at which the "plot" seems to "thicken." The relatively even temper of the opening gives way to a sense of tension. There is an increase in excitement, or perhaps a hint of impending excitement, brought about by a sudden shift in the harmonies, or a darkening of the instrumental colors. Any of these is likely to mark the beginning of the development section. Similarly, the end of the development section and the beginning of the recapitulation may be that point at which the music seems to "come out of the woods," and to give you the sense of being "in the clear" again. After you have let your own emotional responses serve as your guides to the delineation of the large divisions of the forms, all sorts of formal refinements and subtleties will present themselves to you with each new listening.

Let us try to anticipate some of the difficulties you are likely to encounter as you try to follow a movement in sonata form for the first few times. There is a real likelihood that, at first, you may be hopelessly lost. In your desire to discover the various sections, you will tend to grasp at any slight change of pace, of harmony, of mood, and regard that as the beginning of a new section. Then you may imagine—according to your 'Calculations"—that you are at the end of the movement, and be dismayed to find that the movement continues, seemingly endlessly. In reality, you may have come only to the end of the exposition. This simply points up the desirability of your being reasonably familiar with the piece before you try to analyze it. Your knowledge of the music itself will give you a feeling for its length and proportions, and thus help you to avoid such an error.

In spite of your familiarity, there may come times when a composition seems to defy all of your efforts to ascertain its form. At such moments, remember that no two pieces of music—beyond the simplest songs—are likely to be in precisely the same form. Just as there are few persons who can be said to conform to the average in all respects, so with musical compositions. Further, as has been mentioned in connection with the minuet and scherzo, composers often make the joinings between different sections of a movement as unobtrusive as possible. After all, their purpose is to create music that gives a convincing sense of continuity; they are not trying to prove that they know the order in which the sections should occur in the standard forms. Thus, your task of discovering the boundaries of those sections becomes even more difficult.

Remember, too, that composers will sometimes indulge in a certain amount of development in places other than the development section. Moreover, it is not uncommon to find some development during the course of a rondo; thus, we can have a form known as a "rondo-sonata," which partakes of both forms—and incidentally adds to the difficulty of identification.

As you may gather from all this, the composer, thinking in musical terms as opposed to verbal terms, has the freedom to do things that we, using words, can define only with the greatest difficulty. Within the realm of strictly musical thought, we can accept a greater degree of logical freedom than we can in the field, say, of argument. If, during the course of a logical dispute, one person were to introduce an entirely new subject, we should immediately declare his point irrelevant. In music, it is "assumed" that all the themes that will appear in the course of a movement in the sonata-allegro form are expected to make their appearance in the exposition. Beethoven, however, in the first movement of his Third Symphony, introduces a brand new theme in the *development* section. We are told that the first hearers of this symphony were outraged at Beethoven's breaking of the rule, but I confess to taking this story with a grain of salt, finding it difficult to believe that audiences were that much more knowledgeable in 1805 than they are in our own time. I have never noticed any stir among present-day audiences when that unexpected theme appears.

Now, if generations of listeners have accepted that particular movement as one of the most thrilling in all music, without being disturbed by—without even being *aware* of—the fact that a new theme has been introduced where none was expected, does this not suggest that our need to recognize musical form is far less important than the theoreticians would have us believe? It is for this reason that I maintain that we can accept a greater degree of freedom in purely musical thought than we can in other fields. If our emotional needs are met, and if our sense of continuity is satisfied, we are not inclined to be concerned with deviations from the conventional forms. By a reverse logic, we might say that this was precisely Beethoven's motivation. He adapted and extended the sonata-allegro form when he found that the purely classical model no longer served his expressive needs. In other words, what we are observing in his Third Symphony is the trend toward the kind of formal freedom in music that was later to be described as "romanticism."

As you go further into your listening for form, you should draw comfort from the fact that you are certainly not alone in your possible confusion about the various musical structures. Although this statement may sound like heresy, I am convinced, as the result of dealing year after year with the questions of music lovers in classes and seminars, that most of the subtleties of the construction of music are unrecognized even by the sophisticated listener. We might say, therefore, that the composition of an involved musical work is one of mankind's most inefficient undertakings, if by "efficiency" we mean the amount of the "yield" (in this case, the listener's recognition and understanding of subtle relationships), as compared with the amount of thought and effort expended by the composer.

In passing, one wonders that composers continue to create, in view of the fact that such a tremendous proportion of their effort goes unappreciated, even in the cases of those works that attain great popularity and are therefore regularly performed.

Realistically, it is undoubtedly the direct emotional appeals of these works that make them popular, rather than the subtleties of their forms.

In addition to your confusion regarding the intricacies of the various forms, you may at a certain stage find yourself baffled by the common generic titles: "Overtures" and "Preludes" that do not introduce anything; "Intermezzos" that come between nothing; "Capriccios" that are not the least bit capricious; "Waltzes" and "Minuets" that are impossible to dance to; "Scherzos" that are anything but playful and "Etudes," "Fantasias," and "Impromptus" that seem indistinguishable from one another. The very existence of so many titles, and the ease with which they can be confused one with another, suggest that they are not exact, and that the listener therefore ought not to be concerned with their applicability, except as means of identification.

Regardless of title or typical form, the over-all construction of a large work is the composer's means of giving order to his ideas. The design is comparable to the ground plan of a building. Just as architects have found that certain basic forms best meet the needs of people, depending upon the purpose of the building, so composers have found that certain basic musical forms best satisfy us, depending upon the purpose of the music. As long as the form makes for the best expression of what the composer has to say, we will "feel" its rightness.

Because of the nature of our response to music, our tolerance is apt to be very wide indeed. That is why we can be pleased by an endless variety of forms. It accounts for our acceptance of the first movement of a concerto that may have two expositions: one for the orchestra alone, and the second when the soloist enters. It allows us to enjoy a concerto, even though that form usually lacks a scherzo movement.* It also permits us to enjoy a concerto even when one or more of its movements is interrupted by extended passages, called "cadenzas," which are merely vehicles for the display of the soloist's virtuosity.

This latitude in our tolerance to musical form also enables us to enjoy a "sonatina," which is a sonata movement from which the development section has been omitted, or replaced by just a brief episode between the exposition and the recapitulation.

*The Second Piano Concerto of Brahms is an exception.

It enables us to enjoy Liszt's *Hungarian Rhapsody Number Two,* which is in only two large sections, a slow one and then a fast one. And it enables us to absorb all the other digressions from the standard forms, without our thinking about them as digressions. (These are legion, if we judge by the fact that there is hardly a symphony or concerto about which the program notes do not describe one of the movements as being "unusual from the formal standpoint," for one reason or another.)

Our response to form is the least developed of our reactions to music; it really exists only in a broad sense. We can accept works whose form is so loose that the theoreticians can do no better than to refer to them as "free forms," such as the toccata. (Note that they still feel impelled to label them, even when the label negates itself.)

Incidentally, form by itself, no matter how perfect it may be, or how interesting in its digressions from the norm, is not enough to draw people to a piece of music. Consider the fact that a piano sonata or a string quartet may be cast in as fine a form as a symphony or concerto. Yet other factors, such as the greater tonal allure of a full orchestra, or the fascination of watching a famous soloist perform, will make the symphony or concerto far more popular.

As you concern yourself increasingly with listening for form, it will be important to keep in mind a basic fact about musical structure: every musical idea—whether it is a melody, theme, motive, harmonic progression, or simply a rhythmic figure—serves several purposes. First, to some degree, it gives immediate pleasure; second, it may be developed in some way—in other words, it is capable of growth; third, it also serves a structural function in the over-all design, just as a column of a building helps to support the edifice, in addition to being decorative. Regrettably, it is these last two functions that are ignored by the writers who base their appreciation of music on merely calling attention to its "inspired melody."

The very process of discovering the relationships among sections of a piece of music that at first seemed unrelated contributes to our gratification. Therefore, what may seem to be an intellectual process becomes in itself a source of emotional pleasure. Listeners feel a satisfaction as they become aware of the fact that Mozart, in the first movement of his G Minor Symphony, creates so many different emotional states by the way he uses just the first three notes of his opening theme. In other words, they are now following Mozart's *musical thoughts,* as well as the emotional states that he induced.

The ending of the "Funeral March" of Beethoven's *Eroica Symphony is* a very emotional moment, consisting of a whispered melody punctuated with frequent silences. The pauses produce a feeling of extreme pathos. To realize that this moving music, which might almost be said to suggest sobbing, is actually the opening melody of the movement broken up and with the rhythms slightly changed is a source of esthetic wonder. Here, again, as we become aware of the continuity of *musical* thought, we add to our emotional satisfaction.

Music abounds in such relationships. There is no single technique for listening that will point out the subtleties of all music. The technique varies from one kind of music to another. Thus, Debussy's *Prelude to the Afternoon of a Faun* is meant to be listened to less for its over-all structure than for its sensuous, evocative qualities, for the vague, misty characteristics of its harmonies and orchestral coloring. Here thematic development, as such, assumes a subordinate role. The last movement of Mozart's *Symphony Number Thirty-nine,* on the other hand, shows how an entire structure can be generated out of just one simple melodic idea. In deriving from that idea music with a changing emotional coloration, Mozart, in effect, holds the melody up to the light, and shows us what possibilities are inherent in it.

Listen repeatedly. Become familiar with the melodies, preferably to the point where you are able to sing them, but at least familiar enough for you to recognize them. Then watch for their growth and transformations. As you develop your skill in listening, let your ears wander; do not listen only to the "top." Listen to the bass part and to the parts in the middle. At concerts, watching the conductor as he "cues in" the instruments will often give you suggestions as to which instruments have the most important part. Do not expect to hear everything; more is offered than can possibly be grasped.

Almost always you will find that there are portions of a composition that are more appealing than others. It is possible that these will present themselves to you during your early, more casual hearings of a work. By all means, use them for whatever emotional satisfactions they may afford.

When you look forward to hearing those portions, you are truly appreciating that music. It might be well, sometimes, to look further into those moments, and to ask yourself what it is in the music that makes it so affecting. Therein may lie an indication of your own susceptibilities to music.

Repeated listening to a specific work offers still another advantage: the music impresses itself upon our memories, so that we are soon able to anticipate what comes next. Hearing one phrase will then often bring with it the expectation of the next phrase, or of a particular chord or harmonic progression or instrumental effect. The satisfaction of each anticipation is another of the sources of emotional pleasure in listening. Thus, the more intimately acquainted we become with a work, the better we are able to recognize the subtler changes that a composer brings to bear on the themes. It is a never-ending source of gratification to recognize "old friends"—the themes—especially when they show up in unfamiliar guises.

All this is perfectly within the power of the layman to achieve; it is a curious but advantageous fact that, in an art whose creation requires so much technical skill, appreciation of a very high order is possible for the listener with no technical knowledge. Just as it is possible for anyone to enjoy the taste of a fine dish without knowing the recipe, so it is possible for us to appreciate fully the effects of a series of chords without knowing the technical names of the progressions. Similarly, to observe what a composer does with a theme, or the ways in which he combines themes, is well within the grasp of anyone who cares to listen attentively, whether or not one can give the technical nomenclature for what is happening.

(These transformations of the themes are, of course, not to be waved aside as being merely the technical aspect of music, and therefore of interest only to the professional. On the contrary, the development of the themes or of the musical ideas is what the music is "about.")

If our appreciation of music is to go beyond Santayana's all too apt description of what most people derive from music—"a drowsy reverie interrupted by nervous thrills"—then we owe it to ourselves to become familiar with what we are listening to. Roughly, we might say that it is the equivalent of listening for the content of an actor's lines in a play, as well as for the quality of his voice.

Here, incidentally, is another means of expanding one's listening horizons. The novice who has shied away from piano and violin sonatas, trios, quartets, and quintets, just because they do not supply the large-scaled sensuous rewards of orchestral works, may learn to appreciate following a composer's thoughts on a more intimate level. The range of tone colors is smaller with fewer instruments; but the development of the ideas is no less sophisticated in a chamber work than it is in an orchestral work. Although the appeals of chamber music may not be quite as immediate, they may be ultimately more rewarding.

Eventually, as our skill in listening develops, the stage is reached where we do not have to wait for only the "high spots' of a composition, with our minds wandering during the other portions. Instead, a piece of music becomes a discourse that can be appreciated from beginning to end.

CHAPTER 22

Listening to Program Music

Despite what may appear to be a condemnation of program music in Part One, my purpose has not been to evaluate such music, but merely to free the troubled listener from the fear that, because one does not see the pictures or discern the story from the music, one cannot understand or appreciate the music.

For all practical purposes, the process of listening to program music is no different from that of listening to absolute music. In fact, in a philosophical sense, it might be argued t at *all* music is program music. If by program music we mean music that expresses something outside the realm of mere organized sounds, then any music that has even a trace of emotional quality can be said to concern itself with something other than merely the organization of sounds, since it impinges on the realm of human feelings.

But all music has emotional implications, even if in some cases they are of a marginal order. The corollary of this view is that—again, speaking philosophically—there is no such thing as absolute music. Even the most classical work by Mozart, based on themes handled according to purely musical precepts, has its emotional implications. We might say, therefore, that our approach to program music differs from our approach to absolute music only in degree. That degree is determined by the extent to which we admit extramusical concepts into our consideration of the work at hand. So much for the philosophical approach.

Let us now briefly consider two examples, one of absolute music, the other of program music. After determining how each demonstrates the attributes of its category, we shall see how much they have in common.

There are tremendous differences in style between Mozart's *G Minor Symphony, (Number Forty)* which exemplifies the classic spirit, and the *Fantastic Symphony* of Berlioz, which exemplifies the romantic. Mozart deals with a group of abstract musical ideas that have no connection with anything outside the realm of music—except their emotional implications, which are left unspecified. Berlioz, on the other hand, allegedly sets out to illustrate a series of episodes in the life of a young musician who poisons himself with opium in an outburst of amorous despair. Since they start with such different aims, it is inevitable that the two compositions should be quite different. (The process of discovering and exploring such differences, incidentally, constitutes one of the pleasures to be derived from music.)

The Mozart symphony is characterized by relative emotional restraint, traditional patterns of thematic exposition, development, and recapitulation, and a comparatively limited use of the orchestral palette. In its conformity to the molds of its time, much of it can almost be said to have a predictable quality. The Berlioz symphony is much freer in its emotional tone as well as in its structure, and exploits the colors of the orchestral instruments to a much greater extent. It calls for a much larger orchestra; further, it has a larger "dynamic range" (by which is meant the contrast between soft passages and loud), with more numerous and greater dynamic changes. All these features make the *Symphonie fantastique* a much less predictable work than the Mozart. In addition, the Berlioz work is considerably longer, being in five movements instead of the conventional four.

Yet, for all their striking contrasts, the musical differences are ultimately differences of degree rather than of kind. Despite the individual qualities of each work, their similarities are greater than their differences. Both works, being subject to the laws of *musical* organization before anything else, tend toward the condition of absolute music, and can be listened to as such.

It is accepted, even among devotees of the storytelling approach, that any composition must stand on its own feet as *music*, irrespective of its extramusical associations. In other words, no matter how dramatic the implied story is, or how beautiful the suggested pictures, or how ideal the philosophy, these cannot make a bad piece of music better. A piece of good program music must be able to stand the test of being listened to and enjoyed without the necessity of the hearer's reading the story or *even knowing the title.*

As examples, consider any one of the following works, each of which is an acknowledged masterpiece in the realm of program music: Tchaikovsky's *Romeo and Juliet,* Liszt's *Les Préludes,* Moussorgsky's *Pictures at an Exhibition,* Dukas's *The Sorcerer's Apprentice,* and Strauss's *Till Eulenspiegel.* Every one of them can stand the test of being listened to for itself, by a listener who knows neither the title nor the story. Each generates its own excitement, partly because of the effects of the melodies, the rhythms, the harmonies, and the orchestral coloring; each offers a wonderfully imaginative exploitation of the intellectual and emotional possibilities inherent in the themes.

Tchaikovsky's *Romeo and Juliet* overture-fantasy is in sonata form. Listen to the ways in which the opening theme returns later in the work. At the beginning of the composition, the melody is played quietly by the wind instruments at a stately pace. A peculiar beauty is created as a result of the melody's shape, its speed, the chords, and the sounds of the combined wind instruments. (We are told that this is supposed to represent Friar Laurence.) Notice, later on, how this same theme returns. It is no longer confined to the wind instruments, but distributed among the various groups, played faster, and with the previously calm phrases broken up by the interjection of the other accompanying motives. The result is that a sense of excitement takes hold of us. (There is certainly no equivalent transformation of Friar Laurence in Shakespeare's drama.)

Here is the source of the appreciation of that portion of the music—emotionally, in the feeling that each section gives us; intellectually, in the realization that the endless variety of emotional tones have their roots in the same source—the opening melody. The same process takes place with each of the other melodies in the work—melodies which contrast with one another emotionally, and which are also the source of the music's *development.*

This is also the way to appreciate many so-called "character" overtures, such as Beethoven's *Coriolanus* and *Egmont* Overtures, which are also in sonata form. Each might well have served as the opening movement of a symphony. Similarly, Mendelssohn's Overture to *A Midsummer Night's Dream* and his *Hebrides* Overture, as well as Weber's *Oberon* Overture, are in sonata form. Despite the programmatic ascriptions to the various melodies, each of these compositions follows its own musical course, and can be fully understood and enjoyed as abstract music.

Listen to the ways in which Liszt derives an entire work, *Les Préludes*—with its variety of emotional states—out of just two melodies. We are treated to so many different moods that, at first hearing, it seems as if Liszt had used a great number of themes. Yet, as we get to know the work, we find that the long, flowing main melody with its romantic emotional tone is actually used again as the basis for the turbulent section.

Moussorgsky follows a different over-all plan in his *Pictures at an Exhibition.* This is a series of short pieces, each of which is said to be a musical portrayal of a specific painting. (There are ten paintings in all.) Each piece has a different theme and a different emotional coloration, and each is an exploration of its respective melodies. As a way of binding the first five pieces together, the melody with which the work begins reappears before each movement, or each "picture." This is said to be the "promenade" theme, representing the composer (or the listener) walking from one picture to another.

We can use this example to see how much more satisfaction there is in the music than in the story. Granted that we can easily accept the suggestion of the opening melody representing the "promenade." (It suffers, of course, from the limitations of all music, in that it cannot *by itself* convey the idea of a promenade; once the suggestion has been made verbally, however, the theme is certainly appropriate.) But how long can the adult mind maintain interest in such a simple idea as that of walking from one picture to another? Intellectually, there is nothing here that we cannot grasp immediately.

Now consider the music. With each reappearance, the "promenade" theme is musically transformed so that it projects a different mood, a different feeling. Because of the sensuous pleasures to be derived from the sounds, the harmonies, and the rhythms, we can listen to it repeatedly. It is precisely because *it can be dissociated from the programmatic concept*—the never-changing, specific concept of mere walking—that the music can continue to interest us. We derive immediate pleasure from any one transformation of the melody; we also derive another form of pleasure from observing the ways in which each transformation differs from all the others.

The approach to this relatively simple example may be followed even with such supposedly complicated stories as *The Sorcerer's Apprentice* and *Till Eulenspiegel*. The stories themselves do not contain enough substance to warrant *a* great many repetitions; in fact, the point is too seldom made that these particular stories, and any number more that have allegedly prompted the composition of highly sophisticated music, are on a rather childish level.

Probably every program note ever written about *Till Eulenspiegel* states that the music opens with a "once-upon-a-time" feeling. Aside from the fact that the same statement could be made about *any* work that begins softly, and that there is nothing whatsoever in the music that says or even suggests "once upon a time," it is a safe assumption that every one of these explanations fails to mention the important point—which is that the gentle, lyrical first melody contains the seeds out of which much of the music grows.

Till Eulenspiegel is actually in rondo form. Listen for the way in which the quiet opening melody reappears throughout the work in numerous transformations, presented with different instrumental colorings and different harmonies, and creating different moods in the listener each time as a result of the imagination that Strauss shows in the *development* of the music. Here is the source of the true appreciation of one of the masterpieces of orchestral music—the music itself. How much more rewarding that opening phrase becomes when we listen to it both for its momentary effect and with an awareness that the major portion of the entire composition will grow out of it. Let us leave the "once-upon-a-time" approach where it belongs—in the realm of children's stories. It has nothing to do with music.

Now, let me seem to reverse myself slightly and suggest the extent to which we may include the program of a composition in our listening. We are faced with the historical fact that composers have written some of the world's greatest music while motivated (or allegedly motivated) by some extramusical concept. One need not be so lacking a sense of romance as to exclude completely Berlioz's concern for the woman he loved, as she is remembered in his *Fantastic Symphony,* nor so lacking in a sense of humor as not to recognize the lighthearted motivation for Till Eulenspiegel's irreverent roguishness. Our attempt to enlarge our appreciation of music should certainly include a knowledge of the composer's thought processes,as well as the kind of esthetic outlook that was prevalent in his time. Such information serves to fill in the background of our understanding.

The danger lies in the possibility that we may grant too much importance to the programs. Read the story behind the *Fantastic Symphony;* note the subtitles of the various movements. You will then have all the insight into the composer's dramatic imagination that you need. The details of the story are utterly unimportant. His music, not his relationship with Harriet Smithson, is what makes him an important figure. The English authority on Berlioz, W. J. Turner, once said on this point: "I do not need any program—and never did need a program—to understand Berlioz's *Symphonie fantastique,* my pleasure in hearing it being purely musical and precisely of the same nature as my pleasure in hearing any one of Beethoven's quartets."

This attitude is the one that will help you to appreciate any music. Enjoy the *Fantastic Symphony* for its melodies, its moods, its rhythms, and for its imaginative use of the orchestral instruments. Revel in the power of the brass instruments; let yourself be pleased by the coloristic effect of a single loud plucked chord by all the strings, followed by a gentle tap on the cymbals—the contrast in itself is a source of pleasure; let yourself be swept along by the wildness of the climaxes. In addition, as your familiarity with the music increases, discover for yourself how the central melody (the *"idée fixe"*) reappears in each of the movements, transformed in mood.

Similarly—although it is in a totally different style—enjoy the dreamy, atmospheric quality of Debussy's *Nuages* ("Clouds"), one of his three *Nocturnes* for orchestra. Do you find the music indeterminate? Is it difficult to follow a clearcut melody? That is one of the attractions of *Nuages*. Try giving yourself up to the sensuous sounds of the delicately used orchestra; let yourself be carried along by the melting harmonies, the chords used for their coloristic effects, and the feeling of haziness that they create. This is music that fits its title very well indeed. Once you have grasped the musical purposes—and freed yourself from the specific pictorial connotations of the title—there are endless satisfactions to be had from listening to this score. The same points might be made about Debussy's piano pieces—say, the popular "The Girl with the Flaxen Hair" and *Claire de Lune.* These are miniature mood pieces, each one a self-contained musical entity, each with its own particular *musical* theme. In each, watch for the return of the theme, with its gentle, dreamy harmonization.

It is not music's weakness, but its strength, that it communicates to us not through pictures or words, but through the elements of melody, rhythm, harmony, tone color, and form. Thus, whether we are hearing the alleged ticking of a clock in the second movement of Haydn's so-called *Clock Symphony* (Number 101), or the alleged murmuring of a stream in Handel's *Acis and Galatea,* or the alleged swelling of the waves in Debussy's *La Mer,* or the alleged activities of the faun in his *Prelude to the Afternoon of a Faun,* we need to listen above all to the ways in which each composer makes his music germinate and grow. To imitate a clock in music is nothing more than a trick, but to make a ticking motive grow into a meaningful *musical* composition requires genius. Why should we accept less than a musical work has to offer us?

CHAPTER 23

How to Recognize
Composers

Among the many satisfactions to be derived from listening to music, one important one has its roots in our ability to recognize a composer's style. Such recognition gives us a sense of being at home with a composer as we listen to his or her music. The sense of familiarity that we carry over from one of his works to another constantly reinforces our feeling of kinship with him. Then too, the more we know about a composer's style, the better we are able to place him among his contemporaries. Here, incidentally, is another source of pleasure in music—the enjoyment of a work not only for its immediate satisfactions, but in perspective, against the background of its time.

For example, the *Fantastic Symphony* of Berlioz becomes even more fantastic when we stop to realize what an astounding innovator he was, in the coloristic use of the orchestra. Music has long since absorbed his innovations into its main stream, so that today we are, perhaps, hardly conscious of them. In a sense this taking for granted of innovations is a pity, since our present-day background deprives us of the feelings of surprise with which Berlioz's contemporaries heard his music.

Besides, a deepening knowledge of styles enables us to differentiate between the early and late works of the same composer. It is fascinating to compare the Haydnesque music of the young Beethoven with his later creations, some of which (his *Grand Fugue,* Opus 133, for example, or the fugue from his *Hammerklavier Sonata* for piano, Opus 106) sound as if they might have been written in the twentieth century. We can learn to trace many a composer's development from his early stage as an imitator to his emergence as an original creator. Thus we see that familiarity with style can be a source of interest and gratification, over and above the satisfaction that comes from merely being able to identify a composer from his music.

Now, how shall we go about recognizing composers? Let us start by seeing how we differentiate among the largest categories of music.

Any one of us can tell a piece of jazz from a classical work. As simple as this sort of differentiation may seem, remember that our ability to make it depends solely upon our awareness of the ways in which the basic musical elements are used. If you are inclined to say that jazz is easy to spot because it sounds "jazzy," realize what is summed up in that word. You are acknowledging that you recognize certain customary ways of handling melody, rhythm, and the other elements. You no longer have to consider each element separately. It is the "sound" or "feel" of the music as a whole that immediately identifies its style. Similarly, when a work "sounds like" classical music to you, you are bringing to bear a familiarity with a broad musical idiom.

Now let us see how we differentiate among various kinds of music within the same category. Most of us would have no trouble telling that a piece of music was folk music, regardless of the country of its origin; doubtless most of us can recognize the differences among an Italian folk song, a Negro spiritual, a Russian folk song, and a Spanish folk song. We are, of course, influenced by the language in which the song is sung, but so characteristic are the respective styles that the majority of us could probably identify the national origins of these songs even if they were not sung but were played by instruments. It is the rhythm of the spiritual, the contour of the Russian melody, and the nature of the accompaniment of the Spanish song, among many other things, that determine the specific styles.

Our next task is to refine our skill in differentiating among various kinds of concert music. The first broad determination to be made is the period in which any work was composed, since each period has its own characteristic style. In the case of orchestral music, much can be gleaned about the period merely from the size of the performing body. A large orchestra is likely to indicate a nineteenth-century work. The symphonies of Beethoven and of later composers of the romantic period depend for their effectiveness, in part at least, upon the sheer volume of the massed tone. This is particularly true of the music of such composers as Berlioz, Liszt, Wagner, Brahms, Tchaikovsky, and Strauss. The style of their writing—one of the factors that causes us to characterize it as "romantic"—is bound up with the lushness of the sound. Anywhere from sixty-five to a hundred players may be needed for their music. A symphony from the "classical" era of Haydn or Mozart, on the other hand, can be quite well performed with as few as thirty-five or forty players. A baroque work—say from the pen of Bach, Handel, or Vivaldi—will call for an even smaller number.

The size of the performing body is usually related to the texture of the music, thus giving us another means of identifying the period in which it was composed. The smaller orchestra or chorus is more suited to the clear articulation of individual lines, or strands of music, typical of the polyphonic texture of the baroque era, while the more massive, homophonic texture of the romantic era is more readily produced by the larger orchestra.

This is a generalization, however, to which there are many exceptions. As pointed out earlier, there is a good deal of mixture of textures in baroque, classical, and romantic music. Incidentally, many twentieth-century works are composed for small ensembles, not because composers are unwilling or unable to write for giant orchestras, but because the rising cost of engaging large groups of players seriously diminishes the chance of performance. As unglamorous as this may seem, it is one of the reasons contributing to the reawakening of interest in polyphonic music on the part of the modern composer.

Not only the size of the performing body, but also the manner in which the instruments are used, gives a clue to the period. For example, the nature of the bass part varies with the style of the music. The baroque period of Bach, Handel, and Vivaldi, with its emphasis upon the polyphonic style, often allotted to the bass an amount of melodic material equal to that found in the upper parts. With the shift to the more homophonic writing of the classic era, as represented by Haydn and Mozart, the bass was given a subordinate role. It was of extreme importance as the foundation upon which the harmonic structure rested, but it became a generally less interesting part in itself. As the romantic period emerged, the bass part became more prominent again—more interesting, more active, and more independent of the upper parts.

The brass instruments, too, afford an indication of the period in which the music was composed. At the time of

Beethoven, because of the physical limitations of the instruments, the trumpets, and more particularly the French horns and trombones, were given mainly "filler" parts. Frequently these merely emphasized the principal harmonies, and added rhythm to the ensemble. It was not until the first half of the nineteenth century that the technological advances in instrument construction allowed the brasses to assume a more important role. This was manifested both in the number of instruments employed (while three or four horns were enough for Beethoven, the scores of Wagner, Strauss, and Mahler would not infrequently call for eight) and in the increasing technical and expressive difficulties of the music allotted to them.

Another means for the identification of the period of a composition stems from the particular usages to which individual instruments lend themselves. The harpsichord, for example, is known for the clarity and brightness of its sound, but also for the way in which its sound quickly dies away. It was partly in order to make up for this inability to *sustain* tone that baroque composers "decorated" the melodies given to the harpsichord, by means of a standardized repertory of musical ornaments. Particularly in the slower movements, where the dying out of the tone is most apparent, the many ornaments give the effect of a sustained melody. The piano, by contrast, is capable of sustaining tone to a much greater degree, thanks in part to the sustaining pedal (a mechanism unknown to the harpsichord), which allows a struck string to continue sounding even though the finger is no longer depressing the key. However, the musical ornaments in themselves remain a clear indication of the baroque period even when the music is played upon the modern piano.

While Mozart and Haydn were among the first important composers to write for the piano, the instrument they knew was, by today's standards, weak in tone. Not until after their time was a metal frame developed that could begin to support the massive tension exerted by the heavy strings of the "concert grand" we know today. Thus Beethoven was able to write more massively—more "orchestrally"—for the piano, than either Haydn or Mozart, whose keyboard works are, with a few exceptions, characterized by a lightness of sound and of texture. Mozart's piano could not have produced the powerful tone demanded by, say, the opening movement of Beethoven's *Emperor Concerto*. Here, then, is another means of distinguishing the two periods—and the two composers—from one another.

Another insight into the period of the music is given by the freedom with which the orchestral instruments are used. Not only was a noticeable increase in virtuosity demanded of players as the nineteenth century progressed; there was also a markedly freer use of contrasting instrumental colors. The romantic movement, with its increased emphasis upon emotional expression, saw composers making use of the extreme high and low registers of all the instruments, and exploiting novelty of sound for its expressive effects. The search for coloristic variety has continued into our own day, and its results may be heard in some of the extraordinary effects that have been obtained by composers who have turned away from the conventional instruments to make their music out of electronically produced sounds.

It is instructive to listen to a string quartet by Mozart and then to one by Béla Bartók. Even without any attempt to analyze the content of these works, the extreme differences in the kinds of sounds that strike the ear will show the direction—the kind of freedom and diversity of expression—that composers have been seeking over the last century or longer. (And incidentally, if your ears are at first offended by some of the sounds that Bartók employs in his Fourth, Fifth, and Sixth Quartets, it will be well to remember that some of Mozart's works, when they were still new to music lovers, were called the creations of "a piano player with a depraved ear.")

The nature of the melody itself is another way by which periods—and composers—can be recognized. The typical Mozart or Haydn melody stands out prominently against its harmonic background and is thus easy to follow. It is likely to do much of its moving up and down by adjoining scale degrees. Its relatively short phrases are usually of equal length, and thus symmetrical in time. The characteristic melody of Wagner is not only much longer, but also seems to have fewer "breathing places"; it gives the effect of continuous motion. The melodies of many twentieth-century composers seek to do away with symmetry and move up or down by the least expected (and therefore most dramatic) interval. The effect of a typical modern melody—many of those by Stravinsky or Schönberg, for example—is "angularity." Many an ear will hear the notes of such a melody as skipping about rather arbitrarily.

The handling of rhythm offers another clue to both the period of the music, and the composer's identity. The rhythms of the period of Haydn and Mozart are quite regular. Beethoven, on the other hand, is identifiable by his greater rhythmic complexity. Nevertheless, it is a curious fact that the great stream of Austro-Germanic music of the eighteenth and nineteenth centuries is not really venturesome in matters of rhythm or meter. Consider, for example, the opening movement of Beethoven's Violin Concerto, which is admittedly a masterpiece: it continues for twenty-three minutes in an unbroken meter of four beats to the bar. Bach, too, is given to continuing one meter and one rhythm throughout a given movement, thus making for the "mechanical" quality that is sometimes said to characterize his music. It remained for the later nineteenth century, and especially for the twentieth, to witness a real liberation in the use of rhythm and meter. Thus, the music of Stravinsky can often be recognized first of all by the complexity and diversity of its rhythms, and the music of Prokofieff by the boisterousness and power of its rhythms, which impart to them what has been called an "athletic" quality.

Harmony, too, is a clue to style. With a few outstanding exceptions—the madrigals of Gesualdo and Monteverdi, for example—Renaissance composers used a harmonic vocabulary that was relatively simple, as viewed from our vantage point in the twentieth century. Much the same might be said of the music of most Baroque composers. The classic period, while it expanded the harmonic palette, also codified it, so that the harmonic progressions of Haydn and Mozart contain few surprises for us, and have instead a predictable quality. The expressive needs of the composers of the romantic period caused them to expand their concepts of harmonic practices, with the result that chords and chord progressions previously considered inadmissible were used with increasing frequency. It should be remembered that it was during this period that the orchestra was enlarged and compositions became considerably longer. Greater venturesomeness in matters of harmony was required, in order to match the expanding palette of orchestral colors, and in order to sustain the listener's interest over a long time-span in any one work, or in any one movement.

Since the "shocking dissonances" of one period become the commonplaces of another, composers have continually sought new ways of giving spice and interest to their harmonies. One of the ways was to attach additional notes to their chords—a technique which reached its culmination in Stravinsky's *The Rite of Spring,* in 1913. When the harmonic system seemed to be "used up," attempts were made to revitalize it by using other systems. Late in the nineteenth century, Debussy resorted to the "whole-tone scale," in which the smallest interval between notes is a whole step, rather than a half step. This device gave a vague atmospheric quality to his music, which is characterized by the term "impressionistic."

In the music of Beethoven and his contemporaries, the progressions from one key to another, besides supplying an immediate source of emotionalism, had served a structural purpose, helping to determine the form of a composition. As we have seen, the contrast between the tonic and the dominant key was one of the important factors in the sonata allegro form. But with Debussy's whole-tone scale, the sense of tonality was weakened. Harmony was used less for its structural function than simply as a means for supplying sensuous and coloristic pleasure. As a result, the classic forms lost some of their usefulness, and gave way to freer forms, with an increased emphasis upon "color" and "mood."

Another means of enriching the harmonic vocabulary was the use of two or more keys simultaneously—devices known as *bitonality* and *polytonality,* respectively. The French composer Darius Milhaud, in particular, has exploited these devices. In general, the trend has been toward increasing freedom in harmony, so that most contemporary music can be identified almost immediately by the presence of dissonance.

The use of dynamics provides still another indication of the period in which a composition was written. While the earlier composers used a certain amount of dynamic contrast for expressive and dramatic purposes, their range of dynamics, and the suddenness with which they went from one level to another, were relatively limited. A single, unexpected loud chord occurring in a soft passage in one of Haydn's symphonies was so unusual that it caused the symphony to be nicknamed *Surprise.* Beethoven, a generation later, made sudden dynamic changes, by contrast, one of his hallmarks, and composers of the succeeding periods, following his lead, gave their music a highly emotional quality by their use of sudden dynamic contrasts. The trend has continued: one characteristic of modern music is the almost total unpredictability of its dynamic scheme.

It may be argued that the means of identifying styles that have been discussed so far apply mainly to large periods of music, and only to a lesser degree to individual composers. That is perfectly true. Many of our generalizations about the classic period would apply equally to the music of Haydn or Mozart and to that of any number of their contemporaries. Some of the characteristics we have attributed to Beethoven are occasionally to be found in the works of Schubert. Our descriptions of the melodies and the rhythms of Stravinsky and Prokofieff are, by and large, similar. How, then, can we learn to recognize the work of a specific composer? The answer is that, once the broad stylistic marks of a school or a period are determined, we must begin listening ever more closely to the individual works. Each composer has identifying characteristics that are too subtle to be briefly described.

The ability to recognize a composer by his style and his mannerisms is not basically different from our ability to recognize a radio personality by his voice, as we do a friend who calls us on the telephone. We might draw an analogy from the realm of the visual, and liken this to the process by which we immediately recognize, in a crowd of people, someone we know. Just as all music is made up of five basic elements, so all faces are made up of a few basic features. We are able to recognize the face of a friend by the shape and color of these features and by their relationships. As the result of repeated experiences, we do not have to examine a face consciously in order to decide whether or not it is that of someone we know. So it may be in music as well. After we have heard enough music by a particular composer, his style becomes familiar, and we no longer have to consider consciously how he or she manages the individual elements.

Let us consider this phenomenon of aural recognition, noting the complexity of the process that is involved when we chance to hear a known radio personality. First, the communication takes place only by means of sounds—and these often differ only in slight degree from speaker to speaker. To take the more obvious differences first, our previous experience, the result of study or travel, enables us immediately to recognize and distinguish the common foreign languages. But within the English language alone, we are also able instantly to distinguish between an Englishman's speech and an American's. Consider the means by which we are able to tell the difference. Remember that we are comparing two "performances" that, relative to all the possible variations of speech patterns, are quite close; both people are speaking the same language and, for the purposes of this discussion, saying the same words.

So sensitive are our ears that we notice such details as slight differences in rhythm, in the coloration of vowel sounds, in the articulation given to various syllables, and in voice quality—all of which enable us to identify the origin of the speaker. When we identify the English language as spoken with either a German or a French accent, what is this but an awareness of differences in rhythm (the rhythmic characteristics of one language superimposed upon another), in melody (languages have their own melodic qualities, or intonations), and tone color (the vocal quality of French will not be mistaken for that of German)?

In addition to the accent, if a French, a German, and an Italian speaker were all to express approximately the same thought in English, each would reveal his or her national origin with a characteristic sentence structure. Even if the words of each speaker were transcribed and read off by the same neutral voice, we should probably still be able to recognize the national background of the statements by way of their construction. An awareness of language *form,* which is roughly akin to musical form, enters into our ability to identify foreign speech, or a foreigner's rendering of English speech, regardless of its tone color or rhythm.

Moving on from such relatively obvious differences to the subtleties of English as it is spoken in the United States, consider how quickly we can spot the drawl that enables us to identify the Southerner, the twang that goes with some Midwestern speech, the particular kind of broad "a" that colors the speech of the New Englander.

How acute our sense of recognition is, therefore, when we are able to identify a friend after his or her first few words over the telephone! The process of identifying a composer by means of his music is basically no different. Composers "speak" in their music, with the "accents" of their periods and their temperaments. Just as repeated contact enables you to identify your friend by the sound of his or her voice, in the same way, with experience, you can tell a composer by the sounds he produces with an orchestra, a string quartet, or a piano, or even in a vocal work.

Brahms, for example, reveals himself by the "thickness" of his sound, whether he is composing for full orchestra or for the piano, while Debussy reveals himself by a more evanescent sound. Strauss tends toward a flamboyant quality in his orchestral works. The later orchestral compositions of Stravinsky, by contrast with the richly orchestrated works of his youth, project a sparse sort of sound.

Even composers who write in the same basic style "give themselves away" by their individual mannerisms. Mozart, for example, frequently has the solo instrument in a concerto—violin, piano, bassoon—trill at the end of a passage. Beethoven, toward the end of a long, dramatic movement, will sometimes quiet down, just before he ends the piece with a sudden resurgence of power. Mendelssohn has a peculiar lightness of texture in his scherzos that no other composer even approximates. Schumann is given to the habit of repeating his rhythmic patterns for long periods of time. An overture by Rossini is very often identifiable by a long, steady crescendo as it approaches its conclusion. Brahms, when presenting a melody having two notes to a beat, will often accompany it by having the cellos play, *pizzicato* (plucked), three notes to the beat; the resulting rhythmic complexity is one of his identifying mannerisms.

This list of musical thumbprints could be expanded endlessly, but its purpose would be better served by your listening to some of the music we have been discussing. In time, you will notice that composers have their own idiosyncratic ways of saying things, just as we are each given to individual speech mannerisms. The melodies created by any one composer in any given period of his or her life tend to take on a family resemblance, as do the harmonies. There will be a predilection for certain rhythmic patterns and certain orchestral colors.

As the result of our previous experiences with the music of specific composers, our recognition of individual styles will seem to take place so quickly as to appear to require no conscious thought. Repeated listening enables us not only to recognize the period and the nationality of classical works, but also to distinguish the works of Brahms from those of Beethoven, those of Haydn from those of Mozart, those of Debussy from those of Ravel. It should now be clear that only through much listening will anyone learn to differentiate and identify the works of more than a handful of composers. However, there is the comforting fact that stylistic differences among composers can become apparent to the listener without technical training.

CHAPTER 24

A Final Word to the Reader

Although many listeners wish that there were some magic formula by which they could quickly become connoisseurs, no book by itself can transform the beginning listener into a completely sophisticated, knowledgeable music lover. Any book that makes such a claim holds out false hopes, and makes promises that cannot be fulfilled.

It is my sincere hope—and belief—that this book supplies the basis upon which any interested listener can build a true understanding of music, and a genuine enjoyment of the art. With this awareness of what music is, and of what it can do, we can develop and refine the technique of listening, just as a pianist, by other means, can perfect the technique of playing.

Since each of us is in effect the sum of all our experiences—emotional, physical, and intellectual—and the sum is different for every one of us, the effect of any musical experience must also be expected to differ for each of us. In addition, even our own reactions to any given work cannot remain the same, since each rehearing will add to our store of experiences, leading us to approach each subsequent hearing of that composition—and of *all* music—with different ears. Occasionally, the e. effect of repeated hearings of a work will have the result of making us esteem the work less highly. This is one of the concomitants of a constantly improving critical faculty, and it is just as important and valid a part of music appreciation as is the heightening of our admiration for certain other works. In fact, one of the functions of the true appreciation of music is to equip us with the means for distinguishing between the good and the bad, the first-rate and the second-rate.

A final word. Music exists within itself; it does not have to go outside for its subject matter, or for its cause. Music *is* its own subject matter, and it requires no other reason for being. However, listening to music is an integral part of living, and it would be undesirable, even if it were possible, to separate it completely from all other associations.

One purpose of this book has been to help the reader to make the distinction between what he or she brings to music from without, and what the *music* itself is about. But it is my conviction that the satisfactions to be had from *music itself* are so numerous and so great that it is not necessary to resort to extramusical stimuli. To do so deflects our attention from the music, and therefore, actually interferes with our understanding of it.

Once the listener is willing to meet music on its own terms, he will have prepared himself for a wealth of esthetic satisfactions that—in its emotional and intellectual variety—is literally unlimited.

INDEX